JOHN SMITH & SON (GLW) LTD

Strategic Advertising Management

Strategic Advertising Management

Larry Percy

John R. Rossiter

Richard Elliott

OXFORD
UNIVERSITY PRESS

OXFORD

UNIVERSITY PRESS

Great Clarendon Street, Oxford OX2 6DP

Oxford University Press is a department of the University of Oxford.
It furthers the University's objective of excellence in research, scholarship,
and education by publishing worldwide in

Oxford New York

Auckland Bangkok Buenos Aires Cape Town Chennai
Dar es Salaam Delhi Hong Kong Istanbul Karachi Kolkata
Kuala Lumpur Madrid Melbourne Mexico City Mumbai Nairobi
São Paulo Shanghai Taipei Tokyo Toronto

Oxford is a registered trade mark of Oxford University Press
in the UK and in certain other countries

Published in the United States
by Oxford University Press Inc., New York

A catalogue record for this book is available from the British Library

Library of Congress Cataloging in Publication Data
Data available
ISBN 0–19–878232–2

10 9 8 7 6 5

Typeset by RefineCatch Limited, Bungay, Suffolk
Printed in Great Britain
on acid-free paper by
CPI Bath

Preface

In the world of marketing there are many ways of communicating with your target audience. Marketing communication includes everything from packages to advertising in magazines and on television, promotions to signs in stores. But regardless of the form marketing communication takes, or what it is called, it all must follow a very specific strategic direction if it is to be successful. That is what this book is all about. We are concerned with how you effectively develop and use marketing communication to deliver a message about a brand or company.

Over the course of the book you will find that we generally talk about 'advertising,' and use consumer-oriented examples. There is a good reason for this. It does not mean that business-to-business issues are not important or that corporate advertising or trade promotions are not a critical part of marketing communication. In fact, more marketing money is probably spent on trade promotion than anything else. But the strategic *principles* involved are the same, whether we are discussing consumer advertising, business-to-business advertising or trade promotions. And since everyone is familiar with consumer advertising, that is where we focus our discussion.

The very first issue we deal with in Chapter 1 is the definitions of traditional advertising and promotion. We do this because it underscores a critical *strategic* difference. Advertising and advertising-like messages help support the long-term strategic goals of a brand. Promotion and promotion-like messages provide short-term, tactical support. So in a real sense, all marketing communication can be seen as either 'advertising' or 'promotion.' In fact, people generally look at all marketing communication as 'advertising.' From a strategic standpoint, they are right.

Everything really is, or should be, 'advertising,' because everything we do should contribute to the long-term equity of a brand. Even promotions, although their primary task is tactical and short-term, must also contribute to the long-term strength of a brand to really be effective.

Understanding advertising in this strategic sense is what sets this book apart from most advertising texts. It is not enough to simply learn about the different types of advertising and media. We leave that to basic introductory texts. What is important to understand is *how advertising works*, what it is that makes effective advertising.

From a managerial perspective, this is what matters. Most readers of this book will not go on in their professional lives to be part of the 'creative' world that is concerned with the actual production of advertisements. Rather, as a brand manager, marketing manager, a part of senior management (even financial management of a company), or the owner of a small or large business, you will be asked to make *strategic* decisions. Whom should I target for my business? How should I position my brand or company? What should I say? As a manager you will be part of developing or approving strategic plans, and approving the advertising. This book provides the foundation necessary for making these decisions.

The book is divided into four parts, building from a broad introduction to very specific strategic considerations necessary for effective advertising and promotion. In Part One we look at advertising and promotion in a very general way, and provide an overview of a number of issues concerning its role in society and the economy. We also discuss several contemporary perspectives on advertising and its relationship to such diverse disciplines as traditional psychology, feminist and Marxist theory, and post-modernism. In Part Two we discuss planning considerations and introduce a five-step strategic approach to the development of successful advertising and promotion campaigns. Part Three then addresses each of the five steps in the strategic planning process in a separate chapter, and in Part Four we lay out specific tactics for making it all work.

Our goal is to provide background and insight that will stimulate an appreciation for the strategic discipline required if advertising and promotion is to be successful, along with the tools needed for effective strategic advertising management. But perhaps even more importantly, we hope to leave the reader with the sense and understanding that by using a strategic approach, managers will be in a position to make more informed decisions about advertising.

As with all things this book would not have been possible without the help of many people from reviewers and editors to students and others too numerous to mention. But, we are especially indebted to the IPA in London, with special thanks to Lesley Scott and Natalie Swan, who helped us in tracking down many of the adverts used as examples, and to James Best at BMP DDB London who was very generous in securing for us a number of very good adverts to illustrate our points. Peter Field at the IPA was a great help in identifying potential case histories from their extensive database that could be used to reinforce the ideas presented in the text (and which you can review on the book's web site at www.oup.com/uk/best.textbooks/business). Full marks also for Matthew Cotton at OUP who stayed on top of everything, Tina Boatner who managed to read and type all of the first author's handwritten chapters, the patience and encouragement of Mary Walton Percy, and thanks to Chris Elliott for stimulation and toleration.

Larry Percy
John Rossiter
Richard Elliott
April, 2001

Outline Contents

Part One Overview of advertising and promotion

Part Two Planning considerations

Part Three Laying the foundation

Part Four Making it work

Detailed Contents

Part One Overview of advertising and promotion

Part Two **Planning considerations**

Part Three **Laying the foundation**

Part Four **Making it work**

List of Tables

List of Figures

List of Adverts

Part One

Overview of Advertising and Promotion

Chapter 1

What is Advertising and Promotion?

In this first chapter we will be taking a broad introductory look at just what we mean by traditional advertising and promotion, and how it is seen in today's world. This will provide a foundation and perspective for the subject in general before we begin to look specifically at the role advertising and promotion can and do play in support of brands, and how to manage it strategically in order to positively position and build brands.

Defining Advertising and Promotion

If we look up the word 'advertise' in the *New Shorter OED* we find the following definition: 'make an announcement in a public place; describe or present goods publicly with a view to promoting sales'. Right after that we find advertisement defined as: 'A public announcement (formerly by the town-crier, now usually in newspapers, on posters, by television, etc.)'.[1]

This is certainly what most people have in mind when they think of advertising—adverts in the newspaper or magazines and commercials on radio or TV. But this really doesn't begin to tell us much about what advertising actually is. In fact, we are about to spend several hundred pages in effect defining advertising.

A better feel for what advertising is really all about may be gained by looking back to the Latin root of the word 'advertising'. It was Daniel Starch, one of the early pioneers of advertising theory in the twentieth century, who, back in the 1920s, reminded us that the Latin root for advertising is *advertere*. This roughly translates as 'to turn towards'.[2] Returning to the *New Shorter OED*, we find that the word 'advert' is colloquial for advertisement, *and* when used as a verb means 'turn toward'. This definition is more relevant, because it implies more than simply 'an announcement in a public place'.

In a very real sense, advertising is meant to turn us toward a product or service by providing information or creating a positive feeling—something that goes well beyond simply calling our attention to it. Advertising is an *indirect* way of turning a potential customer toward the advertised product or service by providing information that is designed to effect a favourable impression, what we will call a positive brand attitude. This favourable positive brand attitude then helps place the consumer on the path toward seeking out the product or service advertised.

If advertising is meant to encourage consumers to 'turn toward' a brand, what is the traditional function of promotion? Returning to the *New Shorter OED* we see that a promotion 'helps forward.' This definition is quite consistent with the Latin root of promotion, *promovere*. Roughly translated, this means 'move forward.'[3] Contrasting the Latin root of 'promotion', 'move forward', with the Latin root of 'advertising', 'turn toward,' illustrates the fundamental difference between the traditional ideas of advertising and promotion. Advertising is aimed toward the long-term building of positive brand attitude by 'turning' the consumer toward the brand; promotion is aimed at the more short-term tactical goal of 'moving forward' brand sales now.

Advertising and Promotion within the Marketing Plan

It is important to realize that advertising and promotion are only one part of the marketing plan. Other key marketing considerations include product configuration (e.g. making sure the product is offered in the right sizes, shapes, or colours), pricing structure, and distribution—what E. Jerome McCarthy has called the 'Four P's of Marketing' (Promotion, Product, Price, and Place).[4]

In fact, advertising is only one of the elements in the 'promotion' or marketing communication section of the marketing plan. We will be dealing with the idea of the marketing mix again in Chapter 7. In addition to traditional advertising and promotion, the 'promotion' component of the marketing mix also includes public relations and personal selling. We will be discussing the close strategic relationship between promotion and advertising in Chapter 14. This is not to suggest that there is no relationship between advertising and public relations or personal selling; of course there is, especially with industrial and corporate advertisers. However, the budgets and staff involved with personal selling and public relations tend to be separate from those of advertising and promotion.

While a simple definition of public relations is that it is 'unpaid promotion', there is a lot more to it than that, and one can take whole courses in the various aspects of public relations. For our purposes, we need to remember that the position being taken in advertising must be consistent with the story being told through public relations. The same holds true for any collateral material used in personal selling, including catalogues, brochures, and presentations used by the sales force. An added responsibility for advertising is to help pre-sell a prospect for the salesman. To do this, the selling message must be consistent with *all* other aspects of a brand's marketing communication.

A Closer Look at Advertising

Keeping in mind how advertising fits into a company's marketing plan, and our definition of how advertising turns a potential customer toward an advertised product or service, let us look at an example to illustrate how this definition of advertising applies. Remember, we are suggesting that advertising deals indirectly with potential action on the part of someone by providing information or creating feelings that turn them toward the product or service advertised. This will be true regardless of whether we are dealing with fast-moving consumer package goods (fmcgs) like food or household cleaners, industrial manufacturer advertising of heavy equipment, corporate advertisers talking about their company, or non-profit organizations soliciting funds or reminding us to take better care of ourselves.

What do you think Nestlé is trying to do with their advert for Nescafé Gold Blend (Advert 1.1)? What do they wish us to 'turn toward'? We can never really know exactly what an advertiser has in mind without actually reading their marketing plan and creative strategy. But looking at this advert it would appear that Nestlé wants us to think about the aroma of coffee brewing, and to associate Nescafé Gold Blend with this experience. They want us to 'turn toward' the idea that Nescafé Gold Blend creates this pleasant experience better than any other brand of coffee. Of course, much more is *implied*. We are also asked to associate this wonderful 'golden aroma' with rich, good-tasting coffee, a truly satisfying experience, almost sensual.

The point is, this advert is not *explicitly* asking you to buy Nescafé Gold Blend now, but rather is helping to create a positive feeling and attitude for the brand. This positive brand attitude is what will lead to purchase. At the same time, the other components of the marketing mix, mediated by competitive activity in the market, will all contribute to the likelihood of someone actually purchasing Nescafé Gold Blend after seeing this advert. Advertising for a brand only plays a part, but as we shall see through the course of this book, it is a very important, often critical part.

How does Advertising Work?

In a very real sense, the remainder of this book is dedicated to answering this question. But in this section we will provide a very brief introduction and overview of what is involved. Some very basic things must occur if any type of communication is to work. A person must have the opportunity to see or hear the message, they must pay attention to it, understand what is being presented, and then act upon the message in the desired manner. This sequence is the same whether the message is from a parent, a boss, a friend, or an advertiser. In advertising we call these four steps the buyer response sequence, and it is covered in detail in Chapter 3.

Consider the Nescafé Gold Blend advert again. What must happen for this advert to work? It ran in a women's magazine, so the first step is that a potential buyer sees the magazine and at least skims through it. While doing this, they must notice the advert and spend enough time with it to 'get the meaning'. They must then associate a positive

1.1 Advert for Nescafé Gold Blend that illustrates a positive experience with the brand and provides a strong brand identification. Courtesy Nestlé S.A. and McCann Europe

feeling with the brand in response to the idea of a 'golden aroma' and think to themselves, 'I'd like to try Gold Blend.'

Realistically, of course, this is *not* likely to happen all at one go. You may glance at this advert several times without paying much attention to it. But over time, the visual imagery and headline 'Enjoy before drinking' will begin to register and be associated with the brand. As this happens, it will help to build or reinforce a positive attitude for the brand. Then one day while shopping, you see the brand on the shelf and 'remember' the positive feelings and think 'I'll give it a try.'

If someone does pay attention to our advertising, we want them to 'get' something specific. Of course, each advert will have a particular message to deliver, consistent with its creative strategy. But at a more general level, the advertising must satisfy a communi-cation objective. All advertising and marketing communication has the ability to stimu-late four communication effects: need for the category, brand awareness, brand attitude, and brand purchase intention.[5]

In a very real sense, when you pay attention to advertising, all of these effects could run through your mind. While we will later devote a complete chapter to them, at this point it will be helpful to understand briefly what is meant by each of the four communication effects because communications objectives are determined by the communication effect desired.

Category need. Before any purchase decision is made, there must be at least some interest in the product category. This is true of even the most trivial purchase. If you stop to think of it, if there were no 'reason' or need for something, why would you buy it?

Brand awareness. You must be able to identify a brand in order to purchase it. There are two types of brand awareness: recognition and recall. With recognition, at the point of purchase you recognize the brand on the shelf. With recall, you must think of the brand on your own prior to purchase.

Brand attitude. Unless a product is inexpensive or trivial, brand awareness alone will not be enough to drive you to an actual purchase. For purchase to occur, you must have a favourable attitude toward the brand. This attitude will be some combination of what you know or learn about the brand, and any feelings you associate with it.

Brand purchase intention. Someone's mind could be full of different attitudes toward vari-ous brands. And quite possibly, they may hold generally favourable attitudes towards several of these brands. Brand purchase intention refers to such thoughts as 'I think I'd like to try that' or 'I'll buy that', and these follow from favourable brand attitudes.

This discussion should provide you with a brief introduction to what we mean by com-munication effects. As you can see, the effects are simply a reflection of the process your mind is likely to go through prior to almost any purchase. Do you have a need? Are you aware of alternatives? What do you think about those alternatives? Will you buy one? Before you make any purchase you will probably need to give a positive answer each of these questions.

While each of these four communication effects can be part of the response to an advert, they are not all required to be a specific part of the execution. Some may be implied or already understood. Those that are not become communication objectives.

The correct communication objective is critical to effective advertising. We will learn that brand awareness and brand attitude are *always* communication objectives given their importance to a brand, and that under particular circumstances either of the other two communication effects may also serve as a communication objective.

Let us return to the Nescafé Gold Blend advert. This advert assumes that a category need already exists. For this advertising to work, the reader must already drink coffee. But are they aware of the brand? If not, the advert provides good brand name and package visibility, essential for recognition brand awareness, as we shall learn. Earlier we discussed how the advert should stimulate a positive feeling for the brand. This translates to a positive brand attitude, and could also include a positive brand purchase intention.

The actual communication objective for the Nescafé Gold Blend advert cannot be known for sure without seeing the original creative brief, but it appears to reflect the primary communication objectives of brand awareness and brand attitude. There is no attempt to 'sell' the category, to convince people to drink coffee, or to buy soluble coffee (often called 'instant' coffee), and there is no *specific* call to purchase action. Rather, the advert does a good job of creating an impression of a positive experience with the brand, and provides strong brand identity.

Brand Attitude Strategies

We have just suggested that brand awareness and brand attitude are always communication objectives. Obviously, someone must be aware of a brand if they are going to buy it, aware of a service if they are to avail themselves of it, aware of a company if they are going to do business with it. But the real heart of most advertising messages conveys information or communicates a feeling about the product or service being advertised. This is what comprises brand attitude.

There are four brand attitude strategies that we will be concerned with in this text, and they are covered in depth in Chapter 8. These four strategies are based upon two dimensions critical to consumer behaviour: the type of purchase decision, and the motivation that drives the decision.[6]

Type of purchase decision. In terms of the type of decision, we will be classifying all consumer decisions as either low-involvement or high-involvement.[7] When a decision is *low-involvement*, it means that there is very little, if any, risk attached to the consequences of making that decision. For example, if you think you might like a new candy bar, trying it would no doubt be a low-involvement decision because you would not really be risking much money. But when a decision requires a lot of information prior to deciding, and a great deal of conviction that you are making the right decision, it is *high-involvement*. A good example here would be buying a car.

Type of motivation. We will be devoting a lot of time in this book to motivation. For now, in order to begin to understand brand attitude strategies, you need only to know that people do some things because of negative motivations (e.g. to remove or avoid a problem) and some things because of positive motivations (e.g. to make them 'feel good').

Since decisions in the marketplace are governed by type of decision and type of motivation, we know that development of brand attitude strategy in advertising must take this into account. As a result, brand attitude strategies in adverts will reflect one of the four combinations of decision types and motivation:[8]

- low-involvement decisions driven by negative motivations;
- low-involvement decisions driven by positive motivations;
- high-involvement decisions driven by negative motivations
- high-involvement decisions driven by positive motivations

Again, looking at the Nescafé Gold Blend advert, what brand attitude strategy has been followed? Under most circumstances, there will probably be little risk attached to the purchase of coffee. An exception might be if you were entertaining someone very special and wanted a specific brand or blend of coffee in order to impress them. But in most cases, if you try a brand of coffee and don't like it, you will not have lost much. So, we can be fairly safe in assuming that coffee is a low-involvement decision. And what is likely to motivate a person to buy a particular brand of coffee? It is unlikely to be a negative motive. You may buy soluble coffee for its convenience (a negative motive), but that is a *category*, not a brand, decision. Once you have decided upon the type of coffee you want, the *brand* selected is likely to be the one you think you will most enjoy (the positive motive of sensory gratification). This Nescafé Gold Blend advert is a good execution of a brand attitude strategy for a low-involvement decision driven by positive motivations.

As we shall see later, in Chapter 11, the creative tactics differ significantly for each of the four possible brand attitude strategies. If the wrong brand attitude strategy is used, the target audience will not be as likely to pay attention to the advertising or 'get' the message.

What have we learned about brand attitude strategies up to this point? We have seen that one of the jobs of advertising is to generate a communication effect, and that brand attitude is one effect that is always a communication objective. In addition, we know that in order to create advertising that will satisfy a brand attitude communication objective, one of four fundamental brand attitude strategies must be followed. The correct brand attitude strategy will reflect the involvement in the decision by the target audience as well as the likely motivation for their choice. Once the correct brand attitude strategy is selected, the creative and media tactics required to implement that strategy will be more easily identified.

Message Appeal

Now that we have introduced the concept of brand attitude strategies, how does that relate to the appeal that should be used in creating the message? As mentioned, we shall spend a great deal of time looking specifically at creative tactics in Chapter 11, but it is also good to have a general idea about what is meant by 'persuasive appeals' in communication. Persuasion is studied by psychologists interested in attitude-change theory, and obviously what they know about persuasion informs our understanding of how advertising and other marketing communication works.

William J. McGuire, a social psychologist who taught at Yale University, is considered perhaps the foremost authority on attitude-change theory, and he has pointed out that the distinctions Aristotle made in the *Rhetoric* between logos, pathos, and ethos provide a very useful way of classifying the options available for message appeals.[9] Roughly speaking, logos appeals use logical arguments, pathos appeals address our passions, and ethos appeals deal with ethics (in a philosophical sense).

Logos and pathos appeals correspond closely to our brand attitude strategy ideas based upon involvement and motivation. Following Aristotle, logos appeals ask the recipient of a message to draw an inference or conclusion based upon arguments presented in the message. With low-involvement decisions when the underlying motivation is negative, where a problem is to be solved or avoided, this is exactly the appeal that is necessary. When the motive is negative and the decision is high-involvement, the logos requirement—accepting as true what is presented or implied—applies. When we get to Chapter 8, you will see that we call the brand attitude strategies dealing with negative motivation *informational*, because you are providing information to help solve or avoid a problem. In essence, this means using a logos appeal.

On the other hand, a pathos appeal, as characterized by Aristotle, means a persuasive message that involves creating an appropriate *feeling* in the person receiving the message. This is exactly what we are looking for when the brand attitude strategy deals with positive motivations. We will be referring to such strategies as *transformational*, because the message appeal is meant to transform the target audience by creating an authentic emotional experience.[10]

The third message appeal suggested by Aristotle is ethos. By ethos he meant a persuasive message that relied more upon the *source* of the message than the message itself. An example would be a teacher who has the ability to 'persuade' the student because they know the content of the lectures will likely be reflected in the examination. Many years ago Rosenthal made the point that ethos appeals attempt to persuade by forcing the attention of the receiver of a message on the source while logos and pathos appeals focus on message content.[11] We consider a correct understanding of ethos to be very important when using spokespeople in adverts. This is also related to brand attitude strategy, as we shall see in our discussion of the VisCAP model of source effectiveness in Chapter 11. For example, when dealing with logical or logos appeals, *credibility* in the message source is needed, but with a pathos or emotional appeal, *attractiveness* is needed. Aristotle talked about ethos appeals in terms of tapping into someone's 'moral principles'.

Advertising and the Internet

What about advertising and the Internet? There is no question that many people, and many people in advertising, are keen on how the Internet might be used in advertising, and for marketing communication generally. So far we have talked briefly about advertising and promotion, and where they fit within the marketing plan. We have introduced the foundation of the text, the basics of how advertising works. This quite literally outlines what this text is all about.

So where does the Internet fit in this discussion? Unlike many people today, we do *not* see the Internet as something radically new and different, destined to change the face of marketing communication. At this point in time, the Internet is basically another medium, another way of delivering a message. There is an incredible potential for business and communication via the Internet, but is it really different in the sense that it will require new and different ways of thinking about delivering marketing communication? Much as advocates of the Internet would like us to think this is the case, we doubt it very much.

In fact, in many ways there is really nothing 'new' about how you communicate on the Internet. Yes, it does provide the potential for somewhat more specific targeting, but direct marketing already provides a number of ways to target specific individuals in a target audience. The Internet only provides *another* means of directly targeting specific audience members, albeit it more effectively under certain circumstances. In other ways, it is very much like the traditional Yellow Pages on the one hand, and posters and magazines on the other. People use the Internet to search out information, much as they have used the Yellow Pages. They also 'surf' the Internet, just as they browse through magazines or pass by posters. In fact, 64 per cent of all spending on Internet advertising in the UK in 1998 was for banner adverts, and banner adverts are basically posters.[12] With advertising and the Internet we are essentially dealing with a print advert. It is simply being delivered in a new way, and under certain circumstances that offer the potential for increased processing of the message, and even interactive feedback.

The point we are making, and the reason why we are introducing the subject here in the first chapter, is that the success of advertising on the Internet will require attention to the very same strategic and tactical issues that are required for advertising to be successful anywhere. This book addresses the issue of how to identify a target audience and set communication objectives and strategy to maximize the likelihood of effective communication. This holds regardless of where the target audience confronts the message.

This means that advertising on the Internet must follow the same 'rules' and principles as any other advertising if it is to be effective. Adverts on the Internet must attract and hold attention, and quickly communicate a positive benefit for the brand. With more detailed messages, it must also encourage reading and processing the entire advert. Consider the banner advert for amazon.com (Advert 1.2). For it to be effective, it must communicate quickly in very much the same way as a poster. It is unlikely the Internet user has hit this page looking for adverts. The banner advert must say something quickly if the user is going to respond. Just as with a poster, the number of words in the headline must be limited to ensure processing at a single glance, without actually requiring someone to

1.2 Internet banner advert illustrating how pictures and words link together to communicate its message quickly. Courtesy amazon.com

read it. The message and the visual must work together to stimulate quickly a tentatively positive brand attitude, just as with a poster.

In fact, the principal difference between advertising on the Internet and general advertising arises from the initial exposure to the advert. This is not in terms of content, but as a result of the hypertext structure of Internet adverts. Because of the structural difference, we encounter a potential change in the way an Internet advert is processed. While the initial processing of a banner advert is basically the same as that of any print advert, especially posters, further processing will require what Rossiter and Bellman have called a Web ad schema.[13] This Web schema takes over when someone clicks on the banner advert, and this is where the difference lies. We shall explore this idea in more depth when we talk about processing adverts in Chapter 10.

We don't wish to minimize the potential of the Internet as a means of delivering advertising messages. But at the same time it is critical that you not think of Internet advertising as something so new and different that it requires a new way of thinking. With every evolution, or even revolution, in the *means* of communicating, from the printing press to radio to television, and now the Internet, the impulse has been to treat it as something totally new. But as we hope to have shown, while the Internet does provide a new and even exciting potential for reaching people, the execution of the message must still follow the basic principles of communication. And it is these basic principles of communication that we are dealing with in this book. They can and should be applied to advertising on the Internet, just as they must be applied to all forms of marketing communication.

Criticism of Advertising

Advertising seems to be everywhere. Perhaps because of this, many people are concerned with the potential impact advertising has upon society.[14] Critics of advertising raise several concerns about the impact of advertising upon society, and they are worth reviewing. As society has evolved over the last fifty years, so too has the criticism of advertising. The left especially has adjusted its criticism. As Martin Davidson has pointed out, the Marxist critique, for example, now sees advertising as doubly culpable. Not only is it highly suspect in its own right as an image, but it is an image of something even *more* suspect, the commodity.[15]

Perhaps the most widely made criticism of advertising is that it makes people buy things they neither want nor need. We will examine this charge first.

Advertising Creates Unnecessary Desires

To begin with, by the time you have finished reading this book, you will be well aware that communicating with a target audience through advertising is very, very difficult. Even though people are bombarded with messages, they pay attention to very few of them. And even when they do pay attention, that doesn't mean they will actually learn anything from the advert, or be positively influenced by it. In fact, many studies have shown that not only do we not pay much, if any, attention to advertising, but we do not pay much attention to the newspapers, magazines, or television shows where the advertising runs. It is not an easy job to communicate at all with advertising. This is why advertisers go to such lengths to identify a target audience where consumers are already favourably disposed toward their product.

The more philosophical question of whether advertising helps create unnecessary needs is a much more difficult question to answer. Critics of advertising feel that by its very nature advertising stimulates materialism, exaggerating the requirements of a good life. But these needs are driven by other social forces well beyond advertising. A much more serious charge is that advertising creates the desire for unobtainable goals. Again, we doubt that advertising alone must shoulder this charge. This is a problem with society in general. As long as contemporary movies, magazines, and television convey this image of life, some advertising is likely to reflect those images.

Nevertheless, there are areas where the images presented in advertising can and should be realistic. Remember, in advertising you are trying to match the attributes of a product with the perceived needs of the target audience. The problem comes when the perceived need is unrealistic. In the end, the best advertising should be responsible advertising.

Advertising is Misleading

The second most generally made criticism of advertising is that it is deceptive. It seems almost an article of faith that advertising is deceptive, and this has occasioned a rather general scepticism on the part of most people toward most advertising, as we shall see below. In certain cases, especially on the local level, there is no doubt that advertising can be misleading. But think for a moment about the consequences of such behaviour. If a product is misrepresented and you buy it, how likely are you ever to buy that brand again—or anything else from that company? In the long run, if advertising is deceptive, it will kill a brand.

One of the important results of advertising is the creation of brand names. Brand names bring with them almost an implied warranty of quality. Critics will argue that this image is false and that unbranded products are just as good. But are they? Isn't there a social value in enhancing the benefit people perceive in a product? Research has shown that advertised brand names are felt to taste better, last longer, etc. While advertising may have created these images, the products themselves must live up to the expectation. Davidson provides an interesting criticism here. He feels that the 'real objection to advertising is not really that it tells lies, but that it sells objects pretentiously, in terms of values that are more important than it is, and to the detriment of those values'.[16]

The problem with the question of deception in advertising is that it is largely a subjective one. If a claim is truly deceptive, you can be sure that the competition will be quick to let government regulatory agencies know about it. In fact, long before most advertising runs, attorneys for a brand will have considered it, and the censors at the media where it is to run will have taken a hard look at any claim the brand makes. Before a commercial is approved for showing on air or an advert is run in print media, it will require substantiation in terms of valid research for any major claim made for the brand.

In 1991 the European Union created the European Advertising Standards Alliance to provide a mechanism for dealing with false or misleading advertising. While it encourages self-regulation, the EU Misleading Advertising Directive requires member countries to institute powers to protect consumers against misleading claims.[17]

Although advertisers are permitted by law to make *obvious* exaggerations in their adverts, something called 'puffery' (e.g. 'best ever', 'great taste'), any attempt to misrepresent the overall nature of a brand is unlikely. An interesting example of just how restrictive this can sometimes be, even to the point of absurdity, is a commercial that ran in the US several years ago for San Georgio spaghetti. The commercial told the story of 'harvest time' at the San Georgio 'spaghetti farm' where they grow the 'best spaghetti' and featured peasant farm workers harvesting spaghetti from spaghetti trees. The claim 'best spaghetti' was considered puffery, and was acceptable. But the advertiser was required to include a disclaimer that said 'of course you know spaghetti really doesn't grow on trees' before television networks would approve the commercial for use on air.

Responsible advertising will not be deceptive, for the simple reason that it is bad for business. But the grey area of misleading claims or images is more difficult to pin down. In the end, if the media let something slip by, it is unlikely that your competitors will.

Advertising Insults our Intelligence

The charge that advertising is often insulting to the reader's or viewer's intelligence is again one that is frequently heard, but hard to define. What is in bad taste for one segment of the population may not be so for another. There is no doubt that certain adverts will be found to be tasteless, insulting, or offensive to certain people—even large groups of people. If the advertising is seen as tasteless by the intended target audience, however, the advertising will be unlikely to communicate its intended message effectively. So once again we see that to the extent the charge of 'insulting to my intelligence' is true, it will tend to be counter-productive for the advertiser. It is in the advertiser's best interest to provide advertising that will be well received by its target audience. This is one of the reasons you should test adverts before running them.

Advertising and the Economy

Another general area of advertising criticism revolves around the role advertising does or does not play in the economy. Classical economics, as a rule, provides very little comfort for advertising. But most marketers believe advertising does indeed make a positive contribution to the economy—if by no other way than pumping a great deal of money into the economy. For example, it is estimated that spending on advertising in the UK for the year 2000 will be some 15,798 million euros, and in Germany 21,615 million euros.[18]

It is often argued that advertising drives up the cost of products, and that without advertising, most things would cost less. This really is not the case. Of course, the cost of a product does include the cost of the advertising, but dropping the advertising would not necessarily drop the price of the product. Advertising helps increase consumption, which in its turn permits certain economies of scale that help drive *down* prices. For example, consider recent experiences with personal computers. Additionally, an argument can be made that price competition is enhanced by a broader awareness of price, which comes from advertising.

Another very real effect advertising has had on the economy is in the area of new product and new market development. Think of the enormous cost involved in the development of a new market. Without advertising it would be very difficult to generate enough sales fast enough to ensure a realistic payout. Advertising provides a rapid entrée to the consumer, and this encourages innovation on the part of companies. In the same sense advertising helps to expand existing markets, encouraging more and better products for the consumer.

We have already mentioned the idea of brand names and what their role is in today's market. From a business standpoint, a brand name is an *asset*, and is treated as one. In this sense advertising for brand names is often treated by a manufacturer as a long-term capital investment rather than an immediate cost. This is almost universally true of new product introductions. It is advertising that provides relative stability for a brand, building brand equity. There are many examples in almost any field of what happens to a company that does not protect its brand name through advertising. So in a very real sense, advertising is one of the ways in which we are able to provide stability in our economy.

Advertising and the Consumer

There is abundant evidence in the consumer behaviour and social psychology literature which suggests that global attitudes about something will condition how specific messages related to it are received. This is a rather fancy way of saying that if you don't like coffee, you are unlikely to be persuaded to buy a particular brand. This same principle applies to marketing communication. If someone distrusts advertising generally, they will be less likely to trust certain advertising messages. However, this relationship is anything but simple or easily understood.

In an interesting report, Calfee and Ringold reviewed six decades of survey data dealing with consumer attitudes toward advertising.[19] What they found was a core set of beliefs about advertising that has remained relatively constant over time and across a variety of question formats. Roughly 70 per cent of consumers feel advertising is often untruthful, seeks to persuade people to buy things they do not want, should be more strictly regulated, but nevertheless provides valuable information. In fact, despite feeling advertising is more likely to 'seek unduly to persuade' than to 'provide useful information' (when asked to choose between the two), most people tend to feel the benefits of advertising outweigh the deficits. As we remarked, this relationship is not easily understood.

A Question of Trust

One of the key relationships between a brand and its consumer is trust. Unfortunately, in many of today's markets there has been a significant erosion of this critical bond. What is, or has been, the role of advertising in this erosion? One can imagine problems here at many levels. If pricing policies (for example) have led to a certain distrust of a brand, this distrust could significantly affect consumers' perceptions of the brand's advertising. At the same time, a distrust of advertising in general impedes its credibility, and this not only reduces overall marketplace efficiencies, but acts like a cancer, attacking individual advertising messages. As Pollay and Mittal in their analysis of consumer criticism of advertising put it: 'High levels of distrust and cynicism put the professions of marketing and advertising in disrepute and *ultimately require greater advertising spending and creativity to accomplish the same ends*' (emphasis added).[20]

Should we expect this basic distrust of advertising to affect all advertising equally? No, and in fact there is some research available to help us identify types of advertising that are more or less likely to be believed. To the extent that a consumer feels a claim can be verified before purchase, consumer faith in that claim will be stronger than if it can only be verified after purchase ('5-year unconditional warranty,' for example, versus 'tastes great'). Least credible are so-called 'credence claims' which ordinarily can never be verified ('best performance ever').

The alert reader will see that this could be at the heart of the seeming paradox that people often feel advertising is untruthful, yet find it a useful source of information. Some types of advertising are seen as more likely than others to be true. Following this reasoning, as we shall see when we get into this in more detail in Chapter 8, high-involvement brand attitude strategies (i.e. those where there is a psychological or fiscal risk attached to the brand decision) should be seen as more credible than those for low-involvement brand attitude strategies. Again, some support for this has been found, but it is by no means something that occurs as a matter of course. Even if you are advertising a high-involvement product, credibility is far from guaranteed; and consumers are not sceptical of all low-involvement advertising. A lot of other things influence the perceived credibility of advertising in general, as we shall see.

Ippolito has talked about advertising's ability to create a bond, signalling product quality to the consumer. He goes so far as to suggest that this bond can enable an advertiser to induce a useful level of credibility in their advertising simply by advertising heavily![21] The implication here is that if the consumer is exposed to a message repeatedly over time, they will begin to assume that it must credibly reflect experience with the product. Consumers will reason that surely the product must be doing well since they see so much advertising for it. A rather complex notion, to be sure, but if true this would be one way to induce a certain level of credibility into a brand's advertising.

In any event, there certainly are important relationships between trust and advertising credibility, and these relationships should be monitored on a continual basis. The better these relationships are understood, the greater the likelihood of maximizing credibility for one's own advertising.

Regulatory Environment

One of the findings in the Calfee and Ringold review of all that research into consumer beliefs about advertising mentioned earlier is that when asked, some 60 to 70 per cent of consumers will support the idea of stronger regulation of advertising.[22] Somehow they seem to equate regulation with more credible advertising. Unfortunately, a real increase in regulation does not seem to translate into a perceived increase in advertising credibility. While increased regulation and intervention in advertising increased significantly during the 1970s in the US, especially with the implementation of the US Federal Trade Commission's Advertising Substantiation Program, there was no perceived increase in advertising credibility on the part of the consumer. What is really interesting here is that in objective terms, all of the evidence suggests that actual claims made in advertising were indeed more credible after adoption of the substantiation requirements.[23]

Perhaps what we see happening here is another variation on the paradox discussed earlier. While people feel that increased regulation of advertising will make it more credible, as they become aware of the increased regulation, the very knowledge of this activity fuels scepticism. In other words, if it wasn't so bad, there wouldn't be a need for this regulation. One thing is for sure: in the US, when the FTC does publicly act upon a case of false or misleading advertising, the advertiser in question will lose approximately 3 per cent of its share value in the stock market.[24] And the fallout from an action against a particular advertiser for false or deceptive advertising increases consumer scepticism of all advertising, not just that of the advertiser accused.

Understanding Consumer Attitudes toward Advertising

Researchers have for years been surveying the public's attitudes toward advertising and have noticed no significant change in beliefs about advertising. Precisely because there is more to this than meets the eye, and its impact can significantly affect how *individual advertisers'* messages are perceived by consumers, it is important for an advertiser to have a good grasp of general consumer attitudes toward advertising. Beyond this, to the extent that someone in the business of advertising wishes truly to *understand* the business of advertising, it is critical to understand the market's perception of its 'product'. Just as it is important for an advertiser to track response to its specific advertising, it is important to track attitudes toward advertising in general. There are a number of reasons for this, and some should be evident from the paradoxes in consumer beliefs about advertising we have just discussed.

We have seen how trust can play an important role in people's beliefs about advertising, and how external factors such as regulation and publicity about 'false' advertising can influence consumers' feelings of trust. While the relationship among all of these factors is far from clear, monitoring consumer trust in advertising along with things known to influence it puts an advertiser in a better position to understand how their customers and prospects are likely to respond to advertising in general for their brand.

As an example, what is the effect of political advertising upon how people respond to advertising for brands? There is no doubt that people seem fed up with the strident tone of political advertising, and as an article in *Advertising Age* suggests: 'there's a growing concern that they also may be effective in turning off the public from all advertising'.[25] In that article, Sean Fitzpatrick (then a vice-chairman with McCann-Erickson Worldwide) is quoted as feeling that political advertising directly affects any advertising that is running at the same time, even to the extent of effectively blocking it out so that it is not heard. To what extent does political advertising negatively affect regular advertising? And just as important, how long does this negative carryover effect persist? Is it more likely to affect some types or categories of advertising more than others, such as advertising with spokespeople or comparative ads?

Another important question to consider here is the 'universality' of consumer beliefs about advertising. In the Pollay and Mittal article mentioned earlier, they report some preliminary findings that show significant subsets or segments within the population in terms of core beliefs about advertising.[26] As one might expect from the general findings of Calfee and Ringold that 70 per cent of consumers held consistent basic beliefs about advertising, three of the four segments Pollay and Mittal identified reflected degrees of wariness. But one segment (amounting to about a third of the population) did hold positive global attitudes. This sort of segmentation raises interesting questions. Do these segments vary in size over time? Does their make-up differ over time? Do some of the wary segments react differently to external factors such as regulation, 'false' advertising publicity, product recalls, and corporate problems, or perhaps even the vast variety of new media? Is the depth of scepticism related more to some categories or types of advertising than others? These are important issues that could be dealt with tactically in a brand's advertising, given the right information.

At the end of their article, Pollay and Mittal ask the question, *What can the industry do?* They answer: 'The industry can profit from taking the public pulse every so often, utilizing a comprehensive belief inventory.'[27] For many reasons we feel strongly that a continuous reading of consumer beliefs and attitudes is superior to 'taking the pulse every so often', because of the dynamic nature of the factors that mediate those beliefs and attitudes. But however measured, it does make sense to track consumer opinion of advertising in general.

Summary

In this chapter we have defined what we mean by advertising and promotion and introduced the key concepts related to communication effects which will be used to organize our discussions throughout the book. We have discussed some of the common criticisms of advertising and the importance of consumer attitudes towards advertising and the important role played by trust. We have emphasized the vital role of continuous research in tracking consumer attitudes to advertising in general.

Questions to consider

1.1 What is the major difference between advertising and promotion?

1.2 What must occur if any persuasive communication is to be successful?

1.3 What are the four possible communication effects?

1.4   Which of the four communication effects are always communication objectives?

1.5   What are the four possible brand attitude strategies?

1.6   What is the difference between informational and transformational message appeals?

1.7   What does it take for advertising on the Internet to be successful?

1.8   What is 'puffery' ?

1.9   How can advertising contribute to economic stability?

1.10 Why is it important for an advertiser to be aware of trends in public attitudes to advertising in general?

Notes

1   *The New Shorter Oxford English Dictionary* (Oxford: Clarendon Press, 1990).

2   Daniel Strarch, *Principles of Advertising* (Chicago: A. W. Shaw, 1926).

3   Ibid.

4   McCarthy introduces this idea of the so-called Four P's of the marketing mix in his original text, *Basic Marketing: A Management Approach* (Homewood, Ill.: Irwin, 1960).

5   The four communication effects introduced here and discussed extensively in the text were originally described by John Rossiter and Larry Percy in *Advertising and Promotion Management* (New York: McGraw-Hill, 1987).

6   This notion of type of decision, as well as the idea of motivation, is at the heart of the Rossiter–Percy grid, originally introduced in ibid.

7   While we talk about involvement in terms of 'risk', this is a function of the processing required, and this is reflected in traditional models of low- and high-involvement processing. Low-involvement models suggest that advertising and other forms of marketing communication cause brand awareness and a *tentative* brand attitude, but actual brand attitude is not formed until after experience with the brand. Perhaps the best example of a low-involvement model is the one advanced by A. S. C. Ehrenberg in his 'Repetitive Advertising and the Consumer', *Journal of Advertising Research*, 14 (Apr. 1974), 25–34, and 'Justifying Advertising Budgets', *Admap*, 30 (Jan. 1994), 11–13. Low-involvement models have been called the 'weak theory' of advertising by John Phillip Jones in 'Advertising: Strong Force or Weak Force? Two Views an Ocean Apart', *International Journal of Advertising*, 9 (1990), 233–46.

    The generally accepted model of high involvement is the so-called 'hierarchy-of-effects' or H-O-E model. Here marketing communication first stimulates awareness, then affects brand attitude, which leads to brand purchase. In an interesting review of tests of the H-O-E model as applied to advertising, T. Barry and D. Howard suggest the results are 'inconclusive'. This is discussed in their paper 'A Review and Critique of the Hierarchy of Effects in Advertising'. *International Journal of Advertising*, 9 (1990), 121–35. The reason the results are inconclusive, of course, is that the model only applies where high-involvement decisions operate.

8   This follows directly from the Rossiter–Percy Grid referred to in n. 7.

9   McGuire often refers to these distinctions when discussing persuasive message appeals. A good summary may be found in his seminal work on attitude change, 'The Nature of Attitude and Attitude Change', in G. Lindsey and E. Aronson (eds.) *The Handbook of Social Psychology*, vol. 3, (Reading, Mass.: Addison-Wesley Publishing, 1969), 136–314. Another good reference is his 'Persuasion, Persistence, and Attitude Change', in I. deSala Pool *et al.* (eds.) *Handbook of Communication* (Chicago: Rand McNally, 1973), 216–52.

10 Larry Percy and John Rossiter provide a review of the psychological literature associated with logos, pathos, and ethos message appeals in their *Advertising Strategy: A Communication Theory Approach* (New York: Praeger Publishers, 1980), 102–4.

11 P. I. Rosenthal, *Concepts of Ethos and the Structure of Persuasive Speech*, *Speech Memographs*, 33 (1996), 114–26.

12 Juliana Korantegs, 'U.K. Internet Sites Enjoy Big Advertising Boost', *Advertising Age International*, Nov. 1999, 11.

13 John R. Rossiter and Steven Bellman, 'A Proposed Model for Explaining and Measuring Web Ad Effectiveness', *Journal of Current Issues and Research in Advertising*, 21 (1999), 13–31.

14 A good review of many criticisms of advertising may be found in William Leiss, Stephen Klein, and Sut Jally's *Social Communication in Advertising* (London: Routledge, 1997).

15 Martin Davidson, *The Consumerist Manifesto: Advertising in Postmodern Times*, (London: Routledge, 1992), 177.

16 Ibid.

17 Matti Alderson, 'Advertising: Self-regulation and the Law', in Norman Hart (ed.), *The Practice of Advertising* (Oxford: Butterworth Heinemann, 1995), 259–72.

18 These figures were supplied by Zenith Media and reported in *Advertising Age International*, Feb. 2000.

19 John E. Calfee and Debra Jones Ringold, 'The 70% Majority: Endorsing Consumer Beliefs about Advertising', *Journal of Public Policy and Marketing*, 13 (1994), 228–30.

20 Richard W. Pollay and Banwari Mittal, 'Here's the Beef: Factors, Determinants, and Segments in Consumer Criticism of Advertising', *Journal of Marketing*, 57 (1993).

21 P. Ippolito, 'Bonding and Non-bonding Signal of Product Quality', *Journal of Business*, 63 (1990), 41–60.

22 Calfee and Ringold, 'The 70% Majority'.

23 R. Sauer and K. Leffler, 'Did the Federal Trade Commission's Advertising Substantiation Program Promote More Credible Advertising?', *American Economic Review*, 80 (1990), 191–205.

24 Calfee and Ringold, 'The 70% Majority'.

25 Steven W. Colford, 'Fear of Being Painted with Pols' Dirty Brush', *Advertising Age*, (1996).

26 Pollay and Mittal, 'Here's the Beef'.

27 Ibid. 99–114.

Chapter 2

Perspectives on Advertising

For many years all areas of marketing research, and particularly advertising research, have been dominated by the cognitive information-processing perspective. However, in this chapter we review a wide variety of alternative perspectives on how advertising works and its effects on society. Some of these approaches have emerged as explicit criticisms of advertising and are not concerned with advertising as a managerial practice, but some new approaches to visual imagery and meaning-based models, together with an understanding of cultural differences, hold great potential for developing more effective advertising strategies.

Audiences and Individuals

The practice of advertising has for a long time been the butt of attacks from some economists (e.g. Galbraith)[1] and social and political theorists of the Frankfurt School (e.g. Marcuse).[2] But recently sociology and anthropology have started to take consumption seriously as a central element in modern (or postmodern) culture, and together with a developing interest in semiotics, advertising is now studied from a plethora of social science perspectives. To enable us to locate these differing and complex viewpoints we can organize them along two dimensions in relation to their assumptions about the audience (active vs. passive) and to the level of explanation at which they are working (individual vs. cultural) and construct a map of perspectives on advertising (see Fig. 2.1). This provides us with four sectors into which we can slot most approaches to understanding advertising and society: Sector 1, Passive Individuals; Sector 2, Passive Social/Cultural Groups; Sector 3, Active Individuals; and Sector 4, Active Social/Cultural groups.

Sector 1: Passive Individuals

The major theoretical approaches used by marketing academics and advertising practitioners for explaining 'how advertising works' are located in this sector.

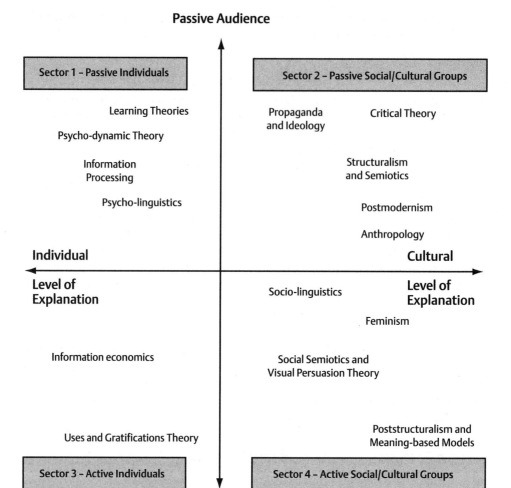

Fig. 2.1 Conceptual Map of Perspectives on Advertising

Learning Theories and Information Processing

Learning theories such as classical or Pavlovian conditioning focus on repetition and the creation of simple associations between elements (e.g. a brand name becomes associated over time with a slogan), while more sophisticated approaches to learning are concerned with how advertising messages are stored in memory. These processes of storage and retrieval are the major focus of the dominant perspective in cognitive approaches to advertising, that of information processing. The approach taken in this text is an information processing approach, which assumes that the audience can be conceived of as largely passive, and managerial attention should be concerned with how individuals move through various stages in making a decision choice (see Chapter 6). Whilst this model does not attempt to reflect the complex reality of communications, it is managerially useful in that it provides guidance for decision-making which other perspectives do not.

Psycho-dynamic Theories

Psycho-dynamic theories of advertising have a long history in both applied marketing research and critical views of advertising effects. The theories of Freud have been most popular in this regard, although Jung's ideas of symbolism and myths have also been used (and some would say abused). In the 1950s motivational research showed that the unconscious mind may play an important role in our responses to advertising,[3] while Vance Packard in his notorious book *The Hidden Persuaders* claimed that advertisers were cynically using hidden messages that were not noticeable consciously but having an irresistible effect on our unconscious minds via such (unproven) processes as subliminal perception.[4] We shall have more to say about this when we talk about processing messages in Chapter 10.

Freudian concepts have been fused with semiotic analysis by Judith Williamson in a sophisticated and insightful analysis of advertisements which claims to have revealed a code by which advertisers can (and do) tap into our unconscious desires and achieve their desired effects on our buying behaviour.[5] If only it was that simple!

Psycho-linguistics

Psycho-linguistics has been applied to advertisements by such people as Cook[6] and Vestergaard and Schroder,[7] who take advertisements as texts which can be studied using conventional linguistic theory. This close reading of language has largely been overtaken by the socio-linguistics approach which falls into Sector 4, and is difficult to square with the rather crucial fact that most advertising uses visual images as well as, or instead of, language.

Sector 2: Passive Social/Cultural Groups

Many of the most negative perspectives on advertising are located in this sector, where society is seen as being at the mercy of the power of organized capital through its vanguard weapon, which is selling the delights of consumer culture to unsuspecting dupes.

Critical Theory, Propaganda, and Ideology

An early approach was that of Raymond Williams, who posited that capitalism could only function with the help of advertising, as rational consumers would be satisfied with purely functional goods.[8] The task of advertising is to imbue them with 'magical' symbolic meaning so that we are never fully satisfied.

A seminal approach is that of the Frankfurt School, who brought a quasi-Marxist analysis to the modern phenomena of consumer society. Earlier concepts such as Gramsci's hegemony (which claimed that the masses were persuaded to accept the self-serving beliefs of the ruling classes through the power of mass communication, and thus could be used to explain why the working class would vote against its own class interest) were brought together with the concept of false needs to build a critique of the entire consumer society.[9] Marcuse describes the consumer as caught within a 'happy consciousness' where their alienation and lack of freedom is balanced with their enjoyment of consumer goods so that they are unable to escape and achieve an authentic existence.[10] In this view, advertising's role is to maintain the hegemonic dominance of consumption as the prime source of human happiness.

Advertising has been analysed by Galbraith as a very powerful form of propaganda which uses seductive imagery to form the ways in which we think about ourselves and society.[11] This view of advertising as ideology (a communication system which supports a vested interest by making the individual believe that his or her conditions are natural, and opposition unthinkable) has been applied to advertising by Goldman, who sees its effects as inescapable.[12] However, as will be discussed in Sector 4, although advertising may be the 'super-ideology' of late capitalism, its persuasive power has to be set against the countervailing effects of polysemy (adverts can have multiple possible interpretations) and oppositional cultural practices, where sub-cultural groups (e.g. gay rights activists) resist the intended meanings of advertisers by such means as parody and distortion.[13]

Structuralism and Semiotics

A structuralist position is taken by Williamson, who maintains that advertising operates as a structure which transforms the language of objects into that of people and vice versa, and that this translation system can be broken down into its structural elements and processes.[14] Based largely on work by Barthes,[15] her approach uses semiotics to analyse sign systems where a sign (such as an advertisement) has two parts, the signifier and the signified. The signifier is a material object (such as a product) and the signified is an idea and/or an emotion (such as excitement). As an analytic system semiotics has been widely used in discussions of advertising to unpack some of its communicative complexity, especially in relation to visual imagery.[16] But as more emphasis has been placed on the ability of active audiences to make their own interpretations of advertisements rather than just accept the semiotic codes they are presented with, semiotics has tended to be replaced by social semiotics and poststructuralism, which will be discussed in Sector 4.

Postmodernism

Writers on postmodernism have had a field day with advertising. Central to postmodern theory is the proposition that consumers no longer consume products for their material utilities but consume the symbolic meaning of those products as portrayed in their images. Products in fact become commodity-signs.[17] 'The real consumer becomes a consumer of illusions', as Debord has put it,[18] and 'the ad-dict buys images not things', in the words of Taylor and Saarinen.[19] Based on semiotic theory, postmodernism points to the uncontrollable disconnection of signifiers and signified, the 'free-floating signifiers' in contemporary consumer culture, where any sign can stand for any aspect of a product.

Advertising is the most visible manifestation of a culture bombarded with commodity-signs, a society where reality and illusion are difficult to distinguish, a society of simulations and even hyperreality which is 'more real than the real'. The phrase 'postmodern condition' depicts a society where media images dominate and construct our consciousness, where the boundary between high culture and popular culture disappears, style dominates substance, and, according to Strinati, 'as a result, qualities like artistic merit, integrity, seriousness, authenticity, realism, intellectual depth and strong narratives tend to be undermined'.[20] Advertising is seen as a major form of popular culture, which people consume as signs and imagery, and adverts can be seen as cultural products in their own right, consumed independently of the product being marketed.[21] As advertising increasingly uses images and references taken from other forms of popular culture such as cinema, television, and pop music it becomes less about telling us why we should buy a product and more about associating the product with style and image, often through a parody of advertising itself.

The complex relationship between the two symbol systems of popular culture and advertising has been explicated by Fowles, who maintains they are the 'two grand domains of public art in these times', if only because of their ubiquity.[22] Many postmodern discussions of advertising are partly a celebration of 'mass culture' in opposition to the Frankfurt School's derision of the way in which the 'culture industries' (cinema, radio, magazines) were 'liquidating' high culture and deceiving the working class into accepting a consumer society and abandoning their heritage of great art. However, other themes in postmodernism seem to be very much informed by critical theory and are really just the Frankfurt School updated for the late twentieth-century media environment. This dialectic continues in the cultural theories discussed in Sector 4.

Anthropology

Anthropology has drawn our attention to the fact that there may be no such thing as universal human nature, all behaviour being determined by culture,[23] and that different cultures have different communication styles. De Mooij has focused on cultural differences in relation to advertising, using Hofstede's 5-D model of culture.[24] This identifies five dimensions of culture that may affect advertising communication: power distance, individualism vs. collectivism, masculinity vs. femininity, uncertainty avoidance, and long-term orientation. If we then add the additional cultural dimension of high vs. low context, we can start to explore the complexity of communicating with people from different cultures. De Mooij points out that all models of how advertising works are culture-bound. In some cultures advertising is assumed to be persuasive in nature, while in others it is assumed to be about building trust. The role of pictures vs. words in carrying information and communicating meaning varies between cultures, as does the way people process information. In Chapter 5 we will discuss de Mooij's analysis of cultural differences in advertising. The overall conclusion is that in order to maximize effectiveness advertising must reflect local cultural assumptions and communication styles, but that advertising effectiveness research must also be culture-sensitive.

Sector 3: Active Individuals

In this section we look at disciplines that consider the audience for advertising as active individuals.

Information Economics

Information economics takes the view that a rational consumer already knows what he or she wants and the task of advertising is simply to inform them of availability and product specifications so as to make their search behaviour efficient.[25] However, only a minority of advertising falls into this information category. The majority of advertising does not appear to carry much information at all. Rather, it conveys implicit information about the brand or company which is advertising.

The fundamental proposition of economic theory is that the most important information which advertising conveys is primarily of commitment to a market and that consumers are active in forming inferences about the product quality of a brand from the amount of money that is spent: 'the persuasive quality arises from the fact, not the content, of advertising', as Kay puts it.[26] This seems to assert that all advertising is equally effective and content-free, and that to beat the competition you only need to spend the most money. We completely reject this perspective and maintain that there is effective advertising and ineffective advertising and the managerial task is to know and manage the difference.

Uses and Gratifications Theory

A very different perspective that also sees the advertising audience as active individuals is Uses and Gratifications Theory. This was the first attempt in communications theory to view the audience as active in their selection of content and messages from the media, and posits that much mass media use is goal-directed. This approach has been applied to advertising by O'Donohoe, who separates the marketing-related uses (information, choice, consumption stimulation, image, vicarious consumption) from a wide range of non-marketing-related gratifications.[27] Some of these gratifications will be discussed in Sector 4 as they are social in nature, but some important individualistic 'things people do with advertising' include: entertainment, escapism, role models, reinforcement of attitudes and values, and ego enhancement.

People often consume advertising as an entertainment form in its own right without any direct relevance to purchase behaviour, and this may also apply to the use of advertising for escapism and fantasy. Advertising may provide consumers with role models or other personal aspirations. This is directly related to the way in which we may also use advertising as a raw material to help us make sense of the world through the social construction of reality, and thus to reinforce our attitudes and our values.[28] Advertising may also help us to sustain our sense of self-worth by keeping us in touch with what is fashionable.

Sector 4: Active Social/Cultural Groups

This sector considers a number of relatively recent applications of theory to advertising. These views take a strong social orientation and assume active participation on the part of advertising's audience.

Socio-Linguistics

The socio-linguistics perspective draws on speech act theory in linguistic philosophy to emphasize the social action aspects of language, and on ethnomethodology to focus on how people use language in everyday situations to make sense of their world. It has extended the study of the use of language to include contextual aspects such as relations of class, power, and gender. The fundamental assumptions of socio-linguistics and its various forms of discourse analysis are that language is a medium oriented towards action and function, and that people use language intentionally to construct accounts or versions of the social world. Evidence for this active process of construction is said to be demonstrated by variation in language. This concept of variability is central for analysis, as discourse will vary systematically depending upon the function it is being used to perform.[29]

Language performs a variety of functions in the world and does not just represent it, for as Foucault pointed out, we are only able to think within the constraints of discourse.[30] Discourse is defined here as a system of statements that constructs an object, supports institutions, reproduces power relations, and has ideological effects. In applying this to advertising, Fairclough suggests that adverts 'help' the consumer to build a relationship with products, evoking an interpretive framework that situates both consumer and product in a 'modern lifestyle'.[31] In a study of overt sexuality in advertising, Elliott and his colleagues have suggested that if consumers could classify overt sexuality within an interpretive framework of 'art', then this 'functioned to legitimate positive interpretations by changing their category from sexual, which would be unacceptable, to art in which the same representation could then be given approbation. This seemed to be related to the product being given very little attention in the advertisement and therefore allowing it to be transferred from the commercial to the artistic realm where moral judgement could be suspended.'[32]

Myers allows more freedom to the audience in the construction of their 'position as consumers', and points to the potential for multiple interpretations of advertising.[33] We will discuss the possibilities for multiple meanings—polysemy—in more detail below when we consider poststructuralism. He also points out that adverts are not consumed alone, but depend on interactions with other people in order to make socially shared meaning.

Feminism

There is a long history of feminist analysis of advertising, almost always from a critical perspective that implicates advertising in maintaining and even enhancing aspects of male subordination of women. In an early empirical study Goffman demonstrated how many print advertisements presented woman in a subservient role to men, the men usually depicted as being above and in control of women.[34] Subsequent content analyses of female images in advertising showed a serious bias towards stereotyped sex-role portrayals of women as primarily homemakers.[35]

A particular focus for analysis has been the extent to which advertising imagery constructs woman's sense of beauty, and may in fact have harmful effects on their sense of worth. Certainly, this seems to be the conclusion from a number of experiments which have shown that exposure to idealized images of women in advertising resulted in women having lower levels of satisfaction with their own attractiveness.[36] Myers suggested that women are more vulnerable to manipulation by advertising than men because their upbringing and social expectations have already been influenced towards accepting gender stereotyping.[37] However, other research has found that women are perfectly able to identify and resist unrealistic gender portrayals in advertising.[38]

Social Semiotics and Visual Persuasion Theory

The recent development of theories of social semiotics, and in particular that of the Theory of Visual Persuasion, is an important development as the vast majority of advertising makes potent use of visual images. Kress and van Leeuwen present an articulated theory that attempts to explain how socially meaningful images can be built into visual narrative systems.[39] In common with socio-linguistics, social semiotics assumes that language varies with social context, and also assumes that the reader of any narrative system plays an active part in its interpretation.

Messaris presented the first comprehensive theory of visual persuasion, in which he utilizes the three semiotic concepts of iconicity, indexicality, and syntactic indeterminacy and applies them to persuasive images.[40] Iconicity relates to the fact that an image not only can represent an aspect of the real world but also comes with a wealth of emotional associations which stem from each individual's unique experiences in addition to the shared influences of culture. These associations are communicated not just by visual content but also by visual form. Indexicality is particularly relevant to photographs, and relates to the fact that a photographic image can serve as documentary evidence or proof of an advert's claims due to its 'authenticity'. He maintains, contrary to the claims of Kress and van Leeuwen, that there can be no precise syntax or explicit propositional system using visual images. It is precisely this relative 'deficiency' of visual syntax that gives images such persuasive power, as not only can they escape explicit interpretation by the audience and thus say what might be slightly unacceptable if fully spelt out, but also they can evade legal and moral restrictions through implicit communication. These are very important issues in relation to advertising and persuasion.

Poststructuralism

Poststructuralism is the final perspective we shall consider here, and this develops from both the Uses and Gratifications approach and from postmodernism. Literary analysis of texts has increasingly seen the growth of reader-response theory, which shows how a text works with the probable knowledge, expectations, or motives of the reader and leads to multiple interpretations of meaning.[41] A basic assumption here is that advertising, like other communicative texts, is subject to polysemy: that is, it is open to multiple interpretations by the audience. A number of recent studies provide empirical evidence of advertising's polysemic status.[42]

Polysemy is a potentially fatal threat to a successful advertising campaign because it can prevent the advertiser from getting the intended meanings across to the target audience. This will pose a significant limitation to a campaign's effectiveness and consequently a brand's future success in the market. In practice (rather than in theory) the interpretation made by the reader or viewer of an advert will be limited in two crucial ways. First, polysemy is limited by the text; some texts are more polysemic than others, being more or less open texts. Secondly, the reader or viewer represents a polysemic limitation in that rather than arriving at a unique, totally idiosyncratic meaning, they will subjectively interpret the text but the end result will be a meaning which is very similar to other individuals' subjective interpretations of the same text.

These individuals form an informal social group called an 'interpretive community'.[43]

Ritson and Elliott identified several interpretive communities within a group of young people, formed around readings of advertising texts, because the proximity of their social location and cultural competencies had led them to interpret the text in a similar way and with similar semantic results.[44] Indeed several groups showed an implicit awareness of their membership in an interpretive advertising community, and used this knowledge as part of their identification with the group.

A recent development in advertising theory is that of meaning-based models, which see advertising not as a conduit of information but as a resource for the construction of personal, social, and culturally situated meanings where human reality is mediated. In this view, consumers construct a variety of meanings from advertising as outcomes of a personal history and subjective interests as expressed through their life themes and life projects. In one study, three brothers had very different interpretations of the same five magazine adverts, each one constructing interpretations which resonated with their subjective interests, goals, and ambitions.[45]

Ritson and Elliott have extended the meaning-based approach from the individual's life world to social contexts, and have shown that advertising texts are often the source for a wide variety of social interactions in which advertising meanings are often changed, transferred, or solidified within the social contexts of everyday life.[46] This suggests an expansion of the concept of advertising context to include the social setting of the viewer alongside the textual setting of the advert. The impact that an advertising execution has on a particular audience and the uses to which it is put are partially dependent on the social context within which the viewer exists.

Implications for Advertising Strategy

The wide range of theoretical approaches to understanding how advertising works that we have discussed raises a number of issues for advertising management. Although the cognitive information-processing approach used in this book is pragmatically the most useful for developing and managing advertising strategy, it tends to ignore the way people interact with advertising in their day-to-day lives. To develop really effective advertising we must pay attention to the rich social and cultural environment in which people consume products, services, and advertisements, and seek to use this knowledge to build connections between individuals, social groups, and brands. Keep this in mind as we now turn our attention to the development and management of effective advertising strategy.

Summary

This chapter has reviewed a wide range of perspectives on how advertising works and on its effects on society. To help in this complex task we have introduced two dimensions which relate to assumptions about the audience (active vs. passive) and to the level of explanation (individual vs. cultural), and used these dimensions to construct a conceptual map. We conclude from this analysis that the cognitive information-processing approach is pragmatically the most useful for advertising management, but we must also pay attention to the broader social and cultural environment.

Questions to consider

2.1   What is meant by hegemony?

2.2   What is the major focus of learning theory approaches to advertising?

2.3   Is advertising an ideology?

2.4   Describe the different semiotic elements of the signifier and the signified in advertisements.

2.5   What are the major propositions of postmodern theory in relation to advertising?

2.6   How are popular culture and advertising interrelated?

2.7   How does economic theory suggest that advertising affects consumers?

2.8   What is meant by polysemy?

2.9   What is an interpretive community?

2.10   Why is the syntactic indeterminacy of visual images a potentially powerful element in advertising?

Notes

1   J. K. Galbraith, *The New Industrial Society* (Harmondsworth: Penguin, 1968).

2   H. Marcuse, *One-dimensional Man* (London: Routledge and Kegan Paul, 1964).

3   For a review of motivational research see P. Martineau, *Motivation in Advertising* (New York: McGraw-Hill, 1957) and E. Dichter, *The Handbook of Consumer Motivation* (New York: McGraw-Hill, 1964).

4   V. Packard, *The Hidden Persuaders* (Harmondsworth: Penguin, 1957).

5   J. Williamson, *Decoding Advertisements* (London: Marion Boyars, 1978).

6   G. Cook, *The Discourse of Advertising* (London: Routledge, 1992).

7 T. Vestergaard and K. Schroder *The Language of Advertising* (Oxford: Basil Blackwell, 1985).

8 R. Williams, 'Advertising: The Magic System', in R. Williams, *Problems in Materialism and Culture* (London: Verso, 1960/1980).

9 A. Gramsci, *The Prison Notebooks* (London: Lawrence and Wishart, 1971).

10 Marcuse, *One-dimensional Man*.

11 Galbraith, *The New Industrial Society*.

12 See R. Goldman, *Reading Ads Socially* (London: Routledge, 1992).

13 See Richard Elliott and Mark Ritson, 'Poststructuralism and the Dialectics of Advertising: Discourse, Ideology, Resistance,' in S. Brown and D. Turley (eds.), *Consumer Research: Postcards from the Edge* (London: Routledge, 1997), 190–219.

14 Williamson, *Decoding Advertisements*.

15 See R. Barthes, *Mythologies* (St Albans: Paladin, 1973).

16 See, for example, G. Dyer, *Advertising as Communication* (London: Methuen, 1982); A. Wernick, *Promotional Culture: Advertising, Ideology, and Symbolic Expression* (London: Sage, 1991); and R. Goldman and S. Papson, *Sign Wars: The Cluttered Landscape of Advertising* (London: Guilford Press, 1996).

17 See J. Baudrillard, 'For a Critique of the Political Economy of the Sign', in M. Poster (ed.) *Jean Baudrillard: Selected Writings* (Cambridge: Polity Press, 1972/1988).

18 G. Debord, *Society of the Spectacle* (Detroit: Black and Red, 1977).

19 M. Taylor and E. Saarinen *Imagologies: Media Philosophy* (London: Routledge, 1994).

20 D. Strinati, *An Introduction to Theories of Popular Culture* (London: Routledge, 1995), 225.

21 See M. Nava, 'Consumerism Reconsidered: Buying and Power', *Cultural Studies*, 5 (1991), 157–73.

22 J. Fowles, *Advertising and Popular Culture* (Thousand Oaks, Calif.: Sage Publications, 1996).

23 See C. Geertz, *The Interpretation of Cultures* (New York: Basic Books, 1973).

24 M. de Mooij, *Global Marketing and Advertising: Understanding Cultural Paradoxes* (Thousand Oaks, Calif.: Sage Publications, 1998).

25 See, for example, P. Nelson, 'Advertising as Information', *Journal of Political Economy*, 81 (1974), 729–54.

26 J. Kay, *Foundations of Corporate Success* (Oxford: Oxford University Press, 1993).

27 S. O'Donohoe, 'Advertising Uses and Gratifications', *European Journal of Marketing*, 28:8/9 (1994), 52–75.

28 See F. Buttle, 'What do People Do with Advertising?', *International Journal of Advertising*, 10 (1991), 95–110.

29 J. Potter, and M. Wetherall, *Discourse and Social Psychology: Beyond Attitudes and Behaviour* (London: Sage Publications, 1987).

30 M. Foucault, *The Archaeology of Knowledge* (London: Tavistock, 1972).

31 N. Fairclough, *Language and Power* (London: Longman, 1989).

32 R. Elliott, A. Jones, B. Benfield, and M. Barlow, 'Overt Sexuality in Advertising: A Discourse Analysis of Gender Responses', *Journal of Consumer Policy*, 18:2 (1995).

33 K. Myers, *Understains: The Sense and Seduction of Advertising* (London: Pandora, (1986).

34 E. Goffman, *Gender Advertisements*, London: Macmillan (1979).

35 A number of studies have dealt with this issue, such as A. Courtney and T. Whipple, *Sex Role Stereotyping in Advertising* (Lexington, Mass.: Lexington Books, 1983); and S. Livingstone and G. Green, 'Television Advertisements and the Portrayal of Gender', *British Journal of Social Psychology*, 25 (1986), 149–54.

36 M. Richins, M., 'Social Comparison and the Idealized Images of Advertising', *Journal of Consumer Research*, 18:1 (1991), 71–91.

37 Myers, *Understains*.

38 See, for example, Elliott *et al.*, 'Overt Sexuality in Advertising'.

39 G. Kress and T. van Leeuwen, *Reading Images: The Grammar of Visual Design* (London: Routledge, 1996).

40 P. Messaris, *Visual Persuasion: The Role of Images in Advertising* (Thousand Oaks, Calif.: Sage Publications, 1997).

41 L. Scott, 'The Bridge from Text to Mind: Adapting Reader-response Theory to Consumer Research', *Journal of Consumer Research*, 21 (1994), 461–80.

42 See, for example, the work of R. Elliott, S. Eccles, and M. Hodgson, 'Re-coding Gender Representations: Women, Cleaning Products, and Advertising's "New Man"', *International Journal of Research in Marketing*, 10 (1993), 311–24; R. Elliott and M. Ritson, 'Practicing Existential Consumption: The Lived Meaning of Sexuality in Advertising', *Advances in Consumer Research*, 22 (1995), 740–46; and D. G. Mick and K. Buhl, 'A Meaning-based Model of Advertising', *Journal of Consumer Research*, 19 (1992), 317–38.

43 See S. Fish, *Is there a Text in this Class? The Authority of Interpretive Communities*, (Cambridge, Mass.: Harvard University Press, 1980).

44 M. Ritson and R. Elliott, 'The Social Uses of Advertising: An Ethnographic Study of Adolescent Advertising Audiences', *Journal of Consumer Research*, 26 (1999).

45 Mick and Buhl, 'A Meaning-based Model of Advertising'.

46 Ritson and Elliott, 'The Social Uses of Advertising'.

Part Two

Planning Considerations

Chapter 3

What it Takes for Successful Advertising and Promotion

Now that we have begun to get some idea of what advertising and promotion are all about, it is time to turn our attention to how advertising works. The first step in learning just how advertising and promotion are meant to communicate a specific message to a particular group of consumers is to understand the various responses we must have to the message if it is to be successful.

If you were to ask most people, even most people involved with advertising, what the function of advertising is, almost everyone will say that advertising's job is to 'sell' a product. While ultimately it is true that advertising should lead to sales (or some other behavioural response, depending on the message—e.g. taking cans to a recycling centre or not drinking when driving), rarely is this the *specific objective* of a single advert or advertising campaign. Nevertheless, a marketer is unlikely to spend money for long on advertising if it does not in the end lead to more sales, and eventually more profit to the company.

Our point here is that advertising in and of itself is rarely meant to have a direct effect on sales. Instead, it usually initiates a series of responses on the part of the consumer, that, if successful, will *lead* to sales.

Communication Response Sequence

Some time ago William J. McGuire developed a theory of attitude change and over the years it has been applied to advertising.[1] If you stop to think of it, more often than not advertising messages deal with the maintenance or changing of attitude. In fact, as we have already mentioned, *brand attitude* is always a communication objective. This being the case, we have a great deal to learn about effective communication from attitude-change theory.

According to McGuire's notion of attitude change, there are six behavioural steps through which the information contained in any persuasive message (advertising and promotion in our case) must pass. At each of these steps, if the message is to be successful, there must be a positive response. The important point here is that if we have failure at *any* of these six behavioural response steps, the communication will not be successful.

McGuire argues that, for any persuasive message to be successful, obviously, the message must first be *presented* to the target audience. Once the target audience has the opportunity of seeing or hearing the message, the next step required is that they *pay attention* to the message. Having attended to the message, it is necessary to *comprehend* what is in the message, correctly understanding the conclusions being urged and, to some extent, the points being offered in support of the conclusion. Now that the target audience understands the message, to be successful the target audience must *yield* to those arguments in the message. Next, assuming we are not asking for an immediate response (e.g. to pick up the phone and order an advertised product straight away), the target audience must *retain* the arguments in the message and the fact that they have yielded to them or accepted them, and intend to behave positively as a result. Finally, if the message is ultimately successful, the target audience will in fact *behave* as urged by the message.

A critical point in understanding this sort of hierarchical model (that is, one where each step is necessary, and must occur in the order presented) is that it reflects *compounding probabilities*. Let us suppose McGuire is correct in his assessment that six behavioural steps are required for a persuasive message to be successful. If that is the case, the probability of actually going out and buying a product as the result of an advertising message would be:

$$P(p) \times P(a) \times P(c) \times P(y) \times P(r) \times P(b),$$

where: $P(p)$ = probability of being presented the message,
$P(a)$ = probability of paying attention to the message,
$P(c)$ = probability of comprehending the message
$P(y)$ = probability of yielding to the message
$P(r)$ = probability of retaining the intention
$P(b)$ = probability of behaving

Given a rather optimistic likelihood of 50 per cent of a target audience responding positively to each of the six behavioural steps, the overall probability of an actual purchase would be less than 2 per cent ($.50 \times .50 \times .50 \times .50 \times .50 \times .50 = .0156$). What this arithmetic exercise underscores is the very difficult job you are confronted with when trying to advertise effectively. Everything must work, and even when it does, you cannot expect to see great changes in consumer behaviour as a direct result of the advertising.

While McGuire's model was designed to explain how communication 'works' from a psychological standpoint, clearly it closely parallels what we know must happen if advertising and promotion are to work. For advertising and promotion to be effective, we must have exposure to the message, processing of the message, the correct communication effect, and target audience action.

Responding to Advertising and Promotion

The very first step that is necessary in order for advertising or promotion to be successful is for the prospective consumer to be *exposed* to the message. This means that it must be placed somewhere that the prospective buyer can see, read, or hear it, as appropriate. The opportunity for exposure to the message takes place through media of one kind or another. Exposure alone, however, is not sufficient. The prospective buyer must next *process* (respond to) one or more elements in the advertising or promotion if it is to have an effect. Processing of the message consists of immediate responses to the various elements in the advert or promotion (the words and pictures). First must come attention, then learning; then in some cases, as we shall see in later chapters, acceptance, and emotional responses.

The immediate responses to advertising and promotion must lead to a more permanent response; and, importantly, this permanent response must be associated with the brand or whatever other subject may be the object of the message, such as a company's image or a particular service. These more permanent, brand-connected responses are the *communication effects* that were introduced in Chapter 1: the two universally necessary communication effects of brand awareness and brand attitude, and category need and brand purchase intention.

If the advertising or promotion message has been correctly processed, the resulting communication effect, associated with the brand, will lead to a particular response when a member of the target audience decides whether or not to take *action* as a result of the message, such as purchasing the brand. More broadly this is called buyer behaviour, although in an advertising context we are generally seeking a response from a particular segment of the market that is known as the target audience.

Exposure corresponds to McGuire's presentation step; *processing* encompasses both the attention and comprehension steps of McGuire's model; *communication effects* encompass both the yielding and retention steps; and *action* corresponds to McGuire's behaviour step (see Table 3.1).

As McGuire has remarked, these sequences are just common sense. Our extension of his work also makes good common sense in understanding advertising. If you do not see the advertising or promotion, it has no opportunity of working. If you do not process the message, there can be no effects; or if you process the message incorrectly, you do not achieve the desired effect. If the correct communication effect and response both follow, then target audience action will result. While Rossiter and Percy provide an interesting argument for referring to these four essential steps as a 'buyer response sequence',[2] we like to think of them as *communication* response steps.

Table 3.1 How the Communication Response Sequence Compares with McGuire's Information Processing Paradigm

Four-step Sequence	Information Processing Paradigm
Exposure	Presented
Processing	Attention / Comprehend
Communication effects	Yield / Retain
Action	Behave

Following through an actual example of what we mean here should help you see why these four steps are necessary for advertising to be successful. Exposure, processing, communication effects, and action are steps you yourself go through when buying a product as a result of having seen or heard some advertising or promotion for it, even if you do not associate the behaviour with the advertising or promotion. Let's think about an ongoing campaign for Nescafé coffee.

Exposure. Assuming you watch TV even occasionally, you have probably been *exposed* to one or more commercials for Nescafé. The Nestlé Company runs a fairly heavy TV media campaign for this brand, along with print advertising and promotion.

Processing. If you were exposed to the advertising, sooner or later you probably paid attention to at least some parts of at least one of the commercials, or saw one of the print adverts. In other words, you *processed* the Nescafé advertising in some fashion, even if it was simply noting the brand name.

Communication effects. If you have learned the brand name 'Nescafé' from the advertising, and remembered what the brand's package looks like, you have responded to one of the core communication effects, brand awareness. If you have also formed an opinion for or against Nescafé, you have responded to the second core communication effect, brand attitude. Brand awareness plus a favourable brand attitude will largely determine whether or not you have actually tried the brand.

Target audience action. The ultimate target audience *action* for Nescafé is purchase. If you have purchased Nescafé, then the advertising has no doubt influenced you positively through the first three steps, leading to a positive behavioural response.

But, as we have already discussed, advertising is rarely responsible for purchase in and of itself. The rest of the marketing mix must contribute too: product performance, such as the coffee's taste (especially important for repeat purchase following trial of the brand); price, assuming the price is competitive with other coffee brands; distribution, assuming you can find the brand where you shop; and other forms of promotion, such as coupons or favourable comments from your friends. But the advertising undoubtedly has played a large part, especially if you were not previously aware of the brand.

Repetition and Response to Advertising and Promotion

Advertising in most cases must repeatedly influence this process in order to initiate trial and maintain repeated purchases of a brand. The one exception to this repetition or 'recycling' of the four steps is direct response advertising. With direct response advertising, the target audience goes through the sequence once, then terminates with action in the form of a single purchase. However, as you might imagine, most advertising tasks require repetition. For example, you may have had a number of opportunities to be exposed to advertising for a brand before you finally paid attention and processed the message sufficiently for the communication effects (probably brand awareness and brand attitude) to work and be strong enough for you actually to try a brand for the first time.

After you have purchased a brand for the first time, the advertiser obviously wants you to purchase it again and become a regular user. This generally requires repeated exposure to the advertising. You now have direct experience with the brand, which will affect your exposure, processing, and communication effects the next time around. This is especially true of brand attitude, which is now being influenced by experience. If you liked the product, positive brand attitudes can develop or be reinforced. But if you disliked it, this negative experience would likely prevent positive processing of future messages, leading to negative communication effects such as declining brand awareness and a change to a negative brand attitude.

While in an ideal world, one could hope that after sufficient numbers of people have formed positive brand attitudes, continued advertising would be unnecessary, this ideal is rarely reached. Not many brands can survive without advertising for any extended period. Communication effects become weaker or are interfered with by advertising for competing brands. Once this happens, the advertiser must begin again, creating new advertising that must be exposed to the target audience, then working through the full sequence.

To summarize, there are four steps in a communication response sequence that must be satisfied before advertising and promotion can be successful. First, the target audience must be *exposed* to the advertising. Next, they must *process* the information. After processing, there must be a *communication effect*. Finally, the target audience must take *action*. If any one of these steps is not influenced positively by the advertising or promotion, and reinforced over time, the advertising simply will not work. And if the advertising or promotion doesn't work here, it obviously cannot contribute to sales or market share, or to profit. All four steps in the sequence must be successfully accomplished if sales, market share, and profit are to increase.

Planning Overview

Careful planning is critical to the success of any venture, and understanding what processes are involved obviously leads to better plans. It is important to understand that overall advertising and promotion planning must correspond to what it takes for advertising and promotion to be successful—the four steps we have just reviewed. After a company sets profit objectives, which are based upon a certain level of sales or market share, a marketing plan lays out how marketing communication efforts will help meet those objectives (*action* sought by the target audience) and what the best message for the brand will be (*communication effects* needed) to maximize those marketing efforts. From the marketing plan the company and its advertising agency are able to develop a creative strategy to execute that message (to ensure *processing* of the message), and finally a media strategy (to ensure *exposure* to the message) to deliver the message.

Interestingly, you will notice that after the marketing objectives have been set, the *planning* sequence is the reverse of the sequence needed for advertising and promotion to be successful.[3] We must begin by thinking of the action we want our target audience to take. Next, we must consider the communication effects we need from the advertising or promotion to help facilitate that action. Then we must be concerned with how the

Table 3.2 Planning Sequence vs. Communication Response Sequence

Planning Sequence		Communication Response Sequence
Stage One	Target Audience Action	Step Four
Stage Two	Communication Effects	Step Three
Stage Three	Processing	Step Two
Stage Four	Exposure	Step One

message will be processed in order to ensure those effects, and finally where to place the advertising and promotion to optimize the likelihood of reaching the target audience (see Table 3.2). Each of these planning stages is discussed next.

Stage One: Objectives for Target Audience Action

Once the overall marketing objectives are set, the manager must decide where, from among all of the people in a market, the brand can expect to find the greatest likelihood of brand trial and usage. This will form the core of the target audience for advertising and promotion. This group of people, however, will not be particularly easy to identify, at least if we are looking for the best group possible. What we want are people who will respond to the advertising and promotion because they recognize something in it that connects, in their mind, the attributes of the advertised product with particular benefits that satisfy the reason or reasons they are interested in products from that particular category in the first place. We will be spending a lot more time with this notion in Chapters 5 and 10.

Depending upon the actual target audience chosen, the action desired will usually be trial for the brand or repeat purchase. For non-users of the brand, the behavioural objective would quite naturally be trial. But for those who have tried the product, we would want to encourage continued or more frequent repeat purchase of the brand. This issue will be dealt with in much more detail in Chapter 5.

Stage Two: Communication Effects

Advertising and promotion work only if they can stimulate a communication effect that will lead to action. The manager, in this second stage of planning, must determine which communication effects (i.e. which associations with the brand) need to be established in the mind of the target audience in order to cause them to take action. Once the manager has determined the most appropriate communication effects, they become communication *objectives* for the advertising and promotion. Those communication objectives are selected from options within the four basic communication effects already introduced: category need, brand awareness, brand attitude, and brand purchase intention. Chapter 8 will cover this subject in depth.

Returning to our Nescafé example, when the brand was first launched, the brand manager probably set a number of communication objectives for Nescafé advertising and promotion.

1. Since Nescafé was the original 'freeze-dried' version of soluble coffee (or 'instant'), the introductory advertising probably tried to stimulate interest in the soluble category as a whole, since Nescafé would benefit from an increase in primary demand for soluble coffee (category need).

2. Potential consumers of Nescafé would also need to learn the new product's name, and learn to recognize the product on the supermarket shelf (brand awareness).

3. Further, before trying Nescafé, potential new consumers would have to develop at least a tentatively favourable opinion of the brand (brand attitude), probably based upon the belief that freeze-drying improves the taste of soluble coffee.

4. Also, a definite intention to try it at the first opportunity would no doubt be a likely advertising communication objective (brand purchase intention).

Stage Three: Processing

Once the communication objectives for a campaign have been determined, the next step in planning is to devise (if in an advertising agency) or approve (if the advertiser) a creative strategy that will achieve the communication objectives. This involves designing specific advertising and promotions that not only meet the communication objective set in the marketing plan, but also maximize its likelihood of then being *processed* by the target audience in the intended manner to produce the desired communication effects. Since it is impossible to know beforehand if a new advert or promotion will accomplish these very important goals, that advert or promotion should be tested. We shall be dealing with creative strategy in some detail in Chapter 8.

At this point it is important to understand that there are many possible creative strategies which could achieve a particular communication effect (i.e. one of our four effects: category need, brand awareness, brand attitude, or brand purchase intentions). Continuing to think about our Nescafé example, if brand attitude was the primary communication objective, their advertising agency may have proposed a creative emphasis on the freeze-dried attribute and its taste advantage as a benefit. Or, the creative strategy could have focused on the same freeze-dried attribute, but directed its emphasis toward 'fresh' as a benefit. Either of these creative strategies (or many others) could probably have been capable of delivering the required communication objective.

We would hope that the actual creative strategy which was pursued was chosen over other alternatives because it was tested among a sample of the target audience and found to work better at stimulating the desired communication response.

Stage Four: Exposure

The last step in the planning sequence requires the managers to decide how best to expose the advertising to the target audience that has been selected. This fourth and final planning stage centres on media strategy. In this stage there are two main decisions to be made: media selection, or *where* to reach the target audience most efficiently; and media scheduling, or *how often* the target audience must be reached in order to produce the intended communication response and ultimate action.

The agency for Nescafé, for example, had to select and then schedule the media for the brand. The Nestlé Company, who markets Nescafé, does most of its consumer advertising on television, so this was no doubt the primary medium selected for the introduction of Nescafé. Additionally, no doubt other back-up or secondary media were used, such as print advertising and coupon inserts in newspapers.

The second media strategy decision, media scheduling, is a lot more complicated. How many times would the Nescafé advertising need to be exposed to the non-user in order to entice him or her to try the brand? And once tried, assuming a favourable opinion of the product, how often, between typical coffee purchase occasions, would the continuing advertising have to be seen or heard in order to keep the consumer aware of and interested in the brand? These problems concern the effective exposure of a brand's advertising. Of course, much more would have gone into this decision, and we will be covering this in Chapter 9.

Once all of these strategic media decisions have been taken, they must be made operational within the budget available. As we shall see, this is not always as simple a job as one might think. Frequently the optimum media plan is too expensive, and trade-offs in the schedule must be made.

The Advantage of Sequential Planning

There is no doubt that the planning process in advertising is complex and often difficult. While we have presented the planning process in terms of four stages that roughly parallel (in reverse) the four communication response steps required for advertising or promotion to be successful, at each of the four stages the manager is confronted with any number of questions that require answers, and decisions that must be made. Just as we saw with the communication response sequence, where the likelihood of success is a series of compounding probabilities, the four stages in developing advertising plans also encounter compounding probabilities. To be truly successful, the plans made at each stage must be as correct as possible, for each shortcoming will be enlarged or compounded at a subsequent stage in the planning process.

But there is a difference. With the four steps of exposure, processing, communication effects, and action, we have seen that for an advertising message to be successful overall *each* step must be achieved in order. In a sense, each step either succeeds or it does not. When one step fails the entire process fails, and the advertising is unsuccessful. For example, if the target audience does not see or hear the advertising, *nothing else will happen*. There will be no processing, no communication effect, no buyer behaviour to lead to sales or profit (at least as a result of advertising). Likewise, if there is exposure, but no processing (or no correct processing) of the message, nothing else will follow.

The planning process, on the other hand, enjoys the benefits of *sequential planning*. If the strategic decision made at a given stage does not work, this does not invalidate the decisions made at other stages (assuming, of course, that they were sound in the first place). Unsuccessful strategies need only be replaced by others that are better designed to meet the objectives set out in the marketing and overall communication plan. Unlike the four steps of the communication response sequence, a failure at one stage does not mean the entire process has necessarily failed.

Let us look at this question a little more closely. Before communication planning can begin, the most critical decision that must be made is: what is our marketing objective, and what will the role of advertising and promotion be in meeting that objective. It is the marketing objective that guides the planner in making decisions regarding target audience selection at the final stage of the planning process. If the wrong target audience is selected, this doesn't invalidate the marketing objectives, but it *will* invalidate any subsequent decisions that are based upon the target audience chosen. For example, if the marketing plan calls for increasing secondary demand for a brand (in other words, more usage from existing customers rather than attracting new users), a reasonable target audience might be brand loyals. But what if brand loyals, assumed to be the easiest to influence, already buy what they see as their limit? This would not mean that the underlying strategy of generating secondary demand for the product is wrong. A change to brand switchers as the target audience may be all that is needed. If brand switchers bought more of our advertised brand than that of the competitors', our sales would increase at our competitors' expense without running into problems with the consumer's self-imposed limit. Consumers would still be buying the same amount, but they would be buying more of our brand.

Similarly, the target audience selected will directly affect the communication objectives, because of their particular behaviour and attitudes. If the wrong communication objectives are chosen, this would not mean the target audience selection was wrong. Advertising based upon the wrong communication objective is unlikely to satisfy the goals of the marketing plan, but this would not be the fault of the target audience selected. In the same way, the communication objectives provide essential guidance for the creative strategy essential to the third stage; and the media strategy developed in the fourth stage will be based upon the target audience and creative strategy. Each stage is sequential, guiding the decisions made at the next stage. But a mistake made at one stage does not affect the *planning* that has gone before.

So, while both the communication response sequence and the planning sequence are hierarchical (remember, that is where one step must precede another), because of the starting point for the four-step communication response sequence, there are no alternatives to the successful execution of the desired response at each step in the sequence. On the other hand, there is room for adjustment in the planning sequence.

Relating Objectives and Goals to the Communication Response Sequence

In the marketing plan certain objectives will be set for the brand, and the manager must be able to relate these brand objectives to their advertising and promotion planning. On the face of it, there are certain obvious reasons for this. With clearly stated objectives, it is possible to coordinate advertising and promotion programmes with the plans of other company units. For example, financial planning and production plans should be matched with the advertising expectations of the brand. If we know our product sells significantly better at certain times of the year, advertising strategy will be geared to those peak selling periods. In terms of cash flow for the company, more money will be required during these periods for marketing expenses, as well as for raw materials and perhaps labour as well. Production will need to plan for greater manufacturing demands for the brand in terms of raw materials, labour, and time. With written objectives, all of the managers involved will know what the demands upon the company will be at any given time.

These written objectives are important for the advertising agency as well. If everyone working on an account—account service, creative, media, planning—knows what the advertiser's objectives are for the brand, there is less opportunity for misunderstandings between the agency and the client advertiser, or between groups within the agency. A third advantage to having written objectives is that they provide something against which both the advertiser and the agency can evaluate the brand's performance.

A distinction often made in marketing management, and an important distinction, is the difference between *objectives* and *goals*. In the broadest sense, objectives define the general ends sought by the company while goals are objectives that have very specific definition. For example, a reasonable objective for a brand might be to generally increase share among a particular target market while a goal would be to specifically increase share from 15 to 18 per cent in the next year. Generally speaking, most companies will have specific goals of one sort or another when they put together their marketing plan. After all, without some estimate of likely sales, not only will it be difficult to determine what money will be available for marketing expenditures, but the company will not be able to plan effectively for things like production schedules, raw material acquisition, etc. If only the vague objective of increasing sales has been adopted, it should be clear that important planning decisions will be very difficult, if not impossible, to formulate.

Having said all this, we must ask ourselves if it is also important to set goals rather than objectives for advertising as well. The answer is that 'it depends'. The reason it depends is that for advertising to be effective it must successfully negotiate each of the four steps in the communication response sequence, and each step makes different demands in terms of planning. Additionally, rarely are we considering the effect of a single advertisement or commercial. We will be much more likely to be considering a campaign made up of several adverts, as well as other marketing communication. In fact, we can actually look at this question of goals vs. objectives for each of the four steps we have been talking about as depending upon whether we are considering a single ad, or an entire campaign. Let us now examine whether or not goals or objectives are more appropriate for each of the steps (see Table 3.3).

Exposure. The first step is exposure and here it makes sense to set *goals* for an individual ad, but only objectives for a campaign. Why? Think about what we are attempting to do in this first step. We have been given a target audience definition, and as we plan for and buy media, we estimate that a particular advert that is a part of the plan will reach a certain percentage of the target audience. Goals for this percentage can and should be

Table 3.3 Setting Goals and Objectives relative to the Communication Response Sequence for Individual Adverts vs. Campaigns

	Setting Goals	Setting Objectives
Exposure	Adverts	Campaign
Processing	Adverts	Campaign
Communication Effects	Campaign	Adverts
Action	Campaign	Adverts

set. But over the course of the entire media planning period, many adverts will run, and run in different media and various media vehicles (e.g. a specific programme or magazine). As a result, more broadly based objectives are made, such as maximizing reach or frequency. We will learn more about these important terms in Chapter 9. For now, simply put, *reach* means the percentage of the target audience likely to be exposed to a message, and *frequency* the number of times these people will have the opportunity to be exposed.

Processing. At the second step, we again find that it is appropriate to set goals for an individual advert, and objectives for a campaign. The reason here is that while we can set goals for message processing, for example that 45 per cent of our target audience should pay attention to the advertising, it would be much more difficult to think of specific goals for an entire campaign. Instead, more broadly based objectives make sense here, like increasing overall attention to our advertising as a whole.

Communication effects. At the third step goals should be set for the overall campaign rather than any specific advert within the campaign. An appropriate goal for communication effects might be to raise overall favourable attitude to our brand from 3.5 to 4.0 on a 5-point attitude scale (where 5 means very favourable). Communication effects are meant to result from a campaign, not from a single advert or commercial within the campaign. Objectives for a single advert might be something like helping to increase positive brand attitude.

Action. To complete the four steps, goals should be set for target audience action only at the campaign level, and not for any single advert within the campaign. For example, a goal for the campaign might be to increase usage of our brand from 50 per cent to 56 per cent, while the objective for each advert is to contribute to this goal.

To summarize our discussion of goals and objectives as related to the communication response sequence, we have seen that objectives are set at every level of planning, but goals are set only where they make sense and can be measured. This means goals are set for an individual advert's contribution to exposure and message processing, and for a campaign when considering communication effects and target audience action.

Summary

This chapter has introduced the communication response sequence of four behavioural steps that are required for advertising to be successful: exposure, processing, communication effects, and action. We have then compared these steps to the sequential stages of strategic planning and emphasized the importance of relating brand objectives and goals to the communication response sequence.

Questions to consider

3.1 What are McGuire's six communication response steps?

3.2 What effect does the concept of compounding probabilities have on actual purchase outcomes of advertising?

3.3 Why is advertising rarely directly responsible for sales?

3.4 What are the four stages of the planning sequence?

3.5 What are the major components of media strategy?

3.6 What are the major benefits of sequential planning?

3.7 How are the objectives in the marketing plan related to advertising and promotion?

3.8 What is the difference between objectives and goals and which is appropriate for which steps in the planning sequence?

Notes

1 Perhaps the definitive work on attitude-change theory is McGuire's original essay, 'The Nature of Attitudes and Attitude Change', in G. Lindsey and E. Aronson (eds.) *The Handbook of Social Psychology*, vol. 3 (Reading, Mass.: Addison-Wesley Publishing, 1969), 136–314. This work and others of McGuire's are reviewed in terms of their implications for advertising by L. Percy and J. R. Rossiter in *Advertising Strategy: A Communication Theory Approach* (New York: Praeger, 1980).

2 J. R. Rossiter and L. Percy, *Advertising Communications and Promotion Management*, 2nd edn. (New York: McGraw-Hill, 1997).

3 This is something originally pointed out by John Rossiter and Larry Percy, in their 1987 text *Advertising and Promotion Management* (New York: McGraw-Hill).

Chapter 4

The Strategic Planning Process

The actual strategic planning process, as you might imagine, is much more specific than the general planning sequence we introduced in the last chapter. While that provided a good way of relating planning overall with the communication response sequence, a good strategic plan must go further. What must we do in order to link the target audience to our marketing objectives? How do we actually decide upon the appropriate communication effects? What determines the optimum creative strategy? What do we need to know in order to deliver our message effectively?

In this chapter we will be considering five specific steps a manager should take in developing a strategic plan for a brand's marketing communication. Then, in the next part of the book we will devote a chapter to each of these five areas as we explore in detail the important issues involved at each step.

As we have seen, the strategic planning process begins with a review of the marketing plan and a determination of what constitutes the target market. While the consumer is ultimately at the heart of any marketing communication programme, there may be many more people involved whom it will be necessary to consider in our planning. Deciding with whom we must communicate is obviously the first step in communication, so the strategic planning process begins there. While a company's marketing plan will have identified (or should have!) the general target market, we must know a lot more about the dynamic at work in the market place as people make decisions to buy or use products and services.

Step One in an effective strategic planning process is to link the general target audience with the overall marketing strategy. Then we can begin to address specific communication issues, taking *Step Two* and determining the best positioning for our brand within its marketing communication. *Step Three* is then to take the information developed in the first two steps and relate it to specific communication objectives. Once specific communication objectives have been established, *Step Four* develops a communication strategy. *Step Five* then considers how best to accomplish the task using available marketing communication options, and selecting the specific advertising or promotion media for delivering the message.

Before discussing these steps in more detail, we will want to consider some of the things managers should be looking for in the marketing plan.

Reviewing the Marketing Plan First

All marketing communication must be consistent with, and in support of, the overall marketing plan. Before a manager even begins to think about specific communication issues, it is important to review the marketing plan. Once this review is completed, it is then helpful to outline briefly 'what we know' about the market and the specific marketing objectives and goals for the brand. This sort of information often has a significant bearing upon what it is that you will want to communicate to your target audience, and it provides important background information for those charged with creating the message.

There are at least five key areas where the manager will want information *before* beginning the strategic planning process for marketing communication. Each of these five areas is discussed briefly below, and outlined in Table 4.1.

Product Description

What are you marketing? This may seem too obvious to think about, but that is precisely the point. While it may be obvious to the manager, it may not be quite so obvious to the target market. Think carefully, and write out a description of the product or service to be advertised or promoted in such a way that someone totally unfamiliar with it will understand exactly what it is. This description will then serve as background for the creative staff who will be charged with executing the brand's marketing communication.

Market Assessment

What is your overall assessment of the market in which you compete? It is important that your source of information here is absolutely up to date. The background information in the marketing plan could be as much as a year old. Be certain that nothing has happened in the market that could possibly 'date' this information. What is needed here is information about the market that might influence the potential success of the brand. How are brands performing relative to category performance? Where does the market seem to be heading? Are there potential innovations or new entries on the horizon? It is important

Table 4.1 Marketing Background Issues in Strategic Planning

Key Areas	Issues
Product Description	What are you marketing?
Market Assessment	What is your overall assessment of the market where you compete?
Source of Business	Where do you expect business to come from?
Competitive Evaluation	What is your competition and how does it position itself?
Marketing Objectives	What are the marketing objectives for the brand?

here to provide enough information to convey a good sense of the market, but only those things likely to have a real impact upon a brand's performance should be included.

Source of Business

Where do you expect business to come from? It is necessary here to consider both potential customers as well as competitors. Do we expect to increase our share of business by attracting new customers to the category, or by attracting users of other brands? What is there about the purchase behaviour of potential customers that we need to know? To what extent does our brand compete with products or services *outside* its category?

Competitive Evaluation

What is your competition and how does it position itself? It is essential to have an accurate understanding of just who your competition is in the *minds of the consumers*. Does the competitive set change depending upon how our brand is used? What are the creative strategies of the competition? It is a good idea to include examples of competitive marketing communication to illustrate the benefits they emphasize and their executional approach. As we shall see in Chapter 13, advertising and promotion must be unique, with its own consistent 'look and feel'. What media tactics are used by competitors? How do they employ advertising and promotion options? We need to have a good understanding of the environment created by our competitors' marketing communication.

Marketing Objectives

What are the marketing objectives for the brand? Here you want to include not only brand marketing objectives, but specific market share or sales goals as well. Usually, these numbers will be available in the marketing plan. If not, you must work them out for the brand. What we want is an estimate of what will happen if our marketing communication program is successful. This is critical for estimating how much will be available for marketing communication.

It is strongly recommended that the manager prepare a briefing document which summarizes each of these key marketing issues. With this review as background, it is time to begin the strategic planning process.

Implementing the Five-Step Strategic Planning Process

In effect there are three broad questions that must be addressed during the strategic planning process. *When* during the decision process should marketing communication reach the target audience in order to have the best chance of positively influencing the

Table 4.2 The Strategic Planning Process

REVIEW THE MARKETING PLAN AND:	
Step One	Select the target audience based upon the overall marketing strategy
Step Two	Determine the best positioning for the brand within its marketing communication
Step Three	Establish communication objectives that are related to steps one and two
Step Four	Develop a communication strategy based upon the communication objective selected
Step Five	Choose the best available communication options to deliver the message and satisfy the communication objectives

choice of our brand? The first two steps of the strategic planning process deal with this question. The second question is: *How* do we create consistent executions of the brand's position in everything we do? The next two steps of the process address this question. The last question asks: *What* are the most effective advertising or promotion media to deliver our message? This question is addressed in Step Five. Table 4.2 summarizes the five-step strategic planning process that addresses these questions. Next, we shall discuss in more detail each step of the process.

Step One: Target Audience

Consistent with what we saw in the last chapter, the first task is to decide upon the target audience. Whom we select must be consistent with the brand's marketing objectives. If part of the marketing strategy is to build the category, this means looking for new users. If the marketing strategy is to increase usage, this means focusing upon existing users. In the next chapter we will deal with the issue of target audience in depth. But for our purposes here as we outline the strategic planning process, we will consider four questions that should be addressed in the planning process (see Table 4.3).

Where are sales or usage to come from?

In our review of the marketing plan we looked at the question of where we expect business to come from. Now we must decide if our primary emphasis should be users or non-users of our brand. While we obviously want a broadly based business, realistically it is either a trial or repeat-purchase target audience objective which will best satisfy a brand's *marketing* objectives. Communication strategy will differ significantly, depending upon which of these target audience objectives is used.

Table 4.3 Key Target Audience Questions

- Where are sales or usage to come from?
- What do we know about the target audience?
- Which participants in the decision must the message reach?
- Where does the trade fit?

A trial objective means a non-user-based target audience, a repeat purchase objective a user-based target audience. But as we shall see in the next chapter, there are further distinctions to be made within each of these groups. With a trial objective, are we interested in new *category* users, or people already in the category but not using our brand? With a repeat purchase objective, are we interested primarily in those loyal to our brand or those who use our brand along with other brands in the category?

In this first step of the strategic planning process the manager should be thinking about the relationship between trial and repeat purchase objectives and which user groups to target.

What do we know about the target audience?

Once the appropriate user groups have been determined, the manager must build a profile of them. Too often this profile only includes demographic characteristics, e.g. 'women, 25–45, with children'. This is not nearly enough. Even when so-called 'psychographic' or 'lifestyle' descriptions are included, descriptions like 'outgoing with an interest in cultural activities', this is not enough. These descriptions are useful, but not often sufficiently discriminating. For marketing communication to be effective it is important also to know those target audience attitudinal and behavioural patterns that are relevant to a brand's marketing communication and media strategies. This means knowing what the proposed target audience's category behaviour is now, or is likely to be in response to our campaign, and how their underlying brand attitudes and motivations effect choices.

Which participants in the decision must the message reach?

Those who study consumer behaviour remind us that in a decision to buy or use a product or service a number of people may be involved, and they may play different roles in that decision process. In Chapter 6, when we discuss how consumers make decisions, we will learn a great deal about this. In that chapter we will introduce a decision grid that helps focus the manager's thinking on the various roles people may play in the decision to buy and use a brand. Basically, there are five possible roles involved:

- *Initiators* who propose purchase or usage;
- *Influencers* who recommend (or discourage) purchase or usage;
- *Deciders* who make the actual choice;
- *Purchasers* who make the actual purchase;
- *Users* who use the product or service.

One person may play all five roles in the decision process, or others may be involved, playing one or more roles. It is critical to understand who is involved and what roles they are playing. When we address our target audience we are talking to them as individuals, but as *individuals in a role.*

Where does the trade fit in?

We must never lose sight of the fact that the trade is almost always a part of our target audience. It is easy to fall into the trap of thinking only about consumers when considering a target audience. But our strategic planning requires a *total* look at the marketing communication task, and when advertising and promotion to the trade is used it must be integrated with advertising and promotion to the consumer. Even if the message is different (as is likely), the 'look and feel', the theme, must be consistent with the overall creative umbrella. An example of why this is so important is seen in relation to the five decision roles referred to above. It would not be unusual for the trade to be either an 'initiator' or 'influencer' in a brand decision, especially for high-ticket consumer goods or in business-to-business marketing.

Step Two: Determining a Positioning

The second step in the strategic planning process is to determine how best to position your brand. While the basic brand positioning will no doubt already be established (except for new products), the strategic planning process must address the particular *communication* positioning that will be adopted for your brand. We must decide whether we want to link the brand in the target audience's mind to the category need in which they already see it competing, or *re*position the brand by linking it to another category need where the brand will have a stronger competitive advantage. In such cases the repositioning rarely involves a drastic change, but rather a switch to another branch or level of the way the overall product category is partitioned in the mind of the target audience.

We shall spend a great deal of time in Chapter 7 discussing the importance of understanding how markets are partitioned. To give you an idea of what we mean by partitioning, think about snacks. What comes to mind? Is it a package of crisps, say, or a candy bar? Clearly both are snacks, but would you position a candy bar against crisps? Unlikely. Candy bars are a different type of snack, and likely to satisfy a different category need. We might imagine the overall snack category dividing (i.e. partitioning) into salty vs. sweet snacks. Sweet snacks might then be seen as splitting into baked snacks like biscuits or pastries vs. confections like candy. Candy bars, then, following our example, would be in the confection category, and positioned against the category need associated with it.

But even within the candy bar category itself there may also be different types of bars that offer various positioning options against more specific category needs. For example, there could be 'luxury' bars to satisfy an exotic indulgence, like Inca in France; or pure chocolate bars, like Cadbury, to satisfy a need for just chocolate; or filled bars, like Lila Parse in Germany. The issue of how the category need is defined for our brand is a critical decision in the strategic planning process.

In addition to establishing the category definition in order to identify the market where the brand or source will compete, positioning also requires us to look for a differential advantage for our brand. How will we present our brand to the target audience? What benefit does our brand offer, or what benefit could our brand be seen as offering, that gives it a unique advantage over its competition? As we shall see in Chapter 7, this will require a thorough knowledge of a target audience's basic attitude toward our brand and its major competitors. What do people believe about the brands in the category? What is important to them, and which brands deliver on these important attributes and benefits? Again, the answers to these questions are critical for successfully positioning our brand, and must be addressed as part of the strategic planning process.

Step Three: Establishing Communication Objectives

In setting communication objectives we are taking the first step in addressing what we want our marketing communication to say about our brand in order to motivate the target audience to take whatever action is required. Communication objectives are quite simply the communication *effects* for which we are looking. In Chapter 1 four communication effects were briefly introduced: category need, brand awareness, brand attitude, and brand purchase intention. It is from this set of possible communication effects that we draw our communication objectives.[1]

Communication objectives will be covered in depth later in Chapter 8. Here we shall look briefly at how each of the four communication effects is likely to translate into communication objectives.

Category Need

It doesn't make much sense to try and sell a brand if there is no perceived need for the product. Most of the time this is not an issue. But for innovative new products, for example, until there is awareness of *the new product as such*, it is almost impossible to create interest in a brand of that new product. Before there were TVs or home computers or CD players, there was really no 'need' in the market for such products. When they were developed, it was necessary to establish the 'need' by introducing the product category itself to the public. Once people understand what this new product category is all about, it is possible to talk about brands.

This does *not* mean that you do not talk about your brand at the same time you are introducing the product category. What it means is that when category need is a communication objective, it is first necessary to emphasize in your marketing communication what this new product category is all about in order to create interest in the category, while also positioning your brand to satisfy this new 'need'.

Category need may also be a communication objective where demand in a category seems to be slackening. This can happen, for example, when something goes out of fashion for a period of time. If this should occur, it may be necessary to *remind* people of a latent category need. This is a particularly appropriate strategy for market share leaders who should reap the benefit of any renewed interest in a category.

Brand Awareness

Brand awareness is *always* a communication objective, regardless of what type of marketing communication you may be using in your campaign. While this is an obvious point for advertising, it is also true for everything from promotion to packaging. Without this essential link between the message and the brand, there is no chance for effective marketing communication. In Chapter 8 we shall see that brand awareness is not as simple a construct as it might seem.

As we briefly mentioned earlier, there are at least two types of brand awareness that the manager must consider: recognition and recall. *Recognition* brand awareness is when someone 'sees' the brand at the point of purchase and is reminded of a need for it. *Recall* brand awareness occurs when someone has a need and must 'remember' the brand as something that will satisfy that need. There are important strategic and tactical issues that must be considered in relation to the type of brand awareness, as we shall see later in the book, depending upon whether recognition or recall is central to how products or services are chosen.

Brand Attitude

Like brand awareness, brand attitude is *always* a communication objective for every type of marketing communication used in a campaign. As we shall see when discussing Step Four, brand attitude strategy is at the heart of developing a communication strategy for advertising and all other forms of marketing communication. Brand attitude itself, as a communication effect and objective, is a complex issue (again, to be covered in some depth in Chapter 8).

While brand attitude strategy is a function of how involved someone is in the decision to purchase or use a product or service, along with what motivates them, the brand attitude itself relates more specifically to the brand. It may be thought of as a summary of what a person knows and feels about a brand, providing the link between the brand and the motive to buy or use it.

Brand Purchase Intention

Too often managers feel that the most important, perhaps the only, objective for marketing communication is to generate sales or usage of their product or service. While this is almost always a *marketing* objective, it is not often a primary communication objective. Of course we want our marketing communication to help contribute to an intention to buy or use the brand, but this is rarely the primary objective. Without brand awareness and brand attitude there can be no brand purchase intention.

Brand purchase becomes a primary communication objective (*always* along with brand awareness and brand attitude) when the principal thrust of the message is to 'act now'. As a result, brand purchase intention is more likely to be a communication objective when using promotion than when using advertising.

Regardless of the types of marketing communications that make up a campaign, whether traditional advertising or promotion, direct marketing, store signs, or even packaging, all have the potential to create any of the four communication effects we have just discussed. But as we shall learn in later chapters, some types of marketing communication are better suited than others to creating these effects. As a result, the choice of communication objectives will *directly* affect the choice of which type of advertising or promotion is to be used.

Step Four: Developing a Communication Strategy

The fourth step in the strategic planning process is to develop a communication strategy. In many ways, most of this book deals with this issue. We have already mentioned that in Chapter 6 we will be discussing consumer decision-making. In addition to helping the manager better identify a target audience, understanding how consumers make decisions also helps in developing a communication strategy.

Looking at consumer decision-making provides a dynamic view of the process which a target audience is likely to go through in making a decision to buy or use a product or service. It provides valuable insight into the likely motives driving behaviour. Understanding *why* people do what they do is critical in establishing an appropriate brand attitude strategy, and the brand attitude strategy is at the heart of successful advertising and promotion, as it is with *any* marketing communication. Additionally, identifying the various people involved in the purchase or usage decision, along with the roles they play, helps target messages more effectively to the appropriate audiences in their appropriate roles.

In effect, understanding consumer decision-making helps answer two fundamental questions the manager must ask in developing a communication strategy: what is the brand attitude strategy, and what do we want the target audience to do as a result of our marketing communication?

What is the Brand Attitude Strategy?

The first question that must be addressed in setting communication strategy is what brand attitude strategy to use. The answer to this question follows from an understanding of the four quadrants detailed in the Rossiter–Percy grid.[2] This concept was briefly introduced in the first chapter, and will be covered in depth in Chapters 8 and 11. As part of their grid, Rossiter and Percy suggest that brand attitude strategy is a function of the two fundamental considerations we introduced in the first chapter: (1) whether there is low or high involvement with the purchase or use decision, based primarily upon the target audience's perceived risk (either in fiscal or psychological terms); (2) whether the underlying motivation that drives behaviour in the category is positive or negative. Combining these two considerations produces the four brand-attitude strategy quadrants of the grid: low involvement with negative motives; low involvement with positive motives; high involvement with negative motives; and high involvement with positive motives.

Understanding these constructs is critical for identifying the appropriate brand attitude strategy, which in turn is critical for creative strategy. That is why we shall spend so much time on this issue later in the book. At this point, all we need is an initial understanding of its importance and where it fits in the strategic planning process.

The creative tactics that maximize the likelihood of an effective message are directly linked to the brand attitude strategy which follows from the appropriate quadrant defined by the Rossiter–Percy grid. These tactics differ significantly for each quadrant. Strategies associated with negative motives require *information* to help solve or avoid a problem, while those associated with positive motives must help *transform* the consumer, for example by gratifying a want by meeting a need for social approval.

As you might imagine, the creative message needed for brand attitude strategies associated with negative motives will be quite different from those associated with positive motives. For the informational strategies, the focus will likely be on attributes associated with a benefit, while for transformational strategies the focus will generally be centered around the emotions associated with attitudes toward the category or brand.

This will all become much clearer in Chapters 8 and 11. For now, the contrast between Advert 4.1*a* and 4.1*b* should help illustrate the point. The advert for Flash (4.1*a*) deals with an informational strategy, and you can see the benefit emphasis is on attributes: 'they clean', 'they kill germs', 'they go on working for up to 12 hours', The advert for Jordan's Luxury Muesli (4.1*b*) reflects a transformational strategy, and you can see that

(a)   (b)

4.1 (*a* and *b*) An example of the contrast between the benefit emphasis of an informational strategy, seen in the Flash advert (4.1*a*), and the more 'emotional' focus of a transformational strategy, seen in the advert for Jordan's Luxury Muesli (4.1*b*). Courtesy Flash and Jordans

the benefit focus is more 'emotional', utilizing a strong visual which projects a very positive feeling, with the copy in the headline reinforcing the overall sense of luxury contentment.

Creative tactics also differ as a function of involvement. Because involvement is defined in terms of risk, when there is low involvement it is not necessary for the target audience to be really convinced before buying. If they make a mistake, they haven't suffered much of a loss. On the other hand, when involvement is high, the potential buyer does not want to make a mistake. In this case the target audience must be convinced by the marketing communication before buying. Consider how much an advert would need to *convince* you that a new snack was 'great tasting' or that a new personal computer was the 'best yet' before you would think of buying. Before buying the computer you would certainly want to know more, but you would probably be willing to take a chance on buying the new snack based only on the feeling that it might be something you would like.

What we have are four potential brand attitude strategies based upon involvement and motivation: low- vs. high-involvement informational strategies and low- vs.

high-involvement transformational strategies. The quadrant that best reflects the decision process of the target audience is what determines the brand attitude strategy.

What do we Want the Target Audience to Do?

What *exactly* do we want people in our target audience to do as a result of our marketing communication? Because there may be a number of people in the decision process, we may want them to do different things. Will this require different messages? Even if there is only one person playing all of the roles in a decision, will different messages or delivery vehicles be needed (e.g. media advertising vs. direct mail or point-of-purchase)? A consumer decision model will help here in identifying exactly what is involved with the roles that people in the target audience are playing in purchase or usage decisions.

For most fast-moving consumer goods (fmcg's), general advertising may be sufficient to handle all of the roles people are playing in the decision process. Fmcg's are generally low-involvement products, so those in a position to initiate or influence a decision probably will not need a specifically targeted message that is different from the message directed to the decider or purchaser. But with high-involvement decisions, the roles people play may indeed require specifically targeted messages.

In addition to this fundamental consideration, the manager must also ask if there is any particular information or incentive the target audience will require if they are to respond to our marketing communication in the desired manner. Do we want people to call or visit for more information, or directly seek out the brand? Do we want to change the timing of their decision process, perhaps accelerating it or breaking a seasonal pattern? Perhaps how the target audience actually goes about making choices should be addressed. For example, the optimum positioning for our brand may require the target audience to reconsider how they currently evaluate category alternatives, placing a higher importance on a benefit where our brand is stronger.

Asking what it is that we actually want the target audience to do helps focus the manager's thinking and provides some of the detail necessary for developing an effective communication strategy.

Step Five: Choosing Communication Options

In this fifth step of the strategic planning process, the manager must select the best communication options to deliver the creative message. This is the first step in considering media selection, and one of the most important things the manager will need to think about at this point is the different relative strengths of advertising and promotion in satisfying the four possible communication objectives. (Remember from our earlier discussion of traditional advertising and promotion that from a practical standpoint we are talking about marketing communication options only in terms of advertising and promotion, while nevertheless realizing that every type of marketing communication should be evaluated in the planning process.)

Basically, both advertising and promotion should have a significant effect upon brand awareness; the primary strength of advertising is brand attitude, while the primary strength of promotion is brand purchase intention, and neither advertising nor promotion can have much of a direct effect upon category need. The relative strength of traditional advertising vs. promotion will be covered in more detail in Chapter 14.

Marketing Communication Task Grid

To help in the selection of the best possible communication options, it is a good idea at this point to summarize just what communication tasks are likely to be required to meet our communication objectives fully. What do we mean by communication tasks? In the broadest sense, it is simply what we want to occur as a result of our marketing communication. This was addressed in Steps Three and Four. What we want to do now is begin to draw things together.

The thinking that went into the first three steps of the strategic planning process provided a solid understanding of the target audience, the best communication strategy to address that target audience, and the communication objectives required to optimize the strategy. A useful way of linking this thinking to the selection of potential communication options is with a Marketing Communication Task Grid.

Basically a Marketing Communication Task Grid looks at the decision stages that consumers go through in making choices, and for each stage details the communication tasks required and the target audience to be addressed. Then, for each stage asks the manager to think through 'where and when' to reach the target audience for maximum effect, and the various marketing communication options available to accomplish this task (see Fig. 4.1).

While we shall look at decision stages in detail in Chapter 6, it will pay to consider some generic decision stages now in order to see how the manager can use the task grid. The first stage in most decisions will be some form of need arousal, after which a brand is selected, purchased, and used. Using these decision stages, how will the manager apply the task grid? For each of these four decision stages, the manager will list the *specific* results desired from the appropriate communication effects serving as communication objectives. Next, again for each of the decision stages, the target audience *at that stage of the decision process* will be detailed. Then the manager must decide the best way of reaching the target audience and the best marketing communication option to do the job, again for each stage of the decision process.

As an example, consider the initial decision stage, need arousal. One obviously needs to stimulate brand awareness and a certain level of brand attitude. But what kind of awareness, and do we need simply to raise or maintain the awareness? In terms of brand attitude, must we teach the target audience something new about the brand; do we need to interest them, stimulate enquiry, give them a good feeling, or underscore a unique feature? As you can see, in detailing the specific results we want from the communication we are going well beyond just the communication effect we are seeking, and thinking through what we want to happen as a result of meeting our brand awareness and brand attitude communication objective.

Next, what specific members of the target audience are we to reach at this need-arousal stage? Most likely it will be those playing the initiator or influencer role, but this information will come from your understanding of consumer decision-making. Which of the possible multiple influencers should be the primary target audience; will we need or want secondary or even tertiary target audiences at this stage; if so, can we afford them?

Decision Stages	Communication Tasks	Target Audience	Where and When	Marketing Communication Options
List appropriate decision stages	List **specific** results desired in terms of communication effects at each stage	Determine primary target audience group to reach at each stage	Determine best way to reach primary target audience group at each stage	List best marketing communication options for accomplishing the communication tasks at each stage

Fig. 4.1 Marketing Communication Task Grid

Source: Adapted from L. Percy, *Strategies for Implementing Integrated Marketing Communications* (Lincolnwood, Illinois: NTC Business Books, 1997)

For most fmcg's, the best way of reaching the target audience will probably be *prior* to purchase in order to build or sustain brand salience (a 'presence' of the brand in the consumer's considered set) and attitude, but also perhaps at the point of purchase for stimulating impulse purchases. In stimulating need arousal for most business-oriented products, the best way to reach the initiators and influencers would most likely be at their place of business.

Questions for the manager to ask, once these issues have been addressed, should deal with identifying the best marketing communication options to effect the desired need arousal (the decision stage we are talking about in this example). What media will best sustain awareness? Should print advertising, billboards, or coupons be used? Will a direct mail campaign aimed at the initiators and influencers of a business decision be best, or would targeted trade magazines make more sense?

In addition to dealing with possible communication options at a general media level, specific media should also be addressed. The point of the Marketing Communication Task Grid is to help *focus* the manager's thinking to optimize the best choice of available communication options. If money were no object, you could proceed to implement everything suggested by the Marketing Communication Task Grid. Unfortunately, that is almost never the case. Rather, realistic budget considerations will require the manager to determine the best mix of communication tasks that can be accomplished with available resources.

We have only dealt with the first decision stage in this example. These same questions will need to be addressed for *each stage* in the decision process. Once a Marketing Communication Task Grid has been completed, listing potential marketing communication options for the various communications tasks associated with each decision stage, the manager must give thought to the *specific* marketing communication media likely to optimize the communication objectives. The work done in completing a Marketing Communication Task Grid provides the manager with an opportunity to review objectively what might be done to exert a positive influence on each stage of the decision process. It does not necessarily provide 'the answer', but it does provide a summary of our best understanding of what should be done to optimize a marketing communication programme.

Matching Media to Communication Objectives

So far we have been looking at media rather generally in terms of communication options. Now we must deal specifically with the appropriateness of particular marketing communication options for specific communication objectives. Direct mail may be a good way of reaching a certain target audience, but is it a good way of delivering the creative message needed to satisfy the communication objective involved?[3] Television advertising offers broad reach, but is it suited to the communication objective? As we shall see below, certain traditional advertising and promotion media will be more or less appropriate for particular communication options for specific communication objectives.

Because brand awareness and brand attitude are always communication objectives, let us focus on them. There are at least three important considerations the manager must look at when selecting media options in order to ensure a proper match with the communication objective (see Table 4.4). The first is *visual content*. To what extent does a particular medium facilitate visual communication? This is critical, for example, when brand recognition is required for brand awareness.

Second, how much *time* is available for the target audience to *process the message*? In some cases, for example when the brand attitude objective involves a high-involvement, informational strategy, which is the case for most consumer durable products (televisions, home computers) and many business purchase decisions, the target audience will

Table 4.4 Considerations for Selecting Media to Match Communication Objectives

Visual Contact	Critical for recognition brand awareness and transformational brand attitude
Time to Process Message	Important for high involvement informational brand attitude
Frequency	Higher frequency is needed for recall brand awareness and low involvement transformational brand attitude

need time to process the message in order to learn enough about the brand. In other cases, such as with most fmcg products, only a brief exposure time is necessary. When more processing time is necessary, broadcast media like television and radio will not do, but they will be very appropriate when only a short time is needed for processing.

The third consideration is *frequency*. Some media, such as broadcasting and newspapers, offer the potential of high frequency. In other words, the creative message can be presented frequently to the target audience. Think of how many commercials for a particular brand you see during the broadcast of a football match. Other media options, for example direct mail or monthly magazines, are much more restricted in terms of frequency. True, a brand could have multiple insertions in a single magazine, but because of the narrow reach of magazines compared to something like television this will not usually be a very efficient way of obtaining higher frequency for your creative message. When the brand awareness objective is recall, higher frequency is required than when it is recognition. When the brand attitude objective involves a low-involvement, transformational strategy, again we need more frequency. *Why* this is necessary will be covered in Chapter 8. The strategic planning process makes it possible to come to more efficient and effective decisions as to how to implement a marketing communication campaign.

Summary

We have now introduced the five decision steps in the strategic planning process: target audience, determining a positioning, establishing communication objectives, developing a communication strategy, and choosing communication options. We have explored each stage at the preliminary level and the following chapters will discuss each stage in depth. We have considered how the Rossiter–Percy grid can be used to guide brand attitude strategy and creative tactics, and this will also be covered in depth in later chapters. We have also introduced the Marketing Communication Task Grid and explained how it can be used to help focus the manager's thinking about communication options.

Questions to consider

4.1   What are the five steps of the Strategic Planning Process?

4.2   What roles may people play in the decision to buy and use a brand?

4.3   When might category need be a communication objective?

4.4   What is the difference between recognition brand awareness and recall brand awareness?

4.5   When might brand purchase intention become a primary communication objective?

4.6 Why is an understanding of consumer decision-making critical in establishing an appropriate brand attitude strategy?

4.7 What are the fundamental considerations that produce the four brand attitude strategy quadrants of the Rossiter–Percy grid?

4.8 How does an informational strategy differ from a transformational strategy?

4.9 What are the components of a Marketing Communication Task Grid?

4.10 What must be considered when matching media options with communication objectives?

Notes

1 John Rossiter and Larry Percy first introduced this idea of establishing communication objectives from the expected effects of communication in their 1987 text *Advertising and Promotion Management* (New York: McGraw-Hill).

2 The Rossiter–Percy grid was originally presented in *Advertising and Promotion Management*, and subsequently summarized in more detail in J. R. Rossiter, L. Percy, and R. J. Donovan, 'A Better Advertising Planning Grid', *Journal of Advertising Research*, 32:5 (1991), 11–21.

3 Rossiter and Percy devote a great deal of their discussion of media selection in their 1997 text *Advertising Communication and Promotion Management* (New York: McGraw-Hill) to the need for a proper correspondence between communication objectives and the specific vehicles needed to deliver such an objective.

Part Three

Laying the Foundation

Chapter 5
Target Audience Considerations

As we saw in the last chapter, the first step in the strategic planning process for marketing communication (or for *any* advertising or promotion programme) is to determine the appropriate target audience. The marketing plan establishes marketing goals and defines the target market. From this target market it is necessary to identify the specific target audience required for a particular marketing communication programme. If we are advertising, are we more interested in attracting new users or encouraging existing users to buy or use more often? If we are running a promotion campaign, is it to reward loyal customers or attract new users?

Selecting the appropriate target audience is not as easy as it may seem. From the examples above, a simple distinction between customers and non-customers may seem to suffice. But this is *not* enough. Much more definition is required. For example, what if someone is a customer only because they haven't yet found something they like better? Or what if they wouldn't think of using any other brand? Obviously it will be important to understand just what type of customers (and non-customers) comprise the market if the manager is to make intelligent target audience decisions.

Target Audience Groupings

There are a number of different ways to think about target audience groups. Gerrit Antonides and W. Fred van Raaij take a broad view of target audience groups, describing them in terms of three levels: general, domain-specific, and brand-specific.[1] At the *general level* they consider target audience groups in terms of descriptive characteristics such as standard demographics (e.g. age, income, geographic location), lifestyle variables (e.g. active in sports, travel), and psychographics (e.g. outgoing, risk-taking).

At the *domain-specific level* target audience groups are described in terms of those characteristics associated with a product or product category. This would include such things as category usage behaviour (e.g. eat a lot of frozen food, own three automobiles), attitudes toward the product category (e.g. I think vitamins are a waste of money), and how decisions are made in the category (e.g. a need is aroused in the product category, a set of brands is considered, one is selected, purchased, and used).

At the *brand-specific level* they describe target audience groupings in terms of such things as brand loyalty (i.e. buys one brand in the category all of the time, or at least most of the time), beliefs about the brand (e.g. Brand A has more cleaning power than Brand B), and brand buying intentions (e.g. I will buy Brand A if it is on special, otherwise I will buy Brand B).

In effect Antonides and van Raaij look at possible target audience groupings in terms of their overall descriptive characteristics, how they behave generally in the product category, and how they behave toward specific brands. Rossiter and Percy, on the other hand, discuss target audience groupings primarily in terms of their brand purchasing behaviours.[2] They suggest a brand could potentially be purchased by any of five buyer groups: *brand loyals* who regularly buy your brand in the category, *favourable brand switchers* who buy your brand but also buy competitor brands, *other-brand switchers* who buy more than one competitor brand, but not your brand, *other-brand loyals* who regularly buy a competitor brand, and a fifth group of *new category users* who are entering the category for the first time or re-entering after a long time.

The Antonides and van Raaij classifications of target audience groupings offer the manager a general-to-specific way of profiling potential target groups. However, this classification screen doesn't really help the manager *select* an optimum target audience. In this regard the Rossiter–Percy notion of looking at brand purchase behaviour is more helpful. In fact, it makes a great deal of intuitive sense. It is a logical refinement of the basic customer vs. non-customer division of the target market.

Obviously, you will want to retain consumers who are loyal to your brand and reinforce that loyalty. This is the hard core of any business. Those who buy your brand along with the occasional competitor brand, however, probably make up the bulk of any business. Here it is necessary to retain these customers and try to encourage less usage of other brands. As we shall see later in this chapter, the objective with these two groups is *repeat purchase*.

If we are looking for new customers, those who buy more than one other brand, but not ours, probably offer the best potential. Since they already buy more than one brand, it should be possible to persuade them to include our brand (either in addition to, or in place of, one of the brands they now buy). The most difficult prospect would be those who tend to be loyal to a competitor brand. But those who do not use the category will not be easy to attract as new customers either. In addition to persuading them to buy your brand you must also persuade them to enter the category in the first place. Again, as we shall see later, the objective for these non-users of your brand is *trial*.

But the real key to identifying an optimum target audience must go beyond basic brand purchase behaviours, even though this does provide the foundation. *Loyalty* to a brand is the key. Those really loyal to a brand will not be tempted by competitor brands. Unfortunately, most people are switchers of some kind. So what exactly is 'loyalty'? Loyalty is the result of people's attitudes, both toward the brand *and* the category.

In recent years the notion of loyalty has become a key issue in marketing. A number of models have been proposed that seek to identify 'loyal' consumers. Perhaps the most familiar is the so-called 'conversion model'.[3] This model looks at consumer attitudes toward brands in a category as well as their involvement with the category. It analyses consumer attitudes on four key dimensions: interest in competitive alternatives, overall satisfaction, category involvement, and intensity or ambivalence. On the basis of a 'black-box' analysis,[4] consumers are assigned to one of four groups based upon their 'vulnerability' to switching brands: the more vulnerable, the less loyal.

We would like to introduce our own loyalty 'model' based upon how involved a person is with the category and how satisfied they are with their current brand. As we discussed briefly in Chapter 1, involvement is a key dimension for defining brand attitude strategy for advertising and promotion. It is also a key dimension in determining brand loyalty. How much 'risk' does a consumer see in switching brands? Obviously, for most fmcg's there will be very little perceived risk in switching brands. But for more durable goods purchases and services such as banking and health care, there can be a good deal of perceived risk. In considering a target audience, if the perceived risk in switching is low, a person *may* be open to switching brands; if perceived risk is high, even if they are open to the idea of switching, it may be seen as too much trouble. If someone is very satisfied with the brand they use, they will be less likely to switch; if they are unsatisfied, they will be more open to switching.

If we combine these two dimensions of perceived risk in switching and satisfaction, we can look at the target market in terms of four loyalty-related potential target audience groupings (see Fig. 5.1). The four loyalty groupings are defined as:

Loyal: highly satisfied with their brand and unlikely to switch;
Vulnerable: satisfied with their brand, but little perceived risk in switching;
Frustrated: not satisfied with their brand, but feel the risk is greater than the potential gain in switching;
Switchable: neither satisfied with their brand nor inhibited from switching.

This model offers more than simply looking at brand purchase behaviours, in that people who regularly buy a brand may be Loyal *or* Frustrated. If they are frustrated, the manager must find out why and address the problem in order to retain them as customers and

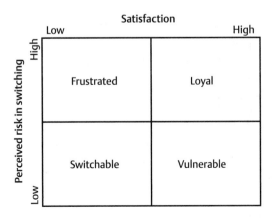

Fig. 5.1 Loyalty Model Groupings

build brand equity. On the other side, someone who regularly buys a competitor's brand, too, may be either Loyal or Frustrated. Those who are frustrated obviously offer more potential for trying our brand if we can overcome their perceived risk in switching.

Looking at consumers who buy more than one brand in a category (e.g. Rossiter and Percy's Favourable Brand Switchers and Other-Brand Switchers), we see that they can be either a Switchable *or* a Vulnerable. Those who buy our brand along with others in the category may or may not be satisfied with our brand. They may see *all* brands as merely adequate, and be open to something better. For our Switchable customers it will be necessary to build a more positive brand attitude; for our Vulnerable, we will want to reinforce the already favourable brand attitude, strengthening brand equity to reduce the likelihood of using other brands. Switchable competitive brand users should be open to trying our brand, given the right message. They already use more than one brand, but are not particularly happy with any of them. Our competitors' Vulnerable's, on the other hand, will be a tougher sell. They do use multiple brands, but are generally satisfied with them. To attract these switchers we must convince them they should also be using our brand.

It might help at this point to think about this idea of brand loyalty with regard to some of your own brand purchase behaviour. Think about some of the things you buy. Do you regularly use the same brand of toothpaste or shampoo? What about candy or snacks? If you do, how open would you be to trying other brands? For most people, they *really* like only a few brands they use, and are not likely to try others in those categories even with a substantial promotional inducement. Those are the brands that have what is known as strong *brand equity* for those consumers. But the vast majority of brands people use are bought more out of habit than from a strong commitment to the brand.[5] This is why it is so important to look beyond brand purchase behaviour and to also determine the degree of loyalty to a brand.

Selecting a Target Audience

When the manager selects a specific target audience, it is not enough simply to look at the projected market share or revenue potential. Equally important is the *cost* of gaining these new customers (e.g. trial objective) or increasing usage (a repeat purchase objective).[6] If our objective is to gain new users for the brand, the cost will be greater than protecting or building on our current business. For potential users who are not new to the category, the cost of attracting them will be substantial, but going after regular users of a competitor brand will be even more so.

In selecting a target audience, one must be consistent with the marketing plan, but the manager must also approach selection with an eye on the ROI (return on investment). Next, we discuss the cost implications of selecting a target audience on the basis of brand loyalty.

Cost Implications and Brand Loyalty

Except in very rare circumstances you should only consider a prospective group as a target audience if the expected return outweighs the cost. The manager must give this matter careful attention. At a very basic level, it will cost less to maintain your business than to build on it, to build on it than attract new business. In selecting the target audience to satisfy the marketing objective for the brand, the manager must consider the *value* of successfully reaching the appropriate target audience group. What is the potential increase in business relative to the cost of the advertising and promotion required to secure it? We will now consider the relative cost-effectiveness of the brand loyalty groups for existing and potential customers.

Loyal

Our brand's loyal customers are relatively inexpensive to maintain at their current level of use. They are quite satisfied with our brand and are not interested in switching. All we really must do is remind them of their positive attitude toward the brand, reinforcing brand equity. But if we want to *increase* their usage, that could be expensive because it means changing an already established and satisfactory behaviour pattern.

Those loyal to other brands are for all practical purposes beyond the reach of a competitor brand, ours included. They are not disposed attitudinally to switching brands, and even if they were the perceived risk is too great. What could we offer? If we literally gave the product away, assuming they would even try it, the likelihood that they would actually then purchase our brand is very low. They simply do not have a sufficiently positive motivation to try our brand. On the other hand, if there is really a significant *demonstrable* difference with our brand such that an immediate positive brand attitude would result from trying it, perhaps it would be worth the cost of giving the product away in a large-scale sampling promotion. But the price would be high, and would need to be carefully looked at in terms of ROI. Generally speaking, this could only be a consideration for fmcg's. Higher-priced products and those with longer purchase cycles would present too high a cost *and* risk.

Vulnerable

Our brand's vulnerable customers have a generally positive brand attitude, but do not see us as necessarily better than some other brands in the category. Maintaining this positive brand attitude is relatively inexpensive, but to retain or increase their usage of our brand will cost more because of the pressure of competing messages and promotions from other brands. Remember, they see no risk in switching even though they are happy with our brand.

Vulnerable competitor brand users who do not include our brand among those they buy, because they are generally satisfied with the brands they are currently using, will tend to be somewhat costly to attract. What keeps them from being very costly is their disposition to switch among different brands in the category. Unless they have tried and rejected our brand, in which case they will be very costly to reach, the cost of addressing the vulnerable competitor brand users relative to our own vulnerable users should only be moderately higher. We need to build a positive brand attitude in their mind for our brand, and provide an incentive for trial.

Frustrated

Because our frustrated users are not satisfied with our brand, even though they regularly use it, maintaining their current level of usage should be relatively inexpensive since they are reluctant to switch (for whatever perceived risk). But our goal should be to build a more positive brand attitude to increase brand equity and satisfaction. This will be more costly.

Frustrated competitor brand users are not happy with the brand they regularly use, but because they perceive some risk in switching, it will be somewhat expensive to get them to overcome this sense of risk. Either marketing or advertising and promotion should be aimed as much at the barriers to switching as at building a positive attitude toward our brand.

Switchable

Our own switchable customers will be somewhat expensive to deal with as a potential target audience. Even though they are currently using our brand, they are not particularly satisfied with it, and they are already using other brands as well. This means they will be receptive to effective advertising and promotion for other brands, especially those they already use. This makes our task that much more difficult. A considerable effort must be made to build a more positive brand attitude (as with our Frustrated users). It will cost even more if we want to increase their usage of our brand.

The cost of attracting competitor brand Switchables should be roughly the same as reaching our own, assuming they have not tried and rejected us. While they do not now buy our brand, they are not particularly happy with the ones they do use; and they are disposed to using multiple brands. In both cases it will be necessary to build a more positive attitude in their minds for our brand.

These cost implications associated with selecting target audiences based upon brand loyalty are summarized in Table 5.1. While we believe that brand loyalty is the best way of looking at target audience optimization, we also understand that there are certain practical limitations. Unlike brand buyer groups, where there is plenty of syndicated research available tying brand behaviour to media behaviour (e.g. the Target Group Index[7]), brand loyalty groups must be determined through basic research conducted by the company. However, the increased effectiveness of the concept of brand loyalty groups over that of brand buyer groups is worth this extra effort.

Table 5.1 Relative Cost Associated with Brand Loyalty Target Audience Selection

	Cost to Protect or Build Users	Cost to Attract Non-users
Loyal	Low	Very high
Vulnerable	Low-moderate	Moderate-high
Frustrated	Moderate	Moderate
Switchable	Moderate-high	Moderate-high

Profiling a Target Audience

Whether we are dealing with brand loyalty groupings or brand buyer groupings, it is usually helpful to have a more detailed understanding of the target audience selected. This means looking at your target audience in terms of those characteristics that Antonides and van Raaij describe as 'general-level' characteristics.[8] They consider general-level characteristics as more or less permanent characteristics of people, and classify them as either objective or subjective. *Objective characteristics* are things like age, education, income, and place of residence—what are known as demographics and geographics. *Subjective characteristics* are things like lifestyle, personality, and values—what are known as psychographics. Next we shall take a closer look at these general-level characteristics.

Demographics

Demographics are perhaps the best-known and most familiar of all target audience descriptions. Because they are objective characteristics, they are not only easy to identify, but conceptually it is quite easy to think about them. If you market laundry soap powder, it is only natural to think in terms of women, especially women with families, as your target audience. But this does *not* describe a target *audience*. Are we really interested in all women with families? Hardly, since some are loyal to other brands, and others use liquid laundry detergents.

It is certainly true that some products or services suggest a very specific demographic group as a target. Toys are for families with young children, baby products for mothers with infants, retirement services for older adults, and Ferraris for people with high incomes. But these are demographic characteristics that define a *target market*, not a target audience.

This is a very important distinction. It may make sense to define a target market in terms of particular demographic characteristics, but then *within* that demographic, we must select the target audience in terms of brand loyalty or brand buyer groupings. Once the target audience has been selected, additional demographics (or geographic or psychographic characteristics) may be looked at in order further to refine the target audience for a particular campaign. Cosmetics may be targeted at women (the target market), but once the appropriate brand loyalty or brand buyer groupings are used to select the target audience, it would not be unusual for a particular campaign to target younger or older women—not all younger or older women, but younger or older women within the appropriate brand loyalty or brand buyer groupings.

One of the major reasons demographics are inappropriate as primary criteria for selecting a target audience is the large amount of individual variation that can exist within a particular demographic. For example, one of the most popular misuses of demographics is with socio-economic classification. This is an attempt to group individuals in terms of their supposed 'social class', related to occupation and education or income. Antonides and van Raaij have defined social class as a 'summary of people's ranking in society with respect to profession and education'.[9] But there are potential pitfalls with such a classification.

Perhaps the most fundamental error is the assumption that all members of a particular class behave in the same way and hold the same basic attitudes about a product or service they use. This is rarely, if ever, the case. In a very interesting study conducted by Nestlé, a group of upper-middle-class shoppers, all with substantial six-figure incomes, were questioned about their use of higher-priced frozen foods. All used frozen foods, but some refused to consider the somewhat more expensive brands. When asked why, they answered that they couldn't afford to *indulge* themselves because of large, pressing expenses such as school fees or dental braces for children. When it was pointed out that the actual difference in price was very small, and in terms of the frozen food they bought would amount to no more than a Euro/dollar or two per month, this simply did not matter. They could easily afford the money. But because of the 'luxury' image of these higher-priced frozen foods, this group of wealthy people felt they could not 'indulge' themselves, even though they could well afford it.

At an even more fundamental level, demographics can be misleading when used to profile a target audience. Someone with a high income may have a lot of expenses while a retired couple with a lower income may nevertheless have significant disposable income. Age, in many ways, is less a matter of actual years than a state of mind. As Robert East has stated so well, 'demographic factors are only loosely connected to the attitudes, beliefs and opportunities that more directly control behaviour'.[10]

Demographics can be useful, but the manager must be very careful how they are used. They should *never* be used as the primary selection criteria for a target audience, but they can often prove helpful in profiling the brand loyalty or brand buyer groupings for particular campaigns.

Geographics

It is always important to understand the geographics of your target audience. But, as we noted with demographics, this is generally a part of the *target market* descriptions. Are we looking at a multi-country marketing programme, or a programme restricted to a particular country or small group of countries, or are we dealing with a regional or local product or service? Geographics can clearly help define the target market, but they can also be useful in better defining a target audience. Because of regional preferences or attitudes (more about this when we discuss culture below), campaigns may be targeted for particular geographic areas. If so, this becomes part of the target audience definition for that campaign.

Geographics, then, can help define a target market area, and can be used (if needed) to help narrow down the *location* of the target audience as defined by brand loyalty or brand buyer groupings. But, just as we saw with demographics, they should *never* be used as primary selection criteria for a target audience. Do we really think that just because people live in a certain area they hold identical attitudes towards, and preferences for, particular products or brands? Of course not. Unfortunately, this is the underlying assumption of something called 'geodemographics'.

Geodemographics

By combining geographic information with demographic information markets can be described in terms of geodemographics. One of the best-known geodemographic systems in Europe is offered by Acorn (which is an acronym of A Classification Of Residential Neighbourhoods).[11] Acorn classifies residential neighborhoods on the basis of postal codes, with certain demographics (usually income or social class) in common.

The assumption here is that people who live in a particular neighbourhood will have similar buyer behaviour patterns. While Acorn does include demographic profiles in their database, this underlying assumption is wrong. There is simply no reason to believe that people living in similar neighbourhoods are going to be loyal to the same brands, or will be more or less vulnerable or frustrated in a particular product category.

What has made geodemographic systems like Acorn (and other systems such as Mosaic and Pinpoint) so popular is that they make it very easy to target direct mail on the basis of postal codes. But the manager must ask, just what is being targeted? Once a target audience has been defined in terms of brand loyalty or brand buyer groups, *if* a correlation is found between the target audience and geodemographic classifications, fine. However, geodemographics should never be the sole or even primary criterion for selecting a target audience.

Psychographics

The word 'psychographics' first entered the vocabulary of advertising in the late 1950s following the introduction of a new technique for studying consumer behaviour called *motivational research*. The father of this technique was a psychologist, Ernest Dichter. The idea behind motivational research was to conduct a number of in-depth personal interviews with consumers in order to discover why they behave as they do in the market. Dichter suggested from one of his studies, for example, that men buy convertibles as a surrogate mistress, reflecting the sublimated desire of the purchaser for the lifestyle of a roué.[12] You can see why creative people in advertising loved this sort of thing.

Today, while still a subjective classification, psychographic or lifestyle variables reflect a broad assessment of non-product-related characteristics that could influence purchase- or usage-related behaviour. Psychographics give you a picture of a person's lifestyle by looking at such things as their general attitudes, interests, and opinions (often referred to as AIO). Some general examples of psychographics would be someone's attitude toward sports or fitness, their willingness to take risks, traditional vs. modern taste, concern with the environment, political opinions, concern with fashion, and innovativeness.

You can see how knowing such things about a target audience would help in better understanding them, but as with the more objective demographic and geographic characteristics, they cannot define the target audience. The primary use of psychographic information is in helping to guide creative development of the message, and possibly to help in selecting specific media vehicles that reflect a particular lifestyle.

One UK advert for a Ford Explorer (Advert 5.1) clearly reflects a 'lifestyle' dimension. It depicts a young, upscale family that enjoys spending time outdoors. But the fact that a Ford Explorer 'fits' their lifestyle does not mean that their lifestyle should define the target audience. There are many people who enjoy an outdoor lifestyle yet have no

WORK LESS

AND YOU'LL BE RICHER.

EXPLORER | Find yourself.

5.1 An example of how an advert can reflect the lifestyle of its target audience, increasing the likelihood of being processed. Courtesy Ford Motor Co.

interest in a sports utility vehicle (i.e. they are not in the category), or if they are interested, may be interested in a different size (e.g. the Mercedes M-Class) or have a loyalty to another brand (e.g. a Land Rover). So while lifestyle can help target a *message*, as is well illustrated in the Ford Explorer advert, the message must be for those *within* the appropriate brand loyalty or brand buyer grouping who have that lifestyle.

Another difficulty with trying to classify people in terms of lifestyle is that it is generally not stable across product categories. At a very general level there tends to be some commonality, but not at the specific level. For example, someone who has a keen interest in outdoor activities may not be interested in some specific outdoor activity.

Social Class

Back in our discussion of demographics we spent some time talking about social class. Practically speaking, it is a demographic variable, but many marketers also consider it a lifestyle variable. As Rossiter and Percy have put it, although social class is measured by *combining demographics*, it functions as a *lifestyle* variable.[13] The assumption is that people in different social classes are likely to have different lifestyles. One of the more popular European classifications of social class is provided by the Joint Industry Committee for National Readership Surveys. They classify people into six groups: (A) Upper Middle Class, (B) Middle Class, (C1) Lower Middle Class, (C2) Skilled Working Class, (D) Working Class, and (E) those at the lowest levels of subsistence.

Even though Antonides and van Raaij feel that social class is an important determinant of consumer behaviour,[14] as we pointed out in our earlier discussion, while there may be a certain *implied* relationship between social class and consumer behaviour, it is more likely to be at the target market, not target audience, level. We may be targeting the upper middle class or middle class for designer clothing, but for our brand marketing communication strategy we must understand the appropriate brand loyalty or brand buyer groupings from the social classes in order to pinpoint the target audience. As Fill has reminded us, relying upon social class can be misleading and prone to excessive generalization.[15]

Values

Another popular lifestyle measure is centred around 'values'. But again, assuming we can find a good summary measure of someone's values, while this may be useful in profiling a target audience or in trying to explain behaviour at a general level, it has more utility in the development of creative *execution* than it does for communication strategy. There are a number of value classification systems used by advertisers, but we would recommend *extreme* caution with all of them.

Perhaps the best-known such value system is VALS, introduced in the late 1970s (VALS-1) and revised in the late 1980s (VALS-2) by SRI International in the US. VALS-2 classifies people into eight groups based upon two dimensions: 'resources' (things like education, skills, and income) and 'self-orientation'. The names of the eight resulting groups are meant to suggest the 'most important value' to that group: Strugglers, Believers, Fulfilleds, Strivers, Achievers, Makers, Experiencers, and Actualizers. Of course, rather detailed descriptions are available for each of these groups.

One of the many problems with VALS has been its inability to be applied across countries—not just, say, between the US and Thailand, but between more homogeneous-seeming countries in Europe like Sweden and Germany. Another problem stems from the fact that a person can only belong to one group. This is always a problem with any rigid system that aims at too much generality.

Another values system is marketed by Synergy Brand Values in the UK and Europe. Their system is based upon Maslow's hierarchy of needs. It utilizes the dimensions of 'inner-directed', 'outer-directed', and 'sustenance-driven' to classify people into seven groups: Self-explorers, Experimentalists, Conspicuous Consumers, Belongers, Survivors, Social Resisters, and the Aimless. These groups vary in size from the Aimless at 6 per cent of the population to Survivors at 23 per cent.

These social value groups, however, have the same problems as those discussed above for VALS, as well as the fact that they are based upon Maslow's work. We are in agreement with the many authors cited by Landy[16] who feel that Maslow's theory is of more historical than functional value, and conclude that there is really no evidence to support the high regard in which his theory seems to be held by many marketers.

Culture

Another important lifestyle characteristic is culture. We have chosen to consider culture as a lifestyle variable rather than a demographic or geographic variable because the idea of 'culture' is not necessarily fixed. To say that someone is from England or France or Germany is not the same thing as saying they are English, French, or German. Antonides and van Raaij have defined culture as 'the entirety of societal knowledge, norms and values', very much as they define lifestyle as 'the entire set of values, interests, opinions and behaviour of consumers'.[17]

Culture is clearly related to how people behave, and for that reason is an important target audience profile variable. But additionally, in Europe as elsewhere in the world, how someone looks at or understands advertising messages is heavily influenced by their culture. In fact, as de Mooij has pointed out, the advertising 'style' of different European countries clearly reflects the cultural values of that country (see Table 5.2). There seems little doubt that culture conditions perceptions, and this influences how people respond

Table 5.2 How European Advertising Style Reflects Cultural Values

Britain	**Reflects a highly individualistic society**
	• Ads show individuals or couples (large groups are rare)
	• Much use of direct address
	• Strong focus on humour
	• Only European country where class differences are recognized in advertising
Germany	**Reflects the need for structure, directness, and facts**
	• Characterized by the need for structure and explicit language to avoid ambiguity
Italy	**Reflects a collectivist culture**
	• Drama and theatre, with strong role differentiation reflected in depiction of males and females
Spain	**Reflects collectivist culture, but takes into account individualistic claims**
	• As a result, less direct than advertising style of Northern Europe
	• Use of visual metaphors
France	**Reflects a need to be different**
	• A propensity for the theatrical and the bizarre
	• Sensual and erotic style
Netherlands	**Strongly reflects the levelling attitude induced by a feminine culture**
	• Softer, more entertaining advertising
	• Hype is not appreciated, nor are pushy presenters
Sweden	**A very feminine culture**
	• Men are shown doing the work in the home
	• Entertainment is frequently used, often within a context of disrespect for authority

Source: Adapted from Marieke de Mooij, *Global Marketing and Advertising: Understanding Cultural Paradoxes* (Thousand Oaks, Calif.: Sage, 1998).

to advertising.[18] A cultural assessment of your target audience provides a very important profile variable, and is essential for multi-country or global advertising.

Personality

Personality is definitely not something ever to consider as a primary characteristic by which to select a target audience—and personality characteristics do not help determine a target market. Then why consider personality as a profile variable? Its importance as a target audience profile variable comes from the effect that personality characteristics have on how advertising and promotion messages are *processed*. This is especially true of the *verbal content* of marketing communication.

Generally, when we think of personality we are thinking about *personality traits*. These are the more or less permanent characteristics of someone's personality that lead them to respond to life in a basically predictable fashion. In the psychological literature, of all the possible mediators of persuasion in communication, personality traits have probably been studied more than any other. But we must also be aware of *personality states*. As Rossiter and Percy have pointed out, a personality state is actually something of a contradiction since personality is an *enduring* predisposition whereas a 'state' is only temporary.[19] Nevertheless, as we all know, in certain circumstances we may exhibit personality traits that are not usual for us—for example undue anxiety during times of stress.

Personality Traits

We mentioned that personality traits are one of the most widely studied variables affecting persuasion in communication. Interestingly, the results of all these studies often produce quite opposite-seeming conclusions. These contradictions mean that you must be very careful when looking at personality traits and their probable effects on how a target audience will process advertising.[20] Three personality traits which particularly influence how advertising messages are processed are self-esteem, intelligence, and introversion/extroversion.

Self-esteem is perhaps the most widely studied personality trait, at least in relation to how susceptible someone might be to a persuasive message. It also illustrates how careful you must be when considering a personality trait in relation to marketing communication. When a message is *simple*, the higher one's self-esteem, the less likely they are to be persuaded; the lower one's self-esteem, the more likely. But when the message is more *complex* or specific, the higher one's self-esteem, the *more* likely they are to be persuaded; and the lower the self-esteem, the less likely.

The difficulty, of course, is how to know if your target audience has high or low self-esteem. Once the appropriate brand loyalty or brand buyer groupings have identified your target audience, a random sample of the target could be given a brief personality inventory to complete. If it is found that they are more likely to have high (or low) self-esteem, your message execution should take that into account. Testing a sample of your target audience is actually the only way for a manager to determine if a personality trait should be considered as a target audience profile variable.

Intelligence is a highly relevant personality trait for advertising, again in terms of the target audience's ability to deal with the complexity of a message. It should make intuitive sense that a more intelligent person will be better able to deal with a complex message, and this is true. Additionally, especially for high-involvement advertising, a more intelligent person should require fewer repetitions to learn the message. Remember that we are talking about the personality trait of raw intelligence here, *not* a surrogate such as education. If the manager is concerned that intelligence could significantly affect the message delivery needed for the brand, perhaps because there is a complicated story to tell, a random sample of the target audience should be given an IQ test of some kind.

Something else to be considered here has been suggested by Rossiter and Percy. When advertising or other marketing communication is *written* in English (or the audio in radio or television is in English), people whose first language is not English, should be thought of as 'less intelligent' as far as processing the message is concerned. It is not that they have lower IQs. They are simply not as competent in English as a native speaker. This means that English-language advertising running in continental Europe (or *any* other non-English-speaking country) should avoid complex messages, and keep the copy simple.[21]

Introversion/Extroversion is one of the few personality traits that is in fact strongly correlated with actual behaviour and attitudes. For example, extroverts have been shown to like novelty and change, even while being realistic and practical in their attitudes. They are adventure-seeking, more likely to use tobacco, and more likely to drink coffee and alcohol. Introverts, on the other hand, value privacy and close friendships, and tend to be anxious in social situations.[22]

You can see how knowledge of someone as an introvert or extrovert could make a difference in how you communicate with them. A number of English psychologists have done extensive work with introversion/extroversion, and the implications of this work offer some interesting insight on how we look at advertising (as pointed out by Rossiter and Percy[23]). Informational appeals (those addressing a negative purchase motive) should be more effective with introverts, while the more outgoing extrovert should be more responsive to appeals addressing positive motives like social approval.[24]

The population is roughly split in terms of whether introversion or extroversion is the dominant trait (with a slight edge to extroverts). But because of the more obvious attitudinal and behavioural associations of this personality trait, for many product categories there is a good likelihood of the target market or target audience being dominated by either introverts or extroverts. Again, a simple testing of a random sample of the target audience with a version of Eysenck's Introversion/Extroversion Scale can alert the manager to the possible relevancy of I/E as a target audience profile variable. The Eysenck scales have been found to be the most useful measure of I/E, and they have considerable equivalence across age groups and cultures.[25]

Personality States

We pointed out earlier that a personality state is really nothing more than a temporary activation of a personality characteristic which is not enduring for that individual. Since it actually operates like a trait when it is activated, we can think of it in much the same way. This means that it can have an important effect upon how the verbal content of communication is processed. As an example, let us look at *anxiety*, a personality characteristic that is often aroused by outside stimulation, acting on a personality state.

If you are planning to drive to the French Alps for a skiing holiday and the day you leave the weather report forecasts heavy snow en route, this could very well raise your anxiety level. What is happening is that the anxiety state is 'warning' you to consider avoiding the storm because it is thought to be potentially threatening. This is really what anxiety is all about, a state that warns you to avoid a future situation.

How might anxiety as a personality state affect the processing of advertising? Anxiety can interfere with the likelihood or the length of time that someone pays attention to your message; and even if they do pay attention, anxiety can interfere with comprehension. If what you see or read in an advert raises your anxiety level, you simply tune it out, either actually by turning away or leaving the room, or mentally. This is something that often happens with some of the more gruesome public service advertising against drug and alcohol abuse. But it can also occur with insurance company or automobile tyre advertising that depicts bad accidents, or health care advertising showing realistic emergency treatment. We don't want to leave the impression that anxiety is always a problem. In fact, if the message makes you anxious, but you still pay attention, you are actually *more* likely to be persuaded. The trick is to make sure the creative execution does not go too far and raise anxiety so high that it interferes with attention.

Unlike personality traits, you can't measure a personality state with a series of scales unless the target audience has been aroused and is experiencing that state. Because advertising itself can occasion a personality state, it is important to pre-test your advertising. You want to be sure that a personality characteristic like anxiety does not arouse a state that will interfere with the processing of the message. On the other hand, you may hope to arouse a particular personality state, such as a warm, nurturing feeling. Pre-testing can help determine if the advertising is activating either desirable or undesirable personality states.

Unfortunately, it is difficult if not impossible to anticipate generally when a particular personality state is likely to be aroused in your target audience. In fact, the likelihood of a *common* personality state being present at one time among a significant portion of any target audience is negligible. While there are a few predictable situations that tend to arouse some personality states (e.g. when a target audience might be tired), the manager's concern should be with the potential of the advertising itself, along with the context within which it is delivered, to arouse a personality state.

Personality and its Relationship with Advertising

Fig. 5.2 provides a simplified idea of how personality traits and states can affect or be affected by advertising and other marketing communication. People's prior experience and their attitudes will always affect how a message is processed, and we will spend a lot of time dealing with this in later chapters.

As we have seen, personality traits, because they are enduring characteristics, can influence how someone processes a message. For example, if someone whose personality reflects a high level of nurturance (a personality trait that suggests a desire to look after and care for people) sees an advertisement for a product positioned as helping you take better care of your family, their naturally high level of nurturance should mean more attention to the advertising and a greater likelihood of positively responding to the message.

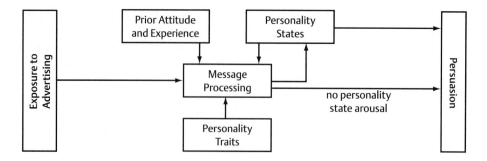

Fig. 5.2 Personality and its Influence on Advertising and Persuasion

Personality states, because they are temporary, can influence message processing in two ways. If some outside event has aroused a personality characteristic, this could influence how a message is processed at that time, or the message itself could arouse that state. Continuing with our nurturance example, while someone may not naturally exhibit a high degree of nurturance, we all occasionally experience it as a state. Think about how you feel when you see a baby, or even a puppy. Suppose you have just watched a particularly heartwarming programme on television and have a warm, contented feeling. This could certainly affect how you process any advertising within the programme or immediately after. On the other hand, a particularly 'warm and fuzzy' advertisement could itself stimulate a temporary warm feeling that could influence how you process the message.

In order to account for the effects of personality in your target audience it makes sense to test a sample of the brand loyalty or brand buyer groups selected as your target audience *if* you feel a particular personality trait might have either a positive or negative effect upon how they process your message. Recall the examples we discussed in the section on personality traits. To address personality states, the manager must pay attention to the context where advertising or other marketing communication is likely to be seen, for example in a situation comedy, on a bus poster, or at a sporting event. Additionally, if a personality characteristic could potentially be aroused by the message, for example positively by a very 'warm and fuzzy' execution or negatively by a 'frightening' message, check for these effects when pre-testing the advertising.

Segmentation

This is a good place to talk about segmentation. Segmentation is a powerful tool for understanding a market and helping to optimize targeting, but we will not spend a great deal of time discussing it in this book. Why not, if it is so important? The reason is that the primary use of segmentation is in defining a target *market*, not a target audience. As noted earlier, this is an important distinction, and one not often made.

Any good marketing or consumer behaviour text will have a chapter on market segmentation (and it should). We like Fill's definition of market segmentation as 'the division of a mass market into distinct groups which have common characteristics, needs, and similar responses to marketing action'.[26] Although this definition is in a marketing communication text, it is in a chapter on *marketing strategy*. This is where market segmentation belongs, in discussions of marketing strategy.

Having said this, segmentation does have a place in better defining a target audience. When we talked about loyalty groups as the best way to select a target audience we pointed out that this is because loyalty reflects the target market's *attitude* toward the category and its brands. Segmentation relevant to marketing communication must be based upon attitude. Attitudes bear directly upon communication strategy because it is attitude that determines how someone is likely to respond to a message, and how they behave.

It is easy to become confused because all of the target audience variables we have just discussed can and are used as *market* segmentation variables. But as we have continually pointed out, knowing that someone is young or old, lives in the country or the town, is outgoing, likes sports, or travels a lot, is simply not good enough to identify a target audience. It may help you to understand the target audience better, but it will not define it.

How segmentation should be used in the development of marketing and communication strategy is illustrated in Fig. 5.3. Traditional market segmentation looks at the entire market, using as a basis for segmentation any and all relevant variables. These could very well be demographics, geographics, or psychographics, what Rothschild has called 'enduring variables' that do not change across product categories, or they could be what he has called 'dynamic variables' such as usage or benefits.[27] It is of course also possible to use attitudes for market segmentation as well.

But once we have set our marketing strategy and selected the target market, we must then identify the target audience. Here the only correct segmentation variable is attitude.[28] We are looking for groups of people in the target market who hold relatively similar attitudes toward category usage and brands within the category. Our primary concern is to identify brand loyalty groups, but it is also important to know how the target market segments generally in terms of other relevant attitudes if we are to optimize

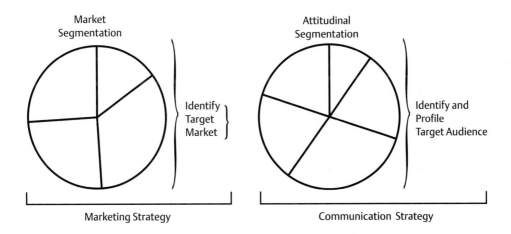

Fig. 5.3 Segmentation and the Development of Marketing and Communication Strategy

communication strategy. Our target audience 'segments' have common attitudes in terms of their brand loyalty, but is what they are looking for, say, in terms of benefits the same?

This is why a communication-based and loyalty attitudinal segmentation is so desirable. Without it, the manager must select the target audience only in terms of brand buying behaviour. While it is easy to select a target audience in this way because brand purchase data is readily available (e.g. from the TGI), to develop the most effective communication strategy and creative executions an understanding of our target audience's category and brand attitudes is essential. It is not enough simply to understand purchase behaviour.

The target audience, whether identified from brand loyalty or brand buyer groupings, is selected to satisfy the objectives of the marketing strategy. But to *communicate* effectively with the target audience, the manager must fully understand what fundamental attitude segments they reflect. This, along with appropriate demographic, geographic, and psychographic profile variables, enables the manager to put together an effective communication strategy, as well as helping in media selection.

Target Audience and Strategy

Once the target audience has been selected and profiled, it remains to link the target audience with the marketing strategy and with the communication strategy. Indeed, the selection of the target market and then the target audience will have followed from the marketing objectives set out in the marketing plan. What we are more concerned with are the specifics of the *behavioural* objectives associated with the target audience that should result from our marketing communication. The selection of the target audience will have determined whether we are looking principally at customers or non-customers (or perhaps both), and this in turn will determine if the behavioural objective is *trial* or *repeat purchase* or use.[29] All of this should be spelled out in the marketing plan, but must now become a part of our strategic communication planning.

Target Audience Links to Marketing Strategy

The marketing objectives as detailed in the marketing plan will generally specify whether new customers or repeat business is to be the principal path for building or maintaining the brand. If a market is growing, the marketing manager is usually looking for new customers; in a more stable market, maintaining share or increasing business is more likely to come from current customers. These marketing objectives clearly help specify the target audience at a macro level—will it be primarily customers or non-customers?

We need to keep this in mind when planning our communication strategy. If the target audience is made up primarily of customers, the behavioural objective will be some level of repeat purchase or use; if the target audience is made up primarily of non-customers, the behavioural objective will be some level of trial. This distinction will hold regardless of whether we are talking about a consumer, business, or trade target audience. Typical examples of trial and repeat purchase objectives linked to a marketing strategy are offered below.

Consumer target audience. The types of trial behaviour sought from consumers include such things as encouraging people to try a brand if it is an fmcg, or to take the first step toward considering higher-involvement, higher-risk purchases. This could be anything from making a phone call to request information to visiting a dealer. When the behavioural objective is repeat purchase, we may be looking for our customers to continue purchasing at the same rate (especially those loyal to the brand), to increase the number of units they buy at a time, or to buy our product more often.

Business target audience. These same general behavioural objectives apply to business-to-business marketing. When we are looking for new customers, the specific trial behaviours desired could include such things as enquiries about a new product, requests for a demonstration or feasibility study, or asking to see a sales rep. If we are looking to customers for repeat business, just as with consumers we may want them to maintain their current level of business, increase the number of units they buy at a time, or use our product more often.

Trade Target Audience. In addition to consumer and business markets, many companies must also market to their trade—the wholesalers or retailers that carry or distribute their products. If you are looking for new trade outlets, this corresponds to a trial behavioural objective. If you are trying to get the trade to maintain premium shelf-space or display, or to move more of your brand, this corresponds to a repeat purchase objective.

Target Audience Links to Communication Strategy

The target audience links to marketing strategy address the fundamental distinction between customers and non-customers, and relate that distinction to the behavioural objectives of trial and repeat purchase. Now we must also consider this same distinction within the context of communication strategy. As you might suppose, the communication strategy which drives trial will be different from that driving repeat purchase. While a target audience based only upon brand buyer groupings already accounts for the distinction between customers and non-customers, brand loyalty groups do not. Both customers and non-customers (with the exception of those not category users at present) can fall within one of the four brand loyalty groupings, and the behavioural objective will vary accordingly. This distinction is summarized in Table 5.3.

All along in this chapter we have been underscoring the importance of *attitude* in selecting and understanding the target audience. Brand loyalty groupings, and at heart even brand buyer groupings, result from an individual's attitude toward the category and its brands. We have pointed out several times that brand attitude (along with brand awareness) is *always* a communication objective. It should be no surprise that the attitude of the target audience toward the brands in the category will be instrumental in formulating the overall communication strategy.

At a very basic level, we can see how the attitudes toward a brand that underlie the brand loyalty groupings will influence strategy. When Loyals are part of a target

Table 5.3 Behavioural Objectives and Target Audience Groupings

Behavioural Objectives	Brand Buyer Groupings	Corresponding Brand Loyalty Groupings
Non-Customers Trial objective	NCU	None
	OBL	L
	OBS	F/V/S
Customers Repeat-purchase objective	BL	L
	BS	F/V/S

NCU: New category users; OBL: Other brand loyals; OBS: Other brand switchers; BL: Brand loyals; BS: Brand switchers; L: Loyal; F: Frustrated; V: Vulnerable; S: Switchable.

audience, it will be essential at least to maintain their already high positive brand attitude. Frustrated and Switchable consumers, because of their lower satisfaction with a brand, will require the building of a more favourable brand attitude. Vulnerables, even though they are generally satisfied with a brand, need to have their brand attitude strengthened, because there are no real barriers to switching. This accounts generally for the underlying attitudes that drive loyalty to a brand, as we discussed earlier in the chapter.

Practically, however, we must deal with brand loyalty groups for both customers and non-customers. Obviously, those loyal to our brand must be treated differently from those loyal to competitor brands. So, while the general brand attitudes will hold for our customers in the target audience, when the target audience includes non-customers as well, the attitudinal assumptions will be different. It is unlikely, for example, that those loyal to a competitive brand will be in our target audience, but if they are, it will be necessary to modify their brand attitude, changing it if negative. For Frustrated non-customers, we need to increase positive attitudes toward our brand (they are currently unsatisfied with the brands they are using), but also to address their barriers to switching. With Switchable non-customers, it will be important to build or increase positive brand attitude, while for the vulnerable we must modify their attitudes, or change them if negative.

Target Audience Member Roles

In the last chapter we briefly introduced the roles people play in the decision process. We pointed out then that it was important to know not just who is involved in the decision, but the *roles* individuals play in the decision to purchase or use a product or service.

This is an important distinction, because when we advertise we are not just addressing the target audience as individuals, but as individuals in a role. To review, in the study of consumer behaviour, there are typically five roles people are seen to play in a purchase decision:

1. *Initiator.* This would be anyone who helps start the decision process by talking about, suggesting, or recommending a brand.

2. *Influencer.* This would be anyone who helps to facilitate or hinder the consideration of a brand.

3. *Decider.* This is the person who actually makes the decision to purchase or use a particular brand.

4. *Purchaser.* This is the person who implements the decision.

5. *User.* Often overlooked as part of the decision process, this is the person *or persons* who actually use the brand.

Why these distinctions are so important will be discussed in some detail in the next chapter. For now, we need only understand that people in our target audience could play all of the roles in the decision themselves (either with or without others involved), or only some of the roles. What roles are involved at different points in the decision process, and whom in the target audience is likely to be involved, must be accounted for when developing communication strategy.

For any target audience the relationship between the roles being targeted and what part of the decision process must be influenced by our message is critical to an effective communication strategy. Consider the relationship between the behavioural objectives of trial and repeat purchase and the role someone plays in the decision process. When the behavioural objective is trial, advertising and promotion are generally aimed at the initiator, influencer, and decider roles. For example, with consumers, are they aware of us so they can initiate or influence a decision favourably for our brand; or with a business target, are we on a vendor's consideration list for the decider? Advertising and promotion aimed at stimulating repeat purchase is usually directed at the purchaser or user roles. For example, we may want the purchaser simply to maintain their favourable behaviour, or perhaps buy more each time they purchase our brand; for users, we may wish them to use our brand more often or in larger amounts.

The importance of the *roles* being played by members of the target audience in the decision process should now be clear, along with its link to communication strategy.

Summary

In this chapter we have explored in depth issues concerning decisions relating to the target audience. We have emphasized the key importance of considering aspects of brand loyalty and have introduced a model which focuses on the role of perceived risk and levels of satisfaction to yield four loyalty groups: Loyal, Vulnerable, Frustrated, and Switchable. We have explained how these loyalty groupings can be used to optimize target audiences. We have discussed the problems with simple demographic segmentation approaches and suggested that the only correct segmentation variable is attitude.

Questions to consider

5.1 What are the four brand loyalty groupings?

5.2 Why is it important to look beyond brand purchase behaviour and examine the degree of brand loyalty?

5.3 What is the difference between a Vulnerable and a Switchable consumer?

5.4 How would you distinguish between a target market and a target audience?

5.5 Why should demographic factors never be used as the primary selection criteria for a target audience?

5.6 How might anxiety affect the processing of advertising?

5.7 Which segmentation variable should be used to identify the target audience?

5.8 Why is it important to distinguish between customers and non-customers when planning a communication strategy?

Notes

1 Antonides and van Raaij talk about target groups in their book *Consumer Behaviour: A European Perspective* (Chichester: John Wiley and Sons, 1998). Interestingly, the subject does not come up until quite near the end of the book in a section on market segmentation.

2 J. R. Rossiter and L. Percy, *Advertising Communication and Promotion Management* (New York: McGraw-Hill, 1997).

3 A number of research institutes in Europe and the US have developed versions of a 'conversion model' to help identify customer loyalty. Charles Moore of Taylor Nelson Sofres-UK discusses their model in 'Linking Market Research Techniques to Database Marketing to Assist Customer Retention', in *The eXperts Report on . . . Database Marketing and Integrated Marketing Communications* (New York: Advertising Research Foundation, 1998), 11–16. A more technical discussion may be found in J. Hofmeyr, 'The Conversion Model: A New Foundation for Strategic Planning in Marketing', unpub. paper presented at the 3rd EMAC/ESOMAR symposium, 'New Ways in Marketing and Marketing Research.'

4 Because conversion models developed by research institutes are considered proprietary to those institutes, *how* the model is applied is not revealed. As a general rule we do not approve of using such 'black-box' models because you have no way of evaluating how valid the model may be.

5 This reflects something John Howard, one of the founders of the study of consumer behaviour, referred to as 'routinized response behaviour'. He considers this the simplest of three stages of consumer behaviour (the other two are 'limited problem solving' and 'extensive problem solving'). This subject is explored in some depth in his book *Consumer Behaviour: Application of Theory* (New York: McGraw-Hill, 1977).

6   Rossiter and Percy discuss this in *Advertising Communication and Promotion Management*, 61–2 in terms of 'leverage', and offer an equation for measuring the return on investment in advertising or promotion expenditure.

7   A good discussion of the Target Group Index (TGI) may be found in P. R. Smith's *Marketing Communication: An Integrated Approach*, 2nd edn. (London: Kogan Page, 1998), 124–5. Basically, the TGI compiles information on brand usage for a wide range of consumer products, and relates that behaviour to the usage, demographic, and media behaviour of the buyer.

8   Antonides and van Raaij, *Consumer Behaviour: A European Perspective*, 548.

9   Ibid. 29 D. K. Oliver, in his book *Marketing Today*, 3rd edn. (Hemel Hempstead: Prentice Hall, 1990) has suggested that the advertising industry was one of the first to combine and use demographic data in terms of socio-economic variables.

10   Robert East, *Consumer Behaviour: Advances and Applications in Marketing* (Hemel Hempstead: Prentice Hall, 1997), 237.

11   Good discussions of Acorn can be found in Chris Fill's *Marketing Communication: Framework, Theories, and Application* (London: Prentice Hall, 1995), 70 and Smith's *Marketing Communication*, 126.

12   See William M. Weilbacken, *Advertising* (New York: Macmillan, 1979), 477.

13   Rossiter and Percy, *Advertising Communication and Promotion Management*, 96. In their discussion of social class, Rossiter and Percy point out how important social class is to retailers. There is a strong positive correlation between the quality image of a store and the social class of its customers, confirmed in a study by J. P. Dickson and D. L. MacLachlan, 'Social Distance and Shopping Behaviour', *Journal of the Academy of Marketing Science*, 18 (1990), 153–61.

14   Antonides and van Raaij, *Consumer Behaviour: A European Perspective*, 30.

15   In his discussion of socio-economic groups in the United Kingdom, Chris Fill provides a good argument for the careful use of social class variables: see Fill, *Marketing Communication*, 69.

16   F. J. Landy, *Psychology and Work Behavior* (Pacific Grove, Calif.: Brooks-Cole, 1989).

17   Antonides and van Raaij, *Consumer Behaviour: A European Perspective*, 39 and 377.

18   A good review of the importance of cultural considerations for effective advertising is found in Mariela de Mooij's *Global Marketing and Advertising: Understanding Cultural Paradoxes* (Thousand Oaks, Calif.: Sage, 1998).

19   Rossiter and Percy, *Advertising Communication and Promotion Management*, 98.

20   Perhaps the best attempt to explain the often conflicting research in this area is offered by McGuire's theory of personality–persuasibility relationships: see his 'Personality and Susceptibility to Social Influences', in G. F. Borgoatta and W. W. Lambert (eds.) *Handbook of Personality Theory and Research* (Chicago: Rand McNally, 1968). In this work he describes five postulates that underlie the complex relationships found in personality trait research: a mediational principle, a compensation principle, a situational-weighting principle, a confounding principle, and an interactive principle.

21   Rossiter and Percy, *Advertising Communication and Promotion Management*, 97.

22 See L.W. Morris, *Extroversion and Introversion: An International Perspective*, New York: Halsted Press (1979).

23 See Rossiter and Percy, *Advertising Communication and Promotion Management*, 97–8.

24 Much of this work can be found in H. J. Eysenck (ed.), *A Model for Personality* (Berlin: Springer-Verlag, 1981).

25 See A. Handel, 'Personality Factors among Adolescent Boys', *Psychological Reports*, 39 (1976), 435–45.

26 Fill, *Marketing Communications*, 68.

27 M. Rothschild, *Marketing Communications* (Lexington, Mass.: D. C. Heath, 1987).

28 The importance of segmenting target markets in terms of attitude for developing a communication strategy which identifies target audiences was pointed out as long ago as the mid-1970s by Larry Percy in a still frequently cited article, 'How Market Segmentation Guides Advertising Strategy', *Journal of Advertising Research*, 16: 5 (1976).

29 While the fundamental behavioural objectives are trial and repeat purchase or use, Rossiter and Percy, in *Advertising Communication and Promotion Management*, 63, point out that there are 'finer gradations' based upon behavioural considerations such as occurrence, rate of purchase, amount purchased, timing, and persistence.

Chapter 6
Consumer Decision-making

The importance of understanding how consumers behave in a category before attempting to develop marketing and communication strategies may seem obvious to us today. Yet oddly enough, the formal study of consumer behaviour as such is a relatively recent phenomenon. It wasn't until the 1960s that consumer behaviour became an academic field of study in its own right, and the first textbooks on the subject were written. From the very beginning, however, researchers and academics have noted the important link between understanding how consumers behave and creating effective marketing and communication strategies.[1]

Also from the earliest days of the study of consumer behaviour as a discipline, those working in the area have been interested in modelling how consumers behave, and have included in these models the important link between how consumers deal with information and how that influences the way they go about making decisions.[2] In Antonides and van Raaij's recent book on consumer behaviour from a European perspective,[3] they devote an entire chapter to the consumer decision process, and one to situation and behaviour. People who study consumer behaviour know how important it is to understand how consumers go about making decisions to buy products or utilize services, and it is *equally* important to the study of the management of advertising and other marketing communication.

While it is beyond the scope of this book to undertake an in-depth study of consumer decision-making,[4] it is none the less important for the manager to have a way of looking at how people in their target market are likely to go about making decisions to buy or use products or services. A very practical tool that can help managers deal with this issue is the Behavioural Sequence Model (BSM) first introduced by Rossiter and Percy in 1987.[5] The BSM is strongly rooted in previous models of buyer behaviour, but it deals much more specifically with the decision *process*, and how that process is likely to be affected by marketing communication. In this chapter we will look at the foundation of the BSM and earlier models of consumer decision-making, and at how this can be used to help guide the development of marketing communication strategy.

Decision Participants

As we begin to consider the decision process consumers use to reach buying decisions, the first question we must ask ourselves is who is involved in that decision. Quite often there is more than one person, even when the decision only involves a fast-moving consumer good (fmcg) such as snacks or toothpaste. The key of course is understanding not just who is participating in the decision, but the *role* each participant plays in the process.

At the end of the last chapter we introduced the topic of how people who study consumer behaviour look at the roles people play in the decision process. You will remember that there are five potential roles for participants to play in the decisions leading up to the purchase and use of a product or service (Table 6.1):

- as the *initiator* who suggests the purchase;
- as an *influencer* who recommends or discourages purchase;
- as the *decider* who makes the actual choice;
- as the *purchaser* who does the actual purchasing;
- as the *user* who consumes or uses the product or service.

The reason it is so important for the manager to understand this idea of roles in the decision process is that advertising and other marketing communication is aimed not just at individuals, but at *individuals in a role*.

Effective marketing communication matches a message with the role (or roles) an individual plays. When we are trying to arouse interest in a product, we are talking to the consumer in their role as an initiator. We want them to initiate the process that will lead to purchase or usage of our product or service. This could be the same message that is also used to address the consumer in their role as an influencer, but it need not be. For example, what if you were introducing a new product, especially a new product when there was no awareness of or experience with the category (think of when CDs were introduced, or cellular phones)? All of your effort initially may be required simply to raise awareness of and stimulate curiosity in the new product. Later messages will begin to build more substantial understanding of the product, addressing consumers in their role as influencers and deciders.

Table 6.1 Likely Communication Objectives for Decision Roles

Role in Decision	Communication Objective
Initiator	Brand awareness, initial brand attitude
Influencer	Brand attitude
Decider	Brand attitude and brand purchase intention
Purchaser	Brand purchase intention
User	Brand attitude

We also need to keep in mind that influencers may exist well outside of the immediate circle of a consumer's family or acquaintances. What if we are advertising a holiday resort? Clearly we will want to make people aware of our great resort and spark an interest (initiating the decision process) as well as begin to influence them positively to consider us as a holiday destination. But at the same time, we will also want to be talking with travel agents, encouraging them to influence their clients to consider our resort. This will surely be a different message from the one directed to consumers.

Basically, no matter how many participants may be involved in a decision process, we want to be sure that initiators are aware of our product and positively inclined to suggest considering it (either to themselves or to others), and that influencers have reasons to recommend it (again either to themselves or others).

In the consumer's role as decider, advertising and other marketing communication must stimulate a positive *intention* to buy or use the product. In later chapters we will discuss in some detail how a consumer's perception of personal risk in buying or using a product is related to how they form intentions. Risk may be defined in terms of fiscal risk because a lot of money is involved, or psychological risk because of personal or social involvement associated with the product. If a consumer perceives risk in a purchase, they will obviously want to be more convinced they are making the right choice in buying or using a particular product or service. When there is this perceived risk, the decision is described as *high-involvement* and when there is little perceived risk present, the decision is *low-involvement*. We have already introduced this idea, and the distinction will be taken up again in Chapter 8, when we talk about brand attitude strategies, and in Chapter 10, when we talk about processing. The reason we are reintroducing the subject here is that it is important to see that it will require more commitment from a consumer in the role of decider when the product choice decision is high-involvement than where it is low-involvement. This will have clear implications for strategic message development.

For most low-involvement purchase decisions, the decider will be a single person. With high-involvement purchase decisions, the decider may be a single person; or for large household purchases, a couple; or for certain major business decisions, a group. Once the decider makes the decision, the person in the role of purchaser actually buys the product or secures the services. It is important to remember that the decider and the purchaser may not be the same person. The significance of this means, especially for low-involvement purchases where there is little or no risk involved, that there is a final opportunity to influence the actual purchase at the point of purchase with some form of marketing communication such as a special promotion or point-of-sale message.

The last role played in the decision process is that of user. You may be wondering why using the product or service is considered as part of the decision process. If the product or service was never to be used again, or nothing else made or offered by that company likely to be bought, perhaps usage would not be a part of the process. But as we know, for most products or services a marketer is looking to encourage *repeat* purchase or usage. This means that in a real sense the user role is really the first step toward repeat purchase.

Roles and Message Objective

Before we proceed further with our discussion of the roles participants play in a decision process, this is a good point to introduce the issue of how *what* you say in your marketing communication is related to *who* you say it to, in terms of the roles they play. We have already suggested that the message needed to stimulate awareness for an initiator may be different from the message needed for other roles. We will of course be dealing at great length with the subject of creative strategy later on in this book, but it is important to understand at this point that messages need to accomplish different things depending upon where you are and what role you are playing in the decision process.

Under some circumstances, the same message may be appropriate regardless of role. This is especially true for low-involvement purchase decisions. For most fmcg's you can think of, communicating brand awareness and positive brand attitude will accommodate all five roles, whether played by a single consumer or multiple individuals. The initiator, influencer, and decider must be aware of the brand, and have at least a tentatively favourable attitude toward it. This will in turn lead to at least an initial positive intention to try, which is required of the decider and purchaser. Continued awareness and a favourable attitude maintains a positive intention to re-purchase, which is the goal for a user.

Because more people are likely to be involved in a high-involvement purchase decision, even though the role may require the same type of message, the *nature* of the role being played may require a different message. Consider the example of potential influencers in a holiday resort destination decision. The potential traveller and their friends or others who may play a role as an initiator or influencer will likely require a different message from travel agents in their role as initiators or influencers. The communication objective is the same: raise brand awareness and build a positive brand attitude for the resort. However, the specific messages directed to the consumer are likely to be different from those directed to the travel agent.

Beyond this difference, with high-involvement decisions, because there is risk, deciders must be *convinced* of their choice prior to a purchase. It is unlikely that a single advertisement for a high-involvement purchase will be able to build the brand awareness and positive brand attitude sufficient to satisfy the initiator and influencer, and also be able to ensure a positive intention to buy. You may see a great commercial for staying at a resort in the Alps and think that it might be a really great place for a holiday. But it is unlikely that you would pick up the phone and book without first learning a lot more about the resort. A specific message keyed to the person in the decider role is almost always required when dealing with high-involvement decisions.

A good example of this may be found when we consider the decision to buy a new automobile. Research into how people go about making a buying decision for an automobile suggests that it is at least a two-stage process.[6] In the first stage a potential buyer must *like* the car. They must see themselves behind the wheel, and feel that this particular vehicle reflects how they want to be seen by the world. This is the 'image' part of the automobile decision, and reflects the positive motives associated with buying a car. Once this is satisfied and the potential buyer is comfortable with the *idea* of owning a particular vehicle, in the second stage they must satisfy themselves that the car meets their more *functional* criteria (gas mileage, service record, features, etc.), reflecting the negative motivations associated with buying a car. (This very important idea of motivation is critical to our view of communication strategy, as we have already suggested.) In our terms, one message is necessary to reach the potential new car buyer first in their role as initiator and influencer (and later as user); a much different, more fact-filled message or messages will be required for them in their role as decider and purchaser.

Decision Participant Grid (DPG)

As you can now see, it is very important to look at the *roles* people play in the decision process leading to the purchase and use of a product or service. There may be only one person involved, playing all of the roles in the decision; or for higher-involvement purchases, a number of different people playing different or multiple roles. To help focus the manager's thinking on all those who might be involved and the roles they are likely to play, it is useful to complete a Decision Participant Grid (Fig. 6.1).[7] For each of the five roles, think about what members of your immediate target market might be likely to be involved. The key, of course, is to see that your potential target audience for marketing communication messages could be wider than simply the person buying the product. Initially you will want to think as broadly as possible. Later, you can refine the list of possible participants. At this point it is not necessary for the grid to be precise.

You will also notice that in addition to consumers there is a column for *providers*. This is to remind us that for many decisions, especially high-involvement ones, various parts of the trade could be involved in the process. In one of our earlier example, we saw where travel agents could play a role as initiator or influencer, as illustrated in Fig. 6.2. Often salespeople can play a role in the decision. You will want to account for these possibilities where members of the trade are dealing directly with the consumer during the decision process.

To help understand how the Decision Participant Grid (DPG) enables managers to stimulate and organize their thinking, let us consider some examples. Perhaps the

Role in Decision	Target Audience	
	Consumer	Provider
Initiator		
Influencer		
Decider		
Purchaser		
User		

Fig. 6.1 Decision Participant Grid

Role in Decision	Target Audience	
	Consumer	Provider
Initiator	self, friends, family	travel agent
Influencer	self, friends, family	travel agent, resorts and other destinations
Decider	self, mate	
Purchaser	self, mate	travel agent
User	self, mate, family	

Fig. 6.2 Decision Participant Grid for a Holiday

simplest case is where a single individual is likely to play all of the roles in a decision. Suppose it is late afternoon, and a student has a 15-minute break between lectures. The student thinks to herself, I need a snack (initiator). What do I want, some chocolate or a salty snack (influencer)? I know, a Mars bar (decider). She goes to a vending machine in the lounge, buys the Mars bar (purchaser), and eats it (user).

You may be wondering why in the world you would need the discipline of a DPG for such a simple case. To begin with, this scenario would only be one of many possible snack scenarios if you were the maker of Mars bars. But even if you could assume that for nearly all relevant confection scenarios one individual would play all of the decision roles, it would still be a good idea to *think about the roles* in filling out a DPG. Earlier in this chapter we talked about how different messages may be necessary to deal effectively with various roles a consumer may play. Suppose you were introducing a new candy bar. You would almost certainly want to use more than one message, keyed to different roles, even though all the decision roles are played by the same person.

We know, for example, that television advertising is probably the best way to introduce a new candy bar, raising awareness and stimulating interest; important for initiator, influencer, and decider roles. But how likely is it that someone seeing an advertisement for our new candy bar will drop everything they are doing and dash out to the shops to find one? Unlikely. What they will do is form a positive intention to try one, and put it out of their mind. For that reason, it makes a lot of sense to offer in-store promotions or use shelf-talkers (those signs or pads sometimes found on the product shelf in stores) to *remind* the consumer of their intention to try the new candy bar (in their role as purchaser). If you were marketing Mars bars and knew a competitor was introducing a new candy bar, you might want to do something to interfere with their message at the point of purchase. By taking time to think through a DPG the manager is forced to focus upon the roles in the decision process and what implications there may be for marketing communication, even in the simplest case where one person plays all five roles.

Let's look at another case that on the surface may seem quite simple, but where a lot more could be going on. In most families the mother is the principal shopper. Continuing our snack scenario, let us suppose that a young child in the family has just seen a commercial on television for the new candy bar we have been talking about and asks the mother to buy some next time she shops (initiator). The father overhears this, and seconds the request, saying he'd also like to try it (influencer). The mother agrees (decider), and makes a note to look for the new candy bar next time she is in the shops. On her next trip, there it is, *but* next to the display is a special offer for the candy bar she usually buys. Too good a deal to pass up; she buys the regular bars (purchaser). At home, she promises to buy the new bars next time, and the family continues to eat the old favourite (users). The same product, but with different people playing multiple roles.

What these examples illustrate is that the underlying communication strategy for the brand will follow from the roles various participants play in the decision. The first scenario assumes that marketing communication is targeted at immediate individual consumption, the second that it is aimed at consumption out of in-home inventory. Can the same message or messages accommodate both strategies? Perhaps, but at this point, in considering the roles being played by the target market, we are not setting communication strategy. What we are doing is considering all of those who might be involved in the decision, and whom we may need to address with the marketing communication.

Both of these examples illustrate why advertising alone, especially for a new product, may not be sufficient even for very simple decisions where one person plays all, or all of the principal, roles. Advertising does a good job of generating awareness of a brand and creating interest in it. But unfortunately, most consumer packaged goods products are purchased out of habit, without giving the product much thought.[8] This is an issue we will examine in some detail later on in Chapter 8 when we talk about brand awareness. While advertising builds interest in a brand, it is often necessary to utilize other means of marketing communication, such as promotion or in-store merchandising where the actual purchase is made, if you want to *change* a consumer's usual, routine purchase behaviour.

Developing a Model of Consumer Decision-making

Up to this point we have concentrated our attention upon those who participate in the decision to buy or use a product or service. Now it is time to see how these participants in the decision and the roles they play relate to the decision process itself. We shall do this by looking at what we have been talking about in relation to the Behavioural Sequence Model. This model utilizes a grid format that requires you first to identify the probable *stages* involved in making a decision, and then for each stage in the process determine: *who* is involved; *where* that stage in the decision is likely to occur; the *timing* of each stage in relation to the other decision stages; and *how* that stage is likely to occur. The result is a detailed flow chart that identifies where potential members of the target market are likely to be making decisions and taking actions that lead to actual purchase and use of a product or service.

The objective of any model of consumer decision-making is to provide a useful format to help managers begin to think of where in the consumer's decision process marketing communication may be expected to influence brand choice. Once the model has been developed it helps the manager identify specific targeting objectives. It is surprisingly easy to construct a consumer decision-making model like the BSM, utilizing what those involved with a brand know about their market. As the manager works through the model, if 'gaps' in the understanding of the brand are uncovered, it will be necessary to conduct whatever research is required in order to feel comfortable that the model does indeed accurately reflect how consumers are making choices in the brand's category.

While it is important that a consumer decision-making model be developed specifically for a particular product category, utilizing the decision stages most likely to be operating for that category, a generic model can be helpful in initiating the process. The generic model shown in Fig. 6.3 illustrates how four general decision stages are combined with the decision roles involved at each stage, where each stage is likely to occur, the timing for each stage, and how each stage is likely to happen. Each of the components of the model will now be discussed.

Decision Stages

From as long ago as the beginnings of consumer behaviour theory the idea of 'stages' of a consumer's decision process has been central to notions of how consumers make choices.[9] Complete models of consumer behaviour have almost always included some step-wise component dealing with the decision model. While these models can often be very intimidating, they do acknowledge the necessity of understanding the consumer's decision process, the stages in the decision, in order to understand consumer behaviour.

Perhaps the most widely known and most enduring of these general models is the one

	Decision Stages			
	Need Arousal	Brand Consideration	Purchase	Usage
Decision Rules				
Where stage is likely to occur				
Timing of stage				
How stage is likely to happen				

Fig. 6.3 Generic Consumer Decision-making Model

originally offered by Engel and his colleagues over thirty years ago. In a recent version of their model we find a five-stage decision process component composed of: need recognition, search, alternative evaluation, purchasing, and outgoings.[10] The similarity of this to our set of decision stages in the generic model is not accidental. Some such 'flow' of thought and action is at the heart of any consumer purchase behaviour, and this is what we want to capture with a consumer decision-making model.

However, the important point to understand is that the exact words we use are not the important thing. What is important is that the manager begin to think about how consumers make decisions in the category, and at what points in this process advertising and other marketing communication can influence what brand is chosen. While the decision stages in the generic model are useful, and can generally be adapted to almost any product category, it is best to develop *specific* decision stages that more closely reflect how you understand decisions to be made in a brand's category. Some decisions may be quite simple, others more complicated. The decision stages for most fmcg products among brand loyals is simply Need Arousal—Purchase—Use. For example, if you have a favourite candy bar that you regularly buy, when you want a candy bar (Need Arousal) you will probably seek out your favourite brand and buy it (Purchase), then eat it on the spot (Use).

But returning to our earlier resort holiday example, the decision stages involved there are likely to be much more involved. Something will get you thinking about your next holiday, and you will begin to look into various alternatives. You will evaluate the options, and decide where you would like to go. Then you will need to check on availabilities and see if you can schedule the trip. You make the arrangements, go on the trip, and hopefully enjoy yourself, then 'relive' the experience afterward with pictures and discussions with friends.

The decision stages in this resort example are much more descriptive than those in the generic model, but they still reflect the basic generic stages. Starting to think about a holiday is Need Arousal; looking into and evaluating places to go is Brand Consideration; checking into availability and scheduling the trip is Purchase; and going on the trip and 'reliving' it is Usage. Modifications of the generic stages to fit specific circumstances enhances the utility of the model. The whole idea is to capture the essence of the decision process in order to facilitate marketing communication planning. Even though we are only at the first step in constructing the model (admittedly the most important), already we can see how laying out the decision stages can help pinpoint opportunities for affecting choice outcomes with advertising and other marketing communications.

Continuing with our holiday example, if we are the marketing manager for a resort on the southern coast of France, we will want to be sure potential guests are aware of us so that we come to mind when they begin to think about a holiday and look into various alternatives. In later chapters we will discuss the importance of building this link between what we call category need (going on a holiday in this case) and brand awareness (our resort). We will want to be sure potential guests have the information they need about our resort to evaluate it favourably. This could mean print advertising in appropriate magazines or direct mail brochures, as well as collateral material for travel agents. To facilitate the decision in our favour, perhaps we will want to offer some sort of incentive (especially at off-peak times of the year). At the resort itself, we will want to remind the guest of what a great choice they have made. The resort will of course need to meet the guest's expectations, but in many ways marketing communication can help reinforce this positive experience. Once guests have returned home, follow-up direct mail and general advertising can continue to reinforce the experience, building a stronger brand attitude, and increasing intentions to return.

It should now be clear that a manager must do more than simply decide they want to advertise and perhaps run the odd promotion or two. Marketing communication must be considered in light of how it is most likely to influence consumers positively as they are going through the process of making decisions. A good understanding of the decision stages is a key element in strategic marketing communication planning.

Low Involvement vs. High Involvement

The alert reader has no doubt already noticed that the distinction we made earlier in this chapter between low-involvement and high-involvement decisions is also related to the complexity of the decision stages associated with a particular product category. The reason is directly related to the fact that with low-involvement decisions, because there is relatively little risk involved in the choice, consumers really do not need to be *convinced* they are making the best choice. With high-involvement decisions, because there is risk attached to the choice, consumers will want to be more certain they are in fact making the best possible choices.

If we consider our generic model, what this means is that for low-involvement decisions, at the Brand Consideration stage there will not be a great deal of serious thinking going on. Using our candy bar example again, once need is aroused, the consumer will look for something to purchase and eat. At the time of need arousal, a brand may come to mind ('I think I'll get a Mars bar'), or it may just be a general category need ('I think I'll get a candy bar'). At the point of purchase the consumer sees what is available and makes a choice from a set of already known favourites. Perhaps there is a new candy bar there that the consumer then remembers seeing an advertisement for and thinks 'I might like that, I'll give it a try.' Because there is very little risk in this decision, at the Brand Consideration stage it is unlikely that the consumer in this case will postpone trial of the new candy bar until she looks into things more, perhaps seeking out friends who have tried it and asking for their opinion.

In consumer behaviour language, there is not a lot of 'information search and evaluation' required for low-involvement decisions. As a result, the decision stages tend to be less involved, even if there are several of them. This becomes evident as we look at the likely decision stages for two typical low-involvement choices: laundry detergent and casual eating out.

- *Laundry detergent*   Notice getting low—Shop—Select brand—Purchase—Use
- *Casual Eating Out*   Need Arousal—Decide what in 'mood' for—Decide on restaurant from that type—Go to restaurant—Eat

Contrast this with high-involvement decisions. Since consumers want to be confident they are making the best choice, there will be a corresponding 'information search and evaluation' to help ensure this. This means, in terms of our generic model, much more attention at the Brand Consideration stage. Suppose you have just bought your first house and with the onset of warm weather begin to notice a lot of bugs. You need an exterminator, but who? You will find out who is supposed to be good, and check them out. What is their reputation? Do they offer a guarantee and if so how long? What do they cost? After convincing yourself that one of them is likely to do the best job, they are engaged. You evaluate the job and decide whether to continue to use their service.

Let us consider another high-involvement decision, this time a business-to-business decision. Suppose you manufacture plumbing fixtures that are distributed through wholesale plumbing distributors. How do these wholesalers decide what fixtures and brands they will stock? A possible set of decision stages might begin with keeping an eye out for better fixtures to maintain an edge over competitors. This would lead to know-ledge about any new lines or items they might wish to stock. Once interest is aroused, the fixtures that caught their eye would be compared with what is currently stocked, and assessed against potential demand. If this evaluation of the potential for the product is positive, contact will be made with the manufacturer and there will be a second evalu-ation, this time in terms of the business arrangement. If the deal with the manufacturer is acceptable, the fixture will be ordered. Once stocked, sales and product reaction will be monitored, and if positive, the fixture will be reordered. Notice in this example that because the wholesaler is in effect the consumer for the fixture manufacturer, the deci-sion stages and BSM are developed around how the wholesaler makes a vendor choice.

It should be quite clear that more attention is given Brand Consideration, and often Purchase and Use, in high-involvement decisions, and our decision stages must reflect this. The decision stages for the two high-involvement examples just discussed might be thought of as follows:

- *Exterminator service*   Need arousal—Identify services—Evaluate services—Decide on service—Contact and schedule service—Evaluate results—Decide whether to retain service
- *Wholesale plumbing distributor stocking*   Monitor manufacturer and wholesale competitors—Identify items to evaluate—Evaluate items—Contact vendor—Evaluate vendor—Order and stock item—Evaluate sales performance—Reorder

Table 6.2 summarizes the various decision stages we have been discussing. As you review them, think about the decision stages in relation to the four decision stages in the

Table 6.2 Decision Stage Examples

Laundry Detergent	Notice getting low—shop—select brand—purchase—use
Casual Eating Out	Need arousal—decide what in 'mood' for—decide on restaurant from that type—go to restaurant—eat
Exterminator Service	Need arousal—verify services—evaluate services—decide on service—contract and schedule service—evaluate results—decide whether to retain service
Wholesale Plumbing Distributor Stocking	Monitor manufacturer and wholesale competitors—identify items to evaluate—evaluate items—contact vendor—evaluate vendor—order and stock item—evaluate sales performance—reorder

generic model. You will see that while the generic model certainly could be used in each case, when you custom-fit the decision stages for a specific product category or situation, you have a much better feel for where advertising and other marketing communication will be likely to have a positive effect upon the outcome of the purchase or usage decision.

Decision Roles

Once we have identified what the likely decision stages are for consumers making choices in a category, we must identify everyone who might play a part in the decision process, and the role or roles they play at *each decision stage*. This is really the first step in determining the target audience for marketing communication. We have already looked at the roles people can play in the decision process. Now we must determine where in the process specific individuals are likely to be involved.

This brings up a very important point. We are looking at *individuals*. In the marketing literature and in the talk of marketing managers today much is made of the notion of 'group decisions'. Important business decisions are rarely made by a single person; important household decisions are made jointly by husbands and wives. While this is certainly true, what we must be concerned with in developing advertising and other marketing communication strategy is the individual and the role he or she is playing in the decision. Advertising and other forms of marketing communication do not influence groups, they influence individuals in their role as part of the group making the decision. Constructing a consumer decision-making model enables the manager to see that many people may be involved in a decision, as we saw earlier, but as individuals in a role.

Let's return to the example of a resort holiday discussed earlier and the DPG in Fig. 6.2 to see how this analysis of decision roles fits into the model. From our earlier discussion, the decision stages for a holiday trip might be seen as:

- *Holiday Trip* Need arousal—Identify possible holidays—Evaluate options—Choose holiday—Book holiday—Take holiday—Post holiday evaluation

According to the DPG, what individuals are likely to be involved at the need arousal stage and in what roles? Because those playing a role as *initiator* get the process started, they are the ones most likely to be involved at this stage. This would include the potential traveller, other family members or friends, and travel agents. All of these people, this time in their role as *influencer*, could be involved in identifying possible holidays and helping to evaluate options. Then the potential traveller and mate (if there is one) in their role as *decider* will both play a part in choosing the holiday, and either they or a travel agent as the *purchaser* will book the holiday. Everyone who goes on the holiday plays a role as *user*, as well as an *influencer* in post-holiday evaluations.

Where the Decision Stages Occur

An important key to effective marketing communication is to identify where in the decision process a message of some kind might make a positive contribution. The better we understand where those opportunities lie, the better our media planning. We need to know where members of our target audience (which at this point is potentially *everyone* involved in the decision process) are likely to be making decisions. These locations are fairly easy to generate, and can range from a single location to many locations spread over a considerable period of time. The important thing is to *think* about likely locations for each stage consumers go through when making a brand choice.

The lower involving the decision, the more concentrated the decision process is likely to be. Generally this will be somewhere prior to purchase where awareness and initial attitudes are formed, then at the point of purchase and time of use. This most likely is simply at home and the store. There are always exceptions, of course. You could be shopping and have someone give you a sample of a new snack. You taste it and really like it, see it on a special rack at the check-out, buy one and eat it on your way out of the store. Everything occurred in the store, but this would *not* reflect the likely location for all decision stages in all snack choices. Do consider exceptions, for possible specifically targeted marketing communication. But in thinking about where decision stages are likely to occur, think more broadly.

Let's continue with our holiday trip example. Where is need arousal likely to take place? For the potential traveller, it could occur at home, while visiting friends (who perhaps are just back from a holiday), or at a travel agency. It could even occur almost serendipitously when the potential traveller sees a poster on the underground or at the train station. *Already media planning possibilities should occur to you.* Broadcast advertising to the home, newspaper advertisements for the commuter, banners and collateral at travel agencies, posters on or near transportation. This is the sort of thinking a consumer decision-making model is designed to encourage.

People might identify possible holidays in any of the places that need arousal occurs, as well as evaluate them there, although they are most likely to evaluate potential destinations at home or with a travel agent. From home or at a travel agent is also where the holiday is most likely to be booked. The holiday itself, of course, occurs at the destination, while the post-holiday evaluation could occur almost anywhere they are reminded of it.

Identifying opportunities for advertising and other marketing communication is, as we have said, a key to effectively implementing a marketing communication programme. Careful attention to where each decision stage in a consumer decision model is likely to occur can be a big help.

Timing of the Decision Stages

Understanding the timing of the decision stages is also very important for media planning, especially for when to schedule media. The timing of most decisions may seem too obvious to occasion much concern. But it can make a critical difference to many products. The timing of most holiday decisions is generally not much more than a few months, unless it is for a very special trip. But what if you are a cruise line? By the time someone is normally at the stage of evaluating options, it is generally too late to book a cruise. This means that a cruise advertiser must do something to stimulate need arousal at a much earlier date relative to expected holiday travel in order to allow for the longer advance booking generally required for a cruise. In this case, knowing the timing of a holiday decision will alert the cruise line manager to the fact that it will be necessary for them to design messages and schedule media such that they are in a position to initiate holiday thinking much earlier among potential travellers.

The timing of a decision can also often play a critical role even in low-involvement decisions. Suppose you are a food company that markets dessert products. You might not think timing would play much of a role in the dessert decision. But, while it doesn't in terms of purchasing dessert products, it is vital to when the decision to *serve* is made. We know from research that the decision stages for desserts are as follows:

- *Dessert decision*   Need Arousal—Purchase for inventory—Decide to serve—Choose
dessert from inventory—Serve and eat

Before moving on, notice that the decision stages include more than the simple low-involvement model of need arousal–purchase–use. Given the nature of this decision, the *usage* stage is more complicated than normal for an fmcg. Working through a consumer decision-making model alerts the manager to special situations such as this that can significantly affect marketing and communication strategies.

The critical timing concern here occurs at the decision-to-serve stage. This stage, for all but special-occasion meals that are planned ahead, occurs *after the meal*. This means the product must be ready-to-eat once the meal is finished and the question is asked: 'What's for dessert?' At this point, it is too late to bake a cake. It is also too late for a product like Jell-O.

Jell-O is a gelatin dessert product that is very popular in the United States, especially among children: when asked if Jell-O would have been a good choice for dessert at last evening's meal, almost everyone will say 'yes'. Unfortunately, when the decision to serve is made, Jell-O is a box of granular crystals. To be ready to serve the box of Jell-O crystals must be dissolved in hot water and left in the refrigerator for some time to set before it is ready to eat. Because the decision of what to serve for dessert is made after the meal, Jell-O is not an option. Knowledge of the timing of the decision, however, led to an advertising campaign called 'early morning reminder to serve'. In this campaign messages were placed in early morning in-home media reminding people they will want Jell-O for dessert that evening, so why not prepare it now while the hot water is at hand for coffee and tea?

Here is an example where the decision itself appears rather simple and straightforward, but where understanding the *timing* of the decision had a significant impact upon increasing usage of the product.

How the Decision Stages Occur

The final step in developing a consumer decision-making model is to consider what is going on at each of the decision stages. In thinking about how each stage happens you are taking one of the first steps toward establishing a *positioning* strategy for your advertising and other marketing communication. The 'how' is your best description of what is happening at each stage of the decision process. What happens to stimulate a perceived need for the product? How is the target market going to behave? Where are consumers likely to find information about brands (if they need it)? What goes on when actually making a purchase? How is the product actually used? Answers to questions like these complete the model.

To finish our example of the decision to take a holiday trip, let us look at how each of the stages in that process are likely to happen. *Need arousal* will occur when the potential traveller is talking with friends about their recent holiday, when they see advertising for a holiday destination, or perhaps when visiting a travel agent. They will *identify possible holidays* at the time their interest is piqued during need arousal, and in the period immediately following by asking friends or family members, paying more attention to advertising on television and in the newspapers and magazines, and perhaps by visiting a travel agent.

In *evaluating options* the potential traveller might ask for specific information from destinations identified in the previous stage, talk about places with friends or family who have been there or know people who have, or ask the advice of a travel agent.

In *choosing the holiday destination* they will no doubt pick the place that best offers what is most important to them for this trip. We mentioned earlier the importance of this 'how' step to positioning strategy for marketing communication. If our example is a good approximation of the actual decision stages and what is involved in making a holiday trip decision (and it is based upon proprietary research conducted by one of the authors), then we can see the importance of *other people* in the evaluation and selection of a holiday destination. Other people will also serve as sources of information to form the basis of beliefs that will help shape the potential traveller's attitudes toward the various destinations under consideration. This insight is critical to the formulation of a communication positioning strategy, as we shall see when we deal with positioning in Chapter 7.

To *book the holiday*, the potential traveller will either call the destination and make their own arrangements or use a travel agent. *They will take the holiday* by travelling to the destination and experiencing what is there. *Post-holiday evaluation* will actually begin as soon as they leave, and reoccur when they talk about the trip with family and friends, when they occasionally just think about the trip and relive the experience, and when they are reminded of the trip by seeing advertising for their holiday site.

This illustrates what forms the foundation of a consumer decision-making model like Rossiter and Percy's BSM, and you can see how it can provide a very detailed look at a target audience in terms of how it actually goes about deciding to buy or use a product or service. Fig. 6.4 summarizes a model for a holiday trip that we have been using as an example. As you review this example, notice how it offers a *dynamic* view of the target market and suggests opportunities for delivering targeted messages to different people who may be involved in affecting the outcome of the decision.

Summary

In this chapter we have examined consumer behaviour in depth by utilizing a consumer decision-making model. We have identified the five roles that participants may play in the decision process and linked this to message objectives. To aid in the analysis process

Decision Stages

Decision Roles	Need Arousal	Identify Possible Holidays	Evaluate Options	Choose Holiday	Book Holiday	Take Holiday	Post Holiday Evaluation
Decision Roles	self, friends, family as initiators and influences travel agent as initiator	self, friends, family as influences travel agent, resorts and other destinations as influences	self, mate as decider travel agent as influence	self, mate as decider	self, mate as purchaser travel agent as purchaser	self, mate	self, mate
Where stage is likely to occur	home, friends travel agency	home, friends travel agency	home travel agency	home travel agency	home travel agency	destination	almost anywhere
Timing of stage	2–4 months before holiday	immediately after need arousal	over 2–4 weeks following need arousal	within 4 weeks of need arousal	within 1 week of choice	2–3 months after booking	after holiday
How stage is likely to happen	friends talk, see adverts, at travel agency	talk with friends, family, see adverts, visit travel agency	call or write destinations, see adverts, talk with friends, family	compare costs, what is offered, when available	call destination, travel agent, internet	travel to destination, experience at destination	tell friends, relatives of experience, reminded when see adverts

Fig. 6.4 Consumer Decision-making Model for a Major Holiday Trip

we have introduced the Decision Participant Grid and illustrated its use. We then went on to analyse the stages of consumer decision-making and related this to high- vs. low-involvement decisions based on perceived risk. We considered the importance of when the stages occur and their timing, and how each stage is likely to happen. We then saw how this information might be used to identify opportunities for targeted messages to different people at different stages of the decision process.

Questions to consider

6.1   What are the five potential roles for participants to play in a choice decision?

6.2   Why is it important to target individuals in a role?

6.3   When might the same message be appropriate regardless of role?

6.4   Why is a single advertisement for a high-involvement purchase unlikely to be effective?

6.5   What is the purpose of the 'Providers' column in the Decision Participant Grid?

6.6   Why do consumers seek more information when making a high-involvement purchase than when making a low-involvement purchase?

6.7   How does advertising influence 'group decisions'?

6.8   How might the timing of a decision affect media scheduling?

Notes

1   One of the first textbooks in the field of consumer behaviour was Francesco M. Nicosia's *Consumer Decision Process: Marketing and Advertising Implications* (Englewood Cliffs, NJ: Prentice Hall, 1966).

2   One of the first and most comprehensive models of consumer behaviour is found in John A. Howard and Jagdish N. Sheth's *The Theory of Buyer Behavior* (New York: John Wiley and Sons, 1969).

3   Gerrit Antonides and W. Fred van Raaij, *Consumer Behaviour: A European Perspective* (Chichester: John Wiley and Sons, 1998).

4   There are a number of recent books on consumer behaviour from many different perspectives, in addition to the Antonides and van Raaij book. Examples include: Robert East, *Consumer Behaviours: Advances and Applications in Marketing* (London: Prentice Hall, 1997); Frank R. Kardes, *Consumer Behaviour and Management Decision Making* (Reading, Mass.: Addison-Wesley, 1999); Michael Solomon, Gary Bamossy, and Søven Askegaard, *Consumer Behaviour: A European Perspective* (New York: Prentice Hall Europe, 1999).

5   In J. R. Rossiter and L. Percy, *Advertising and Promotion Management*, (New York: McGraw-Hill, 1987), and subsequently expanded in their *Advertising Communication and Promotion Management* (New York: McGraw-Hill, 1977), as well as in L. Percy,

Strategies for Implementing Integrated Marketing Communication (Lincolnwood, Ill.: NTC Business Press, 1997).

6   Two-stage choice models can differ significantly from the more usual single-stage choice models. A good review of this issue is found in Dennis Gensch's 'A Two-stage Disaggregate Attribute Choice Model', *Marketing Science*, 6:3 (1987).

7   This idea of a Decision Participant Grid was first introduced in Larry Percy's *Strategies for Implementing Integrated Marketing Communication* (NTC Business Press, 1997).

8   See John Howard's notion of routinized response behaviour in *Consumer Behaviour: An Application of Theory* (New York: McGraw-Hill, 1997).

9   In *Consumer Behaviour*, Howard, one of the fathers of consumer behaviour theory, dealt with the idea of stages in the consumer decision process, integrating how managers, psychologists, and economists view them. This discussion marked an extension of his original work with Jag Sheth (see n. 2).

10 This model was first introduced in J. F. Engel, D. T. Kollat, and R. D. Blackwell, *Consumer Behavior* (New York: Holt, Rinehart and Winston, 1968), and is remarkably similar to the Howard and Sheth model (see n. 2). Authors of consumer behaviour textbooks continue to include this model or a close variation in their books. For example, East, *Consumer Behaviours* includes the most recent version of the Engel *et al.* model. While not completely immune to criticism, principally because of its cognitive nature (see especially A. S. C. Ehrenberg, *Repeat Buying: Theory and Applications*, 2nd edn. (London: Charles Griffin and Co., 1988), this general model of consumer behaviour has proven to be remarkably long-lived).

Chapter 7

Positioning Strategy

Interestingly, most marketing scholars seem to have a rather consistent definition of positioning. In his recent marketing principles book, David Jobber has defined positioning as 'the choice of: target market, *where* we want to compete; [and] differential advantage, *how* we wish to compete' (emphasis his).[1] Compare this with the very similar definition offered by Hooley and Saunders in the preface to their book on competitive positioning, where they describe the two central issues in marketing strategy formulation as: 'The identification of target market or markets, the customers that the organization will seek to serve', and 'The creation of a differential advantage, or competitive edge, that will enable the organization to serve the target market more effectively than the competitor'.[2] And Peter Doyle in *Marketing Management and Strategy* says, 'Positioning strategy is the choice of target market segments, which determine where the business competes, and the choice of differential advantage, which dictates how it competes.'[3]

There would seem to be a consensus that 'positioning' entails identifying the market where you compete, and then seeking a differential advantage. In this chapter we shall look at how to define markets, and then the best way to identify the benefit that will provide a brand with a differential advantage over competitors.

Overall, positioning strategy is generally outlined in the marketing plan, and takes into account all aspects of the marketing mix. While a full discussion of this is well beyond the scope of this book,[4] it would be a good idea, before we get specifically into positioning strategy, to look at just where marketing communication does fit within the marketing mix.

Marketing Mix

To begin with, just what do we mean by the 'marketing mix'? Generally speaking, when one is talking about the marketing mix they are referring to those marketing variables that the marketer controls, and that are used to achieve a company's overall marketing objectives. While there are certainly a great many variables that could be considered here, most people classify them into the four groups popularized by McCarthy which we mentioned in Chapter 1: Product, Price, Place, and Promotion—the so-called 'four P's' of marketing. The key here is that the marketing mix deals with *controllable* variables.

A company certainly decides what product it will manufacture. Clearly they should make a product that corresponds to consumer demand in the category, but it is really up to the company to determine what it will offer. Accordingly, price points are decided upon by the company. Again, while competition within the category will influence pricing strategy, in the end it is really up to the company to decide the prices for their products. Place, McCarthy's 'P' for distribution, is also a marketing variable clearly under the control of the company. Of course the company can't simply 'wish' for distribution and achieve it. But to the extent the company's sales force is effective in gaining and holding distribution, the delivery of the product to the consumer is determined by the company.

This brings us to the final 'P', promotion. McCarthy uses the word 'promotion' in a very generic way: advertising, promotion, public relations, and sales-force selling. Most marketers would agree that in addition to promotion and advertising, personal selling and public relations are also included in the promotion component. Personal selling, while it may account for more actual expenditures from the marketing budget at many companies, is generally a more specialized marketing function and is outside the scope of advertising and marketing communications planning. The overall emphasis a company places upon personal selling vs. advertising and promotion differs markedly from one type of business to another. As you might guess, industrial marketers are more likely to feel that personal selling and trade promotion is more important to their business than advertising, so they concentrate their marketing monies in that area. Companies that manufacture consumer durable goods (heavy appliances, automobiles, and so forth) place about equal emphasis upon advertising and promotion, and personal selling. Consumer package goods companies, of course, rely very heavily upon advertising and promotion in marketing their products. Public relations, on the other hand, is similar in many ways to advertising, and in many cases should be coordinated with advertising strategy. But public relations is implemented in different ways from advertising. The most obvious difference is that much of public relations is 'free' in the sense that the company does not pay to have stories appear in the media. They do, of course, pay public relations specialists to create the stories and attempt to gain exposure for them. There is a great deal to understand about public relations, but this too is beyond the scope of this book.

In this book, we are really only interested in advertising and promotion. But for a company, all of their marketing communication strategies must be coordinated so that expenditure on advertising is reinforced by the money spent on promotion, public relations, and sales, money spent on promotion reinforces advertising, public relations, and sales, etc.

Positioning and the Marketing Mix

McCarthy's broader view of 'promotion' is only one part of the marketing mix, and traditional advertising and promotion only one part of it. Nevertheless, all components of the marketing mix must be understood if effective *marketing plans* are to be developed. How does a company go about determining the strategy that will ultimately affect advertising and other marketing communication planning? Simply put, it must gain as complete an understanding of its market as possible. This means knowing how competitors are positioned, and what benefits consumers are seeking in the market. From this information a marketing plan is developed.

Perhaps an illustration here will help us see just how a company must look at all aspects of the marketing mix before setting a strategic direction. Suppose the brand space shown in Fig. 7.1 reflects the major competitive brands of VCRs in the marketplace, with their relative market shares reflected by the size of their circles.

What this tells us is that of the five leading brands, most consumers tend to see them as differing primarily along two dimensions: price and number of features. The alert reader will immediately see that these two dimensions reflect two components of the marketing mix: price and product. Of course, this need not be the case. Consumers could just as easily compare VCRs along other product attribute dimensions, such as European-made vs. made in the Pacific Rim, or two-track vs. four-track. But as an example, we will look at how price and features might drive strategy.

What we have here is a market where the brand share leader A is seen to be mid-priced, with some features but not a lot. Brand B and Brand C have roughly equal shares, but Brand B is seen as having more features with a higher price, while Brand C is lower-priced with fewer features. Brand D has the smallest share, and is seen as somewhat expensive with few features. Say our brand, Brand E, is the fourth largest and seen as having relatively few features, and a moderate price.

Given these general relationships among the brands in the market, where should Brand E position itself to optimize sales? Practically speaking, it should try to move more to the centre and compete with Brand A, or move toward Brand C's pricing in an effort to attract more buyers. But why should consumers be interested in either new position? There are already products satisfying those segments of the market. Nevertheless, with the proper marketing and communication efforts, along with product modifications, this could be a valid course.

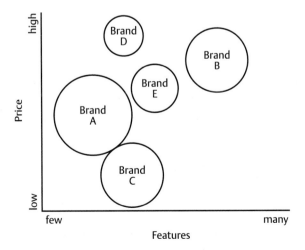

Fig. 7.1 Hypothesized Mapping of VCR Market in Terms of Price and Number of Features

Another course would be to attempt to move alone into the lower right quadrant with a lower-priced VCR that offers a lot of features. If possible, this would be ideal because there are no competitors offering such a product. Of course, there may be good reasons why this quadrant is unoccupied. Brand E's marketing managers must ask themselves whether or not it is possible to manufacture a VCR with a number of features, but still at a low cost. Perhaps the company could put up with lower profit margins, or perhaps the company's research and development could come up with product or manufacturing innovations that would save costs.

In any event, you should by now see that one cannot simply decide upon a positioning for a brand without taking into consideration all of the components in the marketing mix. In this brief example we have seen that price is dependent upon the cost of the features that will be built into the product, and is also perhaps a function of persuading the trade to accept lower margins on the brand (place, or distribution).

Suppose R & D tells marketing that they have achieved a breakthrough which permits them to include all of the features currently available with Brand B, while still maintaining their existing cost structure. Good news indeed for the brand manager, but his positioning options with respect to the marketing mix are still open. For example, one strategy might indeed be price-related, communicating that now the brand offers many new features at the same price. But another strategy could be to upgrade the brand's image by pursuing a quality-feature strategy at higher price points. This would make a lot of sense, since our brand could now offer more features than Brand A at the same price as A, or the same features as Brand B, but at a lower price (while maintaining a higher price than Brand A). Either of these latter two strategies would also permit larger margins at the retail level, pleasing the distribution chain, while at the same time increasing the unit profit for the company.

Although marketing communication is only one part of the marketing mix, all four components interact and must be considered as you begin to think about positioning and communication strategy. Overall, you can think of the marketing mix as providing consumer value. By this we mean that the marketing mix should be construed so as to offer a set of benefits to the consumer, benefits the consumers will relate to their underlying motivations to behave. Of the four components of the marketing mix, the product or service must provide attributes that are seen as offering particular benefits to the consumer; price must be seen within the context of a price–value relationship; place or distribution must provide convenient access to the product, as well as positive store images; and finally promotion will alert the consumer to these potential benefits. These points are summarized in Table 7.1, and this relationship between what the product offers, the benefits perceived by the consumers, and their motivation to respond will be

Table 7.1 Consumer Benefits related to the Four Components of the Marketing Mix

Product	Must provide attributes that are seen as offering particular benefits to the consumer
Price	Must be seen within the context of a price-value relationship
Place	Must provide convenient access to the product as well as positive store image
Promotion	Will alert the consumer to these potential benefits

explored in greater depth in later chapters. In fact, it is this relationship that advertising, and other forms of marketing communication, must forge if it is to be successful.

Understanding How Markets are Defined

As the definitions of positioning offered earlier make clear, one of the most important considerations in the development of a positioning strategy is exactly how you are defining the market where you are competing. This may sound like a very simple question. After all, if you are selling beer, your market is made up of all the brands of beer that are sold along with yours in a particular area, right? Well, this is not necessarily true. For example, what if you were marketing a lower-calorie beer like Amstel Light? You might have a 10 per cent share of the European beer market; or you might be thought of as having a 35 per cent share of the lower calorie beer market; or even a 3 per cent share of the 'light alcoholic beverage' market, which would include wine and other specialty light alcoholic products as well. To establish what category we are dealing with—which will define the important communication effect of category need—requires us to define the market in which our brand competes.

We can see by the Amstel Light example that defining your market is not necessarily a straightforward issue. The actual basis for what defines the true market for a brand is how *consumers* see a group of products or brands competing for the same usage situation. If the majority of consumers regard a group of brands as being close substitutes for each other, or as purchase alternatives, then this group of brands defines the market.

The reason we are so very much concerned about knowing the true definition of a market is that without it the strategic direction for the brand, especially in terms of market share objectives, could well be misleading. If the strategic direction is wrong, you can bet the communication strategy will also be wrong, because it will be based upon a misleading definition of the market.

You may be thinking that the best way to define a market is surely to look for the biggest possible segment, and in a sense you would be right. It is certainly more desirable to have a large share of a big market than of a small market, or at times even a smaller share of a big market than a big share of a smaller market. But this is not the point. It doesn't matter how *we* define the market. The market actually defines itself by how *consumers see the market*. The way in which consumers look at a market will determine how they behave, and for us to develop effective advertising and marketing communication strategy we must understand why and how consumers behave as they do.

Another important reason to understand how markets are defined is that it permits you to make more effective positioning decisions for new products. To the extent that a company positions a new product or brand within the same market as other products sold by that same company it encourages cannibalization. ('Cannibalization' is a term used in marketing to describe a situation where the introduction of a new product takes sales away from existing products the company sells rather than adding incremental new sales.) Again, this could have significant implications for marketing communication.

Let us consider the case of Nestlé, who for many years marketed a frozen pizza product that was made with French bread. First introduced in the US under the Stouffer brand name, it was then marketed in Europe and the Pacific Rim under the Findas brand. This French bread pizza soon became one of the leading frozen pizzas. But a real question arises as to whether or not the consumer saw this product as just another frozen pizza, or as a different pizza-like product. You may feel that it really doesn't matter as long as it has strong sales. But Nestlé obviously considered their product as competing in the frozen pizza market because they referred to it in their advertising as 'Findas Pizza' and not 'Findas French Bread Pizza'.

However, in 1988 Stouffer's introduced in the US a new round frozen pizza similar to other traditional frozen pizzas. At that time, the only frozen pizza they and Findas marketed was the French bread product, which, as we have noted, was referred to in their advertising simply as Stouffer's or Findas Pizza. They had an obvious problem: how to position both products to maximize overall market share. This should help you begin to really appreciate the importance of good market definitions. What should they have done? Reposition the French bread product for a French bread frozen pizza market, or position it simply as one of two types of frozen pizza that they offer? The first position assumes that the consumer looks at French bread pizza products as a different market from traditional round frozen pizzas, but there was no evidence of this. The second position assumes that the consumer looks at all frozen pizza products, regardless of form, as a single market, and would welcome a line extension from Nestlé. The implication for advertising would obviously be different, depending upon how consumers define the market. Nestlé introduced the product under the Stouffer's and Findas brands, but were not successful. The market did not see the need for a 'second' pizza from Nestlé. Perhaps the best way would have been to introduce the round pizza under a new brand name. The problem was that Nestlé did not have a clear understanding of how consumers defined the market where French bread pizza competed.

Ways to Define Markets

Perhaps the most traditional way of describing markets is simply to look at a broad category and then break it down by whatever characteristics of the product make sense. For example, traditionally the beer market is seen as divided first into regular vs. lower-alcohol or -calorie, then price brands, regular, premium, super-premium, imported, and micro-brewed brands. The interesting thing here is that while those who brew and market beer look at the category in this way, consumers are less precise. In fact, if you were to ask the ordinary beer drinker to classify brands like Becks, Budweiser, Heineken, or Miller they would call them regular beers, but these are classified as premium or imported beers (depending upon where you are in the world) by the industry.

Other ways to describe markets *a priori* include defining them in terms of their channels of distribution. For example, especially with industrial products, those sold directly through a manufacturer will be seen as different from those sold through a jobber or distributor. Consumer package goods are often looked at as national brands vs. private label, or advertised vs. unadvertised brands.

The point in presenting these traditional ways in which markets are described is to show that they tend to reflect a product-oriented approach to marketing more than a consumer-oriented approach. Not only are such non-consumer-oriented approaches to market definition likely to lead to less effective advertising and marketing communication strategy, but they can also interfere with effective overall marketing. An interesting case in point was the forced divestiture of Clorox by Procter and Gamble. Some years ago one of the issues raised in support of the antitrust action was the high share of the bleach market controlled by Clorox. Unfortunately for Procter and Gamble, Clorox's market share was defined only in terms of liquid bleach: the definition excluded dry bleaches from consideration.

Cross Elasticity

A rather interesting, if somewhat abstract, way of thinking about defining markets considers the cross-elasticities between products. As you might imagine, this is a method that has been proposed by economists and is price-related. It is not unusual for economists to propose various schemes for dealing with consumer behaviour that are based upon the utilities of time and price. Practically speaking, however, such schemes tend to mask more than illuminate what is going on in the market. Nevertheless, it is useful to at least be aware of some of these ideas.

The notion of using price cross-elasticity to define markets is rooted in the idea that cross-elasticity of price between two products or brands is directly proportional to the shift in sales for one brand as a result of a change in price for another. In other words, to the extent that an increase in the price of one brand brings about an increase in the sales of a second brand, they may be considered substitutable, and therefore part of the same market.

As we have suggested, this is certainly plausible, but rather difficult to measure accurately in the market. Perhaps as scanning data become more widely available, shifts in sales as a function of price changes will be easier to detect. But even if such shifts in market share are reliably measured, there remains the question of controlling for all other variables in the market, especially advertising and other marketing communication.

Perceived Similarity

A much more understandable way of looking at markets is in terms of how similar consumers perceive the brands in a particular category to be. Measures of similarity can range from the very simple to the quite complex. For example, consumers can simply be asked to list all of the products they use for a particular task or in a particular situation. Those products felt to be appropriate for the same usage situation could be thought of as similar, and hence defining a market. For example, in household cleaning consumers may feel that such diverse products as ammonia and soap are appropriate products to clean a counter-top. If so, one could certainly say that they help to define the market for counter-top cleaners.

The alert reader, however, should recognize that while a simple method like this does define a market in a certain way, and it certainly is consumer-based, it does not offer a very precise definition. All this method provides is an aggregate definition of the market, without really telling us how the consumer makes fundamental judgements in the market, and it is these fundamental judgements that are important in formulating advertising strategy. Having said this, it should be noted that this simple idea of perceived similarity is none the less the foundation of category need, which is essential to positioning brands in marketing communication, as we shall see later in this chapter.

A somewhat more advanced version of this simple model permits the consumer to group together products or brands in terms of their perceived relative similarity. There are a number of statistical methods available to deal with this question, and they are usually referred to as perceptual mapping procedures.[5] What these techniques do is take a set of similarity judgements and map them in such a way that those brands which are considered similar to each other end up close together while those which are further apart are seen as less alike.

Let's consider the mapping shown in Fig. 7.2. This represents the actual results of a study where consumers were asked to rank-order all the pairs of brands studied from the two they felt were most alike through to the pair they felt were least alike. While we need not get into the actual way this is done, the results when mapped place those brands close together on the map that consumers see as most alike, and those that are not seen as alike are placed far apart. In this example we can see that brands like Sanka, Nescafé and Nescafé Decaffeinated are seen as unique, whereas other brands—Folgers, Maxwell House, and Taster's Choice regular and Decaffeinated—are seen as alike.

This is a particularly interesting example, because both caffeinated and decaffeinated soluble (or 'instant') coffee brands are included. If consumers initially defined the soluble coffee market by types, we would expect that the caffeinated brands would be mapped separately from the decaffeinated brands. But as we can see, while Sanka and Nescafé Decaffeinated are indeed separate from the caffeinated brands, Taster's Choice regular and Decaffeinated are mapped together, indicating that consumers see them as quite similar. Additionally, Brim (a decaffeinated brand) is also mapped near the regular

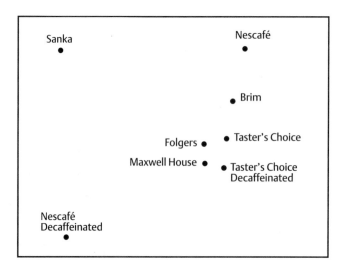

Fig. 7.2 Consumer Mapping of Soluble Coffee Brands

brands. It is simply not clear from this example how consumers are defining the soluble coffee market.

All we can say about the soluble coffee market based upon this similarities mapping is that Folgers, Maxwell House, Taster's Choice, Taster's Choice Decaffeinated, and Brim—two decaffeinated and three caffeinated brands—are seen as similar, and all of these brands are seen as quite different from Nescafé, Sanka, and Nescafé Decaffeinated. While there are methods available to help us determine just why consumers feel these similarities exist, this mapping itself does not offer a very clear understanding of how consumers define this market.

Even though this method is an improvement over the simple aggregate method of looking at similarities in terms of, say, usage, since it does permit us to identify sub-markets, it still is not quite as useful as defining markets *hierarchically*, which we shall look at next. The problem is that we still do not know if, for example, the critical classification is made first in terms of type or brand. Actually, these mappings have much more value in defining the relationship among products or brands than in defining markets.

Hierarchical Market Definition

We encountered the idea of a hierarchical process in our discussion of the four-step response sequence. You will recall that we talked about the compounding problem, where what comes before determines what comes later. One way to look at how consumers define markets is to look at the order in which they consider characteristics of a product in the decisions they make.[6] In marketing terminology this is often referred to as *partitioning* a market.

The thinking that underlies a hierarchical definition of a market is that an overall product category (such as beverages, deodorants, automobiles, etc.) can be divided and then subdivided several times into sub-categories that define narrower markets, and which will tend to end when consumers make their actual choice. Several things are implied in this notion of partitioning markets about the way consumers behave. First of all, as we proceed down the hierarchy, we assume that consumers see different brands in the market as more and more alike, and hence that they are more substitutable. Then, assuming the consumer sees brands as more and more alike, they will be increasingly more willing to switch among brands. This idea is illustrated in Fig. 7.3. You can see that

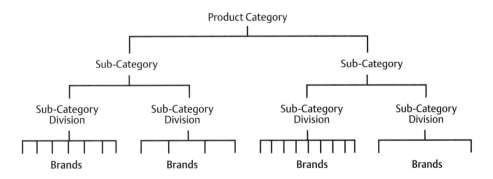

Fig. 7.3 Hierarchical Partitioning of a Product Category

advertising and other marketing communication must be able to deal with this tendency of consumers to view brands as more or less alike as they move down the partitioning hierarchy. It must correctly position the category need in relation to the appropriate decision level in the hierarchy, and work to create a unique positioning for a brand against the competition. This should become clearer soon, when we illustrate hypothetical executions of partitioning hierarchies for the drinks category.

Bases for partitions

When consumers are asked to describe how products in a category differ, they do not make a hierarchical distinction, but they do tend to talk about brands and products in terms of four general characteristics:

- *Type of product*: for example in frozen foods there are full dinners vs. just main dishes, main dishes vs. side dishes, main meals vs. breakfast, etc.

- *End benefit*: for example, aspirin could be taken to ease pain or to help prevent a heart attack, or you could buy an expensive Scotch because you like the taste or because you want to impress your friends.

- *Usage situation*: the end benefit that you are seeking in a product may vary as a function of when or how the product is used, for example 'instant' or soluble coffee only for breakfast, but ground roast for when you have friends over.

- *Brand name*: finally, the brand itself implies many things and could be a key factor in defining markets; for example, we can all think of brands we consider 'quality' brands vs. 'price' brands.

Notice some important things about these characteristics. They could all be used to describe the same product or brand, but the *order* in which they are used by consumers in arriving at a choice is what will determine how consumers define markets. You should be able to see how each factor, depending on which is the final arbiter of choice, will suggest different advertising strategies to deal with it.

Thinking in terms of these four characteristics, if we were to define the coffee market, we would want answers from consumers to questions like these:

- What kind of a product is coffee?

- Why do you drink coffee?

- When do you drink coffee?

- What are the differences among various brands of coffee?

Answers to questions like these begin to explain how consumers see the coffee market, and helps the marketing manager define the market strategically the way consumers themselves do.

If you were the marketing manager for a coffee brand, how do you think the market structure would be defined? This is actually a more complicated question than you might imagine. If you consider simply what coffee 'is', it is something people drink. Fig. 7.4 suggests a reasonable product-based hierarchical partition of the drinks market. If this is an accurate representation (and research suggests it is), then at the product level coffee

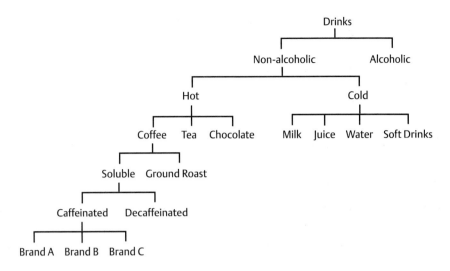

Fig. 7.4 Hypothesized Hierarchical Partitioning of the Drinks Market for Coffee

competes with non-alcoholic, hot drinks. But this is really much too simple, and is actually misleading.

When you ask consumers to talk about coffee, addressing questions like those above, they do talk about it in terms of product characteristics, especially ground roast vs. 'instant' (i.e. soluble). But they are *much* more lively when discussing coffee in terms of end benefits and usage situations.[7] Figures 7.5a and 7.5b illustrate how we might imagine the drinks market partitioned along these lines.

From these partitionings we can see that the market strategy should be aimed at positioning coffee against the end benefits of stimulation and relaxation, or against situational usage. Interestingly, the end benefits partitioning suggests that coffee should be

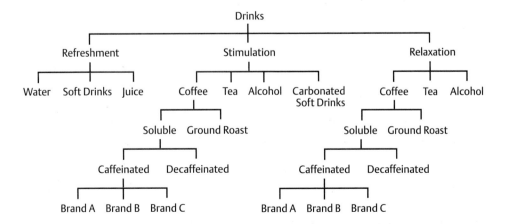

Fig. 7.5a Hypothesized Hierarchical Partitioning of the Drinks Market Driven by End Benefit

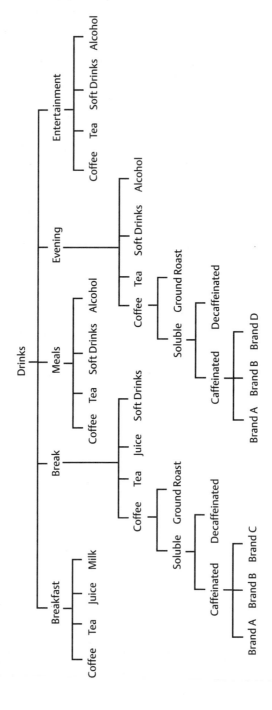

Fig. 7.5b Hypothesized Hierarchical Partitioning of the Drinks Market Driven by Usage Situation

thought of as competing more with alcoholic beverages than with soft drinks. While some perceptions overlap in the consumer's mind, coffee has more in common with tea and alcoholic beverages, and it is not seen as refreshing. Clearly the advertising and marketing communication strategy suggested by this market definition will be much different from that suggested by the product-based positioning.

An interesting use of mappings in conjunction with hierarchical descriptions has been offered by Urban and Hauser.[8] In the method they suggest, you begin with a hierarchical approach, but you define the branches not only in terms of the physical attributes or characteristics of the product, but also by consumer perception. Perceptions are modelled by a map for each branch of the tree generated by the hierarchical definition. Fig. 7.6 illustrates a hypothetical application of this method to the beer market.

What Fig. 7.6 suggests is that consumers first define the beer market in terms of imports vs. domestic beers, then define the domestic market in terms of lower-calorie or 'lite' beers vs. full-calorie beers. Then, within these hierarchical definitions they see brands along taste vs. premium dimensions. If this were a true representation of the beer market (remember, it is only a hypothetical example), it would suggest that for domestic beers it would be important to understand that since consumers make primary distinctions between 'lite' and full-calorie beers, advertising strategy must also take this into account. Specifically, separate campaigns would be necessary for, say, Amstel and Amstel Light. If both types of beer were mentioned in the same advert, as some brewers have done, consumers could be a bit confused because they see these as two distinctly different products.

On the other hand, again assuming our hypothetical example, with imported beers

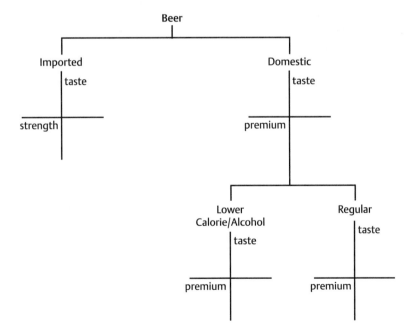

Fig. 7.6 Hypothesized Hierarchical Partitioning and Mapping of the Beer Market

consumers may not distinguish between lower-calorie and full-calorie beers. This would mean that advertisers of imported beers might only be concerned with identifying their brand as imported. How the notion of greater European unity may change ideas of 'imported' beer remains to be seen. The perceptual map of the imported beer market suggests that consumers evaluate *imported* beers in terms of taste and strength.

In summary, you should now see that a consumer-driven definition of markets is essential for the development of effective advertising strategy. Also, the most desirable technique for looking at how consumers define markets is some variation of a hierarchical partitioning.

Benefit Positioning

Up to this point we have looked very broadly at how various components of the marketing mix influence the overall market positioning of a brand, and how markets are defined. Now it is time to look more specifically at how a brand is to be positioned *within* the market definition. In a sense, up to now we have been dealing with the first half of the positioning definitions introduced at the start of the chapter: *identifying the market where you compete*. This is what helps pinpoint the *category* where the brand competes, and frames something we have been calling category need.[9]

Category need defines why the target audience wants the product or service offered by the market. A category, at its basic level, is what people think of spontaneously when asked: 'What is this?' When asked this question, people tend to respond in such terms as beer, coffee, soft drink, or perhaps a brand name. They do *not* talk in terms like 'a beverage', although they may very well describe something like this as 'something to drink', You can see that people tend to think about categories, and as a result category needs, well down the hierarchical market definition. We will be dealing a lot more with this idea of category need in later chapters because it is an important communication effect to consider when setting marketing communication strategy.

What we want to do now is turn our attention to the second half of the positioning definition: *seeking a differential advantage*. This is where we must identify the optimal way of presenting our brand in advertising and other marketing communication, and that means selecting those benefits which will best distinguish our brand from competitors in a way that is important to the target audience. Ideally, these benefits will reflect the underlying motivation that drives purchase behaviour. Again, motivation is something we will be covering in depth in later chapters because it is at the heart of brand attitude communication strategy. What we want to do is be able to 'tap into' the purchase motivation via the benefit presented in the advert or other marketing communication. The difficult question, however, is what benefit should be emphasized in order to get the job done.

We will be looking for a benefit that is *important* to our target audience in influencing purchase, one that our target audience believes our brand can *deliver*, and one that the target audience believes our brand can deliver *better* than other brands.[10] This is what we are looking for, but finding it is not easy. One way is to explore the basic, underlying attitudinal structure used by the target audience in evaluating brands. Perhaps the best way of doing this is to use a multi-attribute model based upon Fishbein's notion of expectancy value.[11]

The Expectancy-value Model of Attitude

What this model suggests is that a person's attitude toward an object (A_o) is the sum of all the things they believe about it (b_i), weighted by how important each of those things are to them (a_i). Mathematically, this is expressed as:

$$A_o = \sum_{i=1}^{n} a_i b_i$$

where: A_o = attitude toward the object,
a_i = importance of belief, and
b_i = belief about the object.

Do not be put off by the mathematical equation, because this is really not very complicated. Think about candy bars. Using the model, how would you determine someone's attitude toward, say, Snickers? What the model says is that a person's attitude toward something, Snickers in this case, will be the sum of its perceived characteristics and how important they are to what *motivates* that person to buy a candy bar.

What are some of the characteristics of candy bars? The obvious attributes are ingredients such as chocolate, caramel, and peanuts, but the characteristics of a candy bar will also include more intangible ones such as 'provides energy', 'is an inexpensive snack', and 'is an indulgence'. While there are clearly more characteristics than these, we will work with this set to see how we can learn something about people's attitudes toward Snickers.

Look at Table 7.2. This hypothetical example shows that people feel that chocolate and a sense of indulgence are essential to a candy bar; that caramel, peanuts, and being an inexpensive snack, while desirable, are not essential; and that it really isn't important that a candy bar provides energy. Their perception of Snickers is that it really delivers chocolate and peanuts, and it is seen as an inexpensive snack, but it only does an okay job in providing caramel and energy, and as an indulgence. Computing an expectancy-value measure of Snicker's brand attitude, using the appropriate numbers and following the model, yields 19.

So what does 19 mean? By itself, very little. The important thing here is to look at *how* the attitude is determined. We can see that for the candy bar attribute most important to people, chocolate, Snickers is seen to do a very good job delivering the benefit. It also delivers well on peanuts, but peanuts are less essential in a candy bar. Caramel is desirable but not essential in a candy bar, and Snickers does an okay job on this attribute.

Looking at the more benefit-oriented characteristics, Snickers is seen as definitely an inexpensive snack, which is desirable, but not essential. People believe Snickers does an okay job in providing energy, even though that is not important. But in terms of being seen as an indulgence, which is essential for a candy bar (in our example), Snickers is only seen as okay.

Table 7.2 Expectancy-value Model of Attitude for a Candy Bar

	Importance weight (a_i)		Beliefs (b_i)		
Chocolate	3	×	3	=	9
Caramel	1	×	1	=	1
Peanuts	1	×	3	=	3
Provides energy	0	×	1	=	0
Inexpensive snack	1	×	3	=	3
Indulgence	3	×	1	=	3
$A_b = \sum_{i=1}^{6} (a_i)(b_i)$					19

3 = Essential	3 = Definitely deliver
1 = Desirable	1 = Does OK
0 = Essential	0 = Does not deliver

Positioning with the Expectancy-value Model

If the expectancy-value attitude doesn't mean much on its own, then why compute it? The reason is that it provides an important *relative* feel for what people's attitudes are likely to be, depending upon how they perceive a brand. This is why the model is so important for positioning.

The strength of people's attitude toward Snickers in this example is that it is seen as having everything important in a candy bar, except for only doing an okay job as an indulgence. But suppose that among chocolate lovers the beliefs about chocolate and caramel were reversed? If that were how chocolate lovers saw Snickers, it would mean it was seen as only doing an okay job on the two things most important to them in a candy bar—chocolate and being an indulgence.

In the first example, where Snickers is seen by the general population as really delivering on the chocolate attribute, the overall attitude score is 19; in this second example, where it only does an okay job on chocolate among chocolate lovers while really delivering on caramel, the overall attitude score is only 13. If the first example reflected general attitudes toward Snickers in the market while the second reflected the attitude of chocolate lovers toward Snickers, how would we need to position Snickers to attract the chocolate lover?

Looking only at the attitude scores, we know that attitudes toward Snickers in the general population are much more favourable than they are among chocolate lovers: 19 vs. 13. But even more importantly, as we look at the beliefs and their weightings, we know that the reason for this less favourable attitude among chocolate lovers is their perception that Snickers is more about caramel and peanuts than it is about chocolate. This suggests that if Snickers is to attract chocolate lovers, they must be positioned more strongly against that benefit. Since we know (again in our hypothetical example) that in a candy bar chocolate is more important than caramel or peanuts, taking a strong chocolate positioning would reinforce the already held beliefs of the general population while building this perception among chocolate lovers.

Let us take this idea one step further and look at hypothetical beliefs about two candy bar brands, Snickers and Cadbury. Assume that consumer attitudes toward these brands are the results of the weighted beliefs shown in Table 7.3. These figures suggest that the overall attitudes toward Snickers and Cadbury, as measured by an expectancy-value model, are roughly equal, although the edge goes to Cadbury.

If you were the brand manager for Snickers, what would you do to position the brand more strongly against Cadbury? The two most important benefits are chocolate and indulgence. Cadbury delivers both, while Snickers lags behind on the indulgence benefit. In other words, Snickers doesn't deliver as well as Cadbury on this important benefit; Cadbury does it better. One way for Snickers to build a more positive brand attitude would be to position itself more as an indulgence. If it were to succeed, its overall attitude score would jump to 25, better than Cadbury at 21. Another option would be to *drive down* the importance of indulgence, while playing up the 'extra' taste of caramel and peanuts. If the importance weighting of indulgence were to drop from essential to desirable, Snickers would enjoy a slight edge in overall attitude (17 vs. 15). Add to this a heightened awareness among candy bar buyers that Snickers really delivers on caramel, and the advantage becomes even stronger (19 vs. 15).

We must remember that in these examples the numbers have been made up in order to illustrate the points, and also that there could be many other important benefits we have not considered. But the important thing to understand is that you can use an expectancy-value model to identify the importance of benefits to your target audience, the degree to which they perceive that you and your competitors can deliver those benefits, and which benefits one brand is seen to deliver better than its competitors.

In using the model, include those benefits seen by the target audience as being important or potentially important, and have the target audience evaluate your brand and two or three key competitors. Remember that this exercise must be done for the *appropriate target audience*, not the population at large (unless, of course, that happens to be your

Table 7.3 Comparative Expectancy-value Model of Attitude for Two Candy Bars

	Importance weight (a_i)	Beliefs (b_i)	
		Snickers	Cadbury
Chocolate	3	3	3
Caramel	1	1	0
Peanuts	1	3	0
Provides energy	0	1	1
Inexpensive snack	1	3	3
Indulgence	3	1	3
$A_b = \sum_{i=1}^{6} (a_i)(b_i)$		19	21

target audience). As you work out the numbers, it will be possible to evaluate positioning options in terms of:

- reinforcing or building a uniqueness for your brand on important benefits;
- capitalizing upon competitive weaknesses on important benefits;
- emphasizing important benefits your brand delivers better than others;
- increasing the importance of benefits your brand delivers better than others (if not already seen as essential);
- decreasing the importance of benefits your brand does not deliver better than others.

Benefit Emphasis in Positioning

One final consideration in benefit positioning is how to focus on or emphasize the benefit. This will depend upon the motivation associated with purchase in a category. As we shall discuss in the next chapter, brand attitude communication strategy depends upon understanding the correct underlying purchase motivation. We shall defer a detailed discussion of this to then. For now, we only need to know that some advertising and marketing communication strategies are based primarily on providing 'information', others on addressing 'feelings'. When the motive is negative, information in some form is provided in order to address a problem of some kind: how do I get my clothes looking better, what is the best washer, what can I take for real pain? When the motivation is positive, messages must address the target audience's 'feelings' in some way: I want a car everyone will notice, I want to indulge myself, etc.

The way the brand positioning in the message addresses the benefit should reflect this fundamental distinction between purchase motivations. When the motive is negative and the advertising and other marketing communication is basically providing information, the emphasis should be *directly* on the benefit. This can be accomplished in three ways. You can draw attention to the benefit either by way of an attribute of the product or of the emotion associated with the problem, or you can simply state the benefit without specific support. Let's look at the examples of negative motives we listed above. If your problem is 'how do I get my clothes looking better?', GloWhite suggests in their adverts that they are '30% brighter', a simple statement of the benefit. If you are shopping for the best washer, Busch Maxx suggests in their adverts that 'Thanks to a 20% bigger drum it's like having an extra pair of hands,' where the attribute, 'a 20% bigger drum', supports the benefit claim, 'it's like having an extra pair of hands.' What can you take for real pain? In an advert for Advil, a woman remarks, 'Once a month I'm doubled over in pain. No one comes near me until I've taken my Advil.' Here we have an example of the negative emotion occasioned by real pain being relieved by the benefits of taking Advil.

When the motive is positive and the advertising and other marketing communication is addressing the target audience's 'feelings', the emphasis should be on the *emotional consequences* of the benefit. This can be accomplished in two ways. You can draw attention to the emotional consequences through the benefit, or simply refer to the emotion. Again, using our previous examples of positive motivations, if you are looking for social approval and want a car everyone will notice, a Mercedes-Benz advert offers a picture of

Table 7.4 Benefit Emphasis in Positioning

	Benefit Emphasis	Example
Negative Motivation		
	Benefit without support	'30% brighter' (GloWhite)
	Attribute supports benefit	'Thanks to a 20% bigger drum it's like having an extra pair of hands' (Busch Maxx)
	Emotions related to problems identified by benefit	'Once a month I'm doubled over in pain. No one comes near me until I've taken my Advil.' (Advil)
Positive Motivation		
	Benefit leads to emotion	'Without equal' (Mercedes-Benz)
	Emotional consequence alone	'Enjoy a drop of tranquility' (Twinings)

the car with the simple statement, 'Without equal.' Here is an example of the benefit, 'Without equal', stimulating the desired emotional consequence for the target audience—a car everyone will notice. If you want to indulge yourself, Twinings tea suggests in an advert that you 'enjoy a drop of tranquillity', where the focus is entirely on the emotional consequence of using the brand.

These benefit focuses are summarized in Table 7.4. The correct benefit emphasis in positioning a brand through advertising and other marketing communication is essential to maximizing a brand's position within its market.[12]

Summary

We have now considered in detail how positioning strategy can be developed, and have emphasized the importance of market definition in this process. After discussing the market mapping approaches we suggested that hierarchical market partitioning offers a number of advantages for the development of positioning strategy, and that this can be used in conjunction with data on consumer perceptions. We introduced the expectancy-value model of attitude as a tool to investigate underlying attitude structures and explained how it provides guidance on the relative importance of benefits to the target audience. We then went on to discuss how to emphasize benefits depending on the underlying motivation for purchase.

Questions to consider

7.1   What is meant by positioning?

7.2   What is the best basis for defining a market?

7.3   How can measures of perceived similarity be used in positioning a brand?

7.4 What four characteristics do consumers use to distinguish between brands?

7.5 How can defining a market by hierarchical partitioning help in developing advertising?

7.6 What is meant by category need?

7.7 How can the expectancy-value model of attitudes help in positioning a brand?

7.8 What are the two fundamental motivations for purchase?

Notes

1   David Jobber, *Principles and Practice of Marketing* (New York: McGraw-Hill, 1998), 193.

2   Graham Hooley and John Saunders, *Competitive Positioning: The Key to Market Success* (London: Prentice Hall, 1993), p. xi.

3   Peter Doyle, *Marketing Management and Strategy* (London: Prentice Hall, 1994), 79.

4   A discussion of the marketing plan may be found in any number of marketing textbooks, and is covered in detail by W. A. Cohen in his book *The Marketing Plan*, 2nd edn. (New York: John Wiley and Sons 1998).

5   Perceptual mapping was developed in the late 1960s at Bell Laboratories in the US. One of the best books on the subject is still Paul Green and Vilhala Rao's *Applied Multidimensional Scaling: A Comparison of Approaches and Algorithms* (New York: Holt, Rinehart and Winston, 1972).

6   See J. R. Bettman, *An Information Processing Theory of Consumer Choice* (Reading, Mass.: Addison-Wesley, 1979).

7   This finding comes from research conducted by Larry Percy for a major multinational coffee company. The company was so disturbed to learn that their traditional view of the market, based upon a product definition, was wrong that they refused to complete the project.

8   Glen Urban and John Hauser, *Design and Marketing of New Products* (Englewood Cliffs, NJ: Prentice-Hall, 1980).

8   In J. R. Rossiter and L. Percy, *Advertising Communication and Promotion Management* (New York: McGraw-Hill 1997), they discuss the first half of this definition in terms of product *location*—how a brand can be located within the product category with either a central or differentiated position. Simply put, a central location requires the brand to be positioned to deliver all those benefits associated with the category (generally a positioning for market leaders), while a differentiated location means finding a unique or differentiated positioning. Generally speaking, most brands should pursue a differentiated positioning.

10   For a more detailed consideration of a model that deals with this point, see Rossiter and Percy's discussion of what they call an I-D-U (Importance, Delivery, Uniqueness) model of benefit emphasis in *Advertising Communication and Promotion Management*.

11   While it can be argued that Harry Triandis actually developed the idea of an

expectancy-value model of attitude, Martin Fishbein is generally credited with its development. See M. Fishbein and I. Ajzen, *Belief, Attitude, Intention, and Behaviour: An Introduction to Theory and Research* (Reading, Mass.: Addison-Wesley, 1975).

12 See Rossiter and Percy, *Advertising Communication and Promotion Management*, for a similar but more detailed discussion of benefit focus.

Chapter 8

Communication Strategy

We are now going to deal with creative strategy, and the first thing we must consider as we address this issue is the development of communication strategy. We have been through our initial planning stages—selecting a target audience, developing a model of consumer decision-making, and positioning our brand. Now it is time to decide how to put together our message. Clearly, before we can create advertising or other marketing communication executions we must have an overall communication strategy, and this begins with setting communication objectives.

In this chapter we will be looking at how to go about selecting communication objectives, with a special emphasis on brand awareness and brand attitude, which are *always* communication objectives. Chapter 10 will take this a step further and look at how understanding the way people process messages can lead to more effective creative strategy, and then in Chapter 11 we will look specifically at creative tactics.

Setting Communication Objectives

We have already briefly introduced four communication effects discussed in the work of Rossiter and Percy, and it will be from these effects that we draw our communication objectives: category need, brand awareness, brand attitude, and brand purchase intention.[1] In this section we will see how and when each of these effects may become an objective for advertising and other marketing communication. Depending upon where a product or brand stands within the market, as defined by the consumer, we will have various options open to us that will guide the selection of the desired communication effect. Once this is done, we will be in a position to choose the appropriate effect for a communication objective (see Table 8.1).

Category Need

Category need refers to the target audience's feeling that they would like a particular product or service in order to satisfy a specific need. It is important to remember here that category need is a *perception*, and therefore it can be established by the advertiser. By successfully establishing a belief in the target audience's mind that links the product

Table 8.1 Potential Communication Objectives

Category Need	When it is necessary to **remind** the target of their need for the category or when you must **sell** the target audience the need
Brand Awareness	**Always** an objective in order to enable the target audience to identify the brand in enough detail to purchase or use the brand
Brand Attitude	Also **always** an objective because there must be some other reason to select one brand over another
Brand Purchase Intention	Not often a specific objective except when brand attitude is positive and a 'reason to buy' now is required

category and a felt need, the advertiser can stimulate *primary demand* for the product category. Category need is the communication effect that causes primary demand. But note that category need, and the primary demand it can stimulate in the marketplace, applies to *all brands* in the category. To stimulate secondary or selective demand, the advertiser must also influence brand-level communication effects like brand awareness, brand attitude, and brand purchase intention.

Because different consumers may be looking for different things in a product, category need can be seen differently, given the particular perceived needs of various segments of the target market. As an example, with the introduction of compact discs, people needed first to be informed about this new category, and interest in CDs stimulated. However, interest in CDs can very easily be different among various consumer groups. One group may be interested because they are always interested in being first with anything new. A second group may be drawn to CDs because of their better sound quality. A third may become interested later because they can't find records any more. Category need in each case will be stimulated by different perceptions, and hence can require different communication strategies.

How do you decide when category need should be a communication objective? Category need must be present at full strength before purchase of a brand within that category can occur. In other words, the potential consumer must be in the market for the product (category). Category need is not very often required as a communication objective, because most brands are marketed in categories where the perceived need is well established. But when circumstances dictate it, it is absolutely essential. There are two cases when category need must be one of your communication objectives: when it is necessary to remind the target audience of their need for products in the category, or when you must sell the target audience on a need for the category.

Reminding the Consumer of the Category Need

The first situation in which category need becomes a communication objective is when you must remind the prospective consumer of a latent or forgotten (but previously established) category need. A Campbell's soup campaign in the US during the mid-1980s and again in the mid-1990s provides a perfect example of reminding prospective buyers of the category need. The campaign was built around the category benefit 'soup is good food'. Here was a case where soup sales had been soft, and by reminding the consumer about the category need, eating soup because it is good food, Campbell's was able to renew interest in serving soup. They were able to support such a campaign because they dominate the category. As interest in soup increased, so would sales of the Campbell's brand.

Usually, however, reminding the target audience of a category need applies to product categories that are infrequently purchased, such as pain remedies. It also applies to one-time-purchase products that are infrequently used, at least in the opinion of the advertiser. Traveller's cheques are another good case where it is important to remind people of the category need because of infrequent use. Category need reminder campaigns can generally be achieved without devoting a lot of copy specifically to the category need. The purpose is merely to re-establish a previously held need. There is plenty of opportunity to address the brand. This is in sharp contrast to when it is necessary to sell a category need.

Selling the Category Need

When a category need has not yet been established in the target audience's mind, the advertising campaign, often with promotional support, must sell the need. Selling category need is a communication objective for all new products and also for established products aimed at new users. If the target audience has not bought within the category before, advertising must include selling the category need as a communication objective. While it is easy to see that new product categories obviously must be sold to the consumer, you should also see how it is important to sell the category to anyone who has not yet purchased products in the category. This is why advertising always relies upon category need as an *effect* in communication, but selling category need only becomes an objective when the target audience is made up of people who have no experience with the category.

In order to sell the category to someone new to it, the content of the advertising requires the selling of *category* benefits in addition to brand benefits. Selling the category involves creating, in the potential consumer's mind, *category communication effects*. As a result, just as we have brand communication effects, we will have category awareness, category attitude, and category purchase intention. When selling category need, these category-level communication effects must be addressed *in addition to* brand-level communication effects. This is not an easy job, and almost impossible within a single execution. It requires a campaign.

Category awareness, category attitude, and category purchase intention, which must be addressed when selling the category, are no different conceptually from their brand counterparts—brand awareness, brand attitude, and brand purchase intention. But they are separate communication objectives which must be decided along with brand-level communication objectives.

Brand Awareness

Brand awareness is the target audience's ability to identify a brand within a category in sufficient detail to purchase or use it. There are at least two ways in which to identify a brand. You can either *recognize* the brand or you can *recall* it. As we shall see below, this is a very important distinction to understand when setting brand awareness objectives.

The reason we say that the brand must be identified in sufficient detail is that brand awareness does *not* always require identification of the brand *name*. For the consumer, brand awareness may be stimulated by a familiar package or an even more general stimulus such as colour. Think of the long-running Silk Cut cigarette advertising in the UK, where the brand name does not even appear, but the distinctive royal purple colour always dominates. Identifications such as these still enable brand response even though no brand name is mentioned.

You may not even need to remember beforehand the brand name or be able to describe the package or colour. Instead, brand awareness may occur through simply recognizing it at the point of purchase. When a package is recognized in a supermarket (e.g. the bright blue box of Persil) or when a fast-food restaurant sign is recognized on a trip (e.g. McDonald's golden arches), brand awareness does not require brand recall.

We have already seen that at the product category level consumers will not buy unless there is a perceived category need. At the brand level, consumers *cannot* buy unless they are first made aware of the brand. As a result, brand awareness must always be considered first, before any other communication effect.

Recognition or Recall: An Essential Difference

Brand awareness is widely misunderstood even by the most experienced people in advertising. The difficulty relates to the essential difference between recognition and recall, a difference that is fundamentally important to advertising and all other forms of marketing communication.[2] Brand recognition and brand recall are two different types of brand awareness. The difference depends upon which communication effect occurs first in the consumer's mind: the need for the product (i.e. category need) or seeing the brand in the store (i.e. brand awareness).

Recognition brand awareness is when the awareness of the brand reminds you of the category need. In many brand decision-making situations, especially in supermarkets or large chemists or pharmacies, the brand is quite literally presented to you from the shelf. As you look over the shelf and spot familiar brands, you *then* decide whether or not you are in the market for something in that category.

Recall brand awareness is when the category need occurs and you must remember brands which will satisfy that need. When recall awareness is required, the brand is not present. For example, if you catch a cold and are looking for some relief, you must remember which cold remedy is likely to help. Even better examples of recall-dominant decisions are airline reservations or ordering beer in a restaurant when you don't know what brands they carry. Unlike when you catch a cold and recall could be offset by recognition of another brand at the point of purchase, with product categories such as these you do not have the benefit of a point-of-purchase reminder of the airlines or the brands of beer available. The first-recalled brand (given also a favourable attitude) will usually get the business.

When setting advertising strategy the key is to assess the most likely decision situation for the brand. You can find this out by questioning consumers about the situations they find themselves in when buying, or by common knowledge of how people buy the brand.

Brand Attitude

Just as with brand awareness, brand attitude must always be a communication objective. If there is no brand attitude present among the target audience, there is very little likelihood they will want to purchase the product. Why? If you think about it, for most product categories most people are aware of more than one brand. Unless we believe that brand choices are made randomly from among the brands people are aware of, there must be something about the brands that lead a person to purchase one rather than another. That something is a brand attitude.

The study of attitudes is really based in psychology, but those who work in the area of consumer behaviour have adapted various theories of attitude as to why people behave as they do. It is from this body of knowledge that we borrow our definition of attitude. While the definition that follows may at first seem heavy going, as we get into discussing its various components and applying it to how advertising works within its context later in the chapter, it should all become quite clear.

We look at brand attitude as the understanding a person has in terms of how they evaluate a particular brand and its ability to satisfy what the consumer is looking for in the product. There are four important characteristics about brand attitude that we need to understand. First of all, brand attitude depends upon what the potential buyer wants *now* from the product, which is the motivation that drives someone's behaviour. Second, brand attitude is made up of what someone knows about a brand (cognitions or beliefs) and what they feel about the brand (affect or feelings). Thirdly, someone's knowledge is usually made up of a number of different beliefs about a brand. And finally, brand attitude is a *relative* concept.

Because of the importance of brand attitude to effective communication, we will explore these four points in more depth later in this chapter.

Brand Purchase Intention

Brand purchase intention is the communication response that relates to the target audience's *decision* to purchase a brand or use a service. It does not refer to the actual behaviour of buying the brand or using the service, but only the *intention*. The target audience, as a result of processing an advert or other marketing communication, say to themselves: 'I think I'll try that brand' or 'I want to pick that up again next time I shop.' Remember, in the communication response sequence, the final step *after* communication effect is actual behaviour. All advertising or other marketing communication can do, if correctly processed, is generate either a low-level curiosity to try (with low-involvement product decisions) or a definite intention to buy (for a high-involvement product decision).

We should also take note here of the potential ways in which brand purchase intention may be influenced by advertising. It may not always be the same person who both intends to buy as a result of the advertising and actually makes the purchase, as we saw when we discussed the roles people play in the decision process. A common example of this would be advertising to children for such things as toys or breakfast cereals. The advertising may be aimed at children in their role as initiator and influencer, stimulating a brand purchase intention for Cocoa Puffs or some other child-oriented breakfast cereal, but the mother will actually buy the product. You can surely imagine other cases where the intention to purchase is really only a recommendation or proposal to someone else who will actually make the purchase decision. Nevertheless, for our purposes we will consider all of this under the communication objective of brand purchase intention.

In those situations where the strategy is to build or reinforce an image for a brand, and there is very little risk involved in the purchase decision, brand purchase intention will almost surely be delayed, and therefore should *not* be considered as a communication objective. This situation occurs with products like beer and soft drinks, certain well-established food products, and other generally inexpensive, routinely purchased packaged-goods products.

Let us see if we can illustrate what we mean here. If you see an advertisement for ice cream or beer or soft drinks, it is unlikely that you will say to yourself immediately that you're going to buy that brand. What is more likely is that after you have seen the advertising a few times you will begin to feel good about the brand and begin to identify with it. Then if you are passing the ice cream section of the store, or see the advertised brand of beer or soft drink when shopping, you will remember the feeling and then, at the *point of purchase*, decide to buy.

Contrast this with other advertising you are familiar with, where there is 'information' provided. Advertising for such things as cold remedies, for example, provides you with a 'reason to buy' right then, if you are suffering from a cold or cough: 'relieves sore throat pain' or 'helps you sleep'. You learn the information and form a tentative decision to try the brand because of what you have learned about it. In cases like this, brand purchase intention can be a communication objective.

Brand Awareness and Brand Attitude Strategy

How do you decide which awareness response and which aspect of brand attitude should form the basis of your communication objectives? We have seen that both brand awareness and brand attitude are *always* communication objectives. But with brand awareness, should it be recognition or recall? How do we look at the various aspects of brand attitude in developing an optimum communication strategy? In this section we will look into these questions as we take a more in-depth look at brand awareness and brand attitude strategy.

Brand Awareness Strategy

There are three possible ways for brand awareness to be used as a communication objective. As we have seen, brand awareness may be executed as brand recognition or brand recall, or in certain cases both may be appropriate.

Recognition Brand Awareness

Recognition brand awareness is where the awareness of the brand reminds you of the category need. The primary reason for selecting brand recognition as a communication objective is that consumers buy the advertised brand because they recognize it *at* the point of purchase. This is a very frequent occurrence, especially with supermarket products. Think about most people's shopping behaviour. They don't really have in mind all the brands they are likely to buy when they go shopping, even if they use a list. Instead, as they shop, when they go past, say, the cereal section and see all of the brands, they *recognize* the brand they usually buy and are reminded that they need cereal. In effect, what is happening here is that the awareness or recognition of the brand reminds them of the category need. Again, even if they were using a list, it would probably only serve as a reminder that they needed, in our example, cereal. The *brand* choice would probably not be made until it was recognized at the point of purchase.

Advert 8.1 provides a good example of how you can deal creatively with recognition awareness. Because the Budweiser label has *evolved* rather than changed completely over time, by showing this evolution they not only reinforce the image of the package label for point-of-purchase recognition but also communicate that the brand has been around for a long time. This, of course, helps build positive brand attitude, and does so in a unique way.

Recognition awareness can function in another way. What we have just discussed is really visual recognition. In other words, you *see* a package and recognize the brand. But recognition can be auditory as well. For example, suppose you get a phone call from someone trying to sell you insurance or financial services. If you don't recognize the name of the insurance company or brokerage house, how likely are you to be interested in what they have to say? This is a case where the brand name is *heard* and recognized rather than seen and recognized.

When visual brand recognition is our objective, in almost all cases we will want to feature the package in a dominant position. For both print adverts and television commercials, a close-up in colour of the package should be presented in order to offer the best possible cue for consumers when they later confront the package in the store. Because a visual representation of the package is required, quite obviously only visual media can be used. As a result, when visual brand recognition is the brand awareness communication objective, radio cannot be considered.

Recall Brand Awareness

As discussed, recall brand awareness is when category need occurs first, and you must remember one or more brands which you think will satisfy that need. The circumstance under which you would choose brand recall as a communication objective is when the potential buyer must remember the brand name prior to the point of purchase. These are all those situations where a problem or need comes up, and the solution is thought about in terms of a brand name. For example, if you have an upset stomach, you must decide on what products you are aware of that might help (e.g. Pepto Bismol or Alka Seltzer). If your brand is not in the consumer's mind when the problem comes up, it has very little

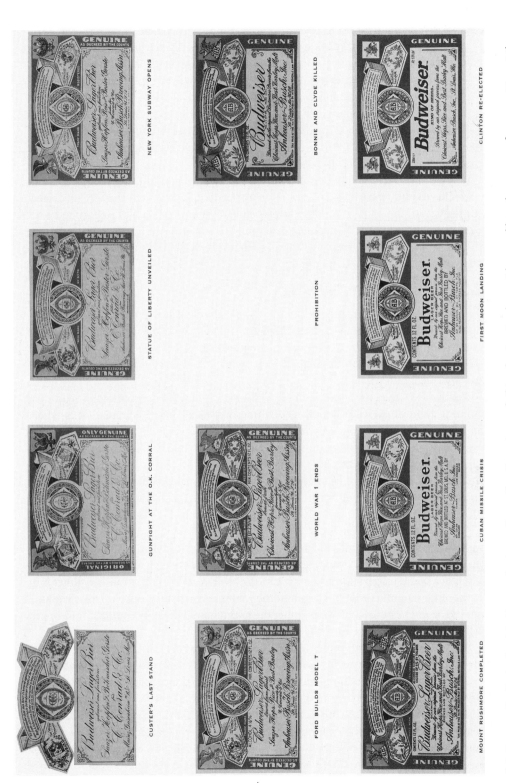

8.1 Because the Budweiser label has evolved over time rather than changed, this advert not only provides good brand awareness for recognition at the point-of-purchase, but also helps reinforce a positive brand attitude. Courtesy Anheuser-Busch

likelihood of being purchased. Another example might be if you are thinking about a trip to Sydney, and wonder what airline to call. Here is another case where the need (the trip to Sydney) occurs and you must think of a solution (the airlines that fly there).

There is an important point to understand here. When we refer to a brand recall objective for advertising we do not mean recall of the actual advertising. The reason we point this out is that many advertisers try to test their advertising with day-after recall experiments where people are called the day after a commercial has run on television and asked if they remember seeing it. Our concern is with *brand* recall, regardless of whether or not the consumer can remember the advertising.[3]

When we have decided that brand recall should be our communication objective, our advertising should repeat the name as often as possible, linked with the category need. With television, the name should not only be heard often, but seen as well. In radio, of course, the name can only be heard, and in print adverts only seen. But the critical point is that the brand is always *linked to the need*, so that when the need occurs in 'real life', our brand will come to mind.

Brand Recognition and Brand Recall

Occasionally one may feel that both brand recognition and brand recall should be considered as communication objectives. However, this is a very difficult objective to effect since it requires two different types of creative execution tactics, and, as we have just seen, may also require different media (since, for example, radio is unable to communicate visual recognition).

None the less, there are two circumstances where it may be appropriate to set a dual communication objective of brand recognition and recall. The first situation is where your target audience is generally made up of two major segments, one of which makes their brand choice prior to shopping, the other at the point of purchase. We should understand, however, that this is a very rare occurrence.

The second case where a dual brand awareness communication objective may be called for is when the average member of the target audience finds themselves frequently in both decision-making situations. This case is far more common than the first, but it too is not likely to occur often. An example of what we mean here would be the brand choice for liquor. Frequently the potential buyer of vodka, say, will recognize a brand name like Absolut at the store when shopping and be reminded of their need to buy, a situation calling for a brand recognition communication objective. When this same consumer is in a bar or restaurant and orders a martini, if the waiter asks whether any particular vodka is preferred, it will be necessary to remember the brand name, a situation calling for a brand recall communication objective.

If the makers of Absolut vodka feel that both situations are important to the sales of their product, then both types of awareness must be utilized in developing the advertising. But, again, careful planning and a full knowledge of the consumer's behaviour and attitudes must be available before this decision can be made. While it could be true that the scenario of a waiter asking for a customer's brand preference is a common occurrence, it may still only account for a very small proportion of the average vodka drinker's consumption. If that were the case, we would be wise to ignore the brand recall situations and concentrate only on the single brand awareness objective of recognition. As the long-running campaign for Absolut Vodka featuring unique presentations of the bottle implies, this is probably the case.

Brand Attitude Strategy

Again, brand attitude will always be a communication objective. There are several possible specific communication objectives related to brand attitude. Depending upon what beliefs the target audience holds for our brand, the brand attitude options are to: create, increase, maintain, modify, or change their brand attitude. We can see that without a prior knowledge of the target audience's brand attitude, we will not know which option will be best for the brand. So our first step is *always* to understand fully the attitudes of our target audience toward both the category in general and the specific brands which the target audience feels compete in that category.[4]

We need to *create* a brand attitude for new category users or when introducing a new brand. It is hard to imagine any other case where someone in the market has no attitude at all toward a brand, always assuming they are aware of it. When we find that our target audience has a moderately favourable brand attitude, our brand attitude communication objective will be to *increase* the already favourable brand attitude. Almost anyone who at least occasionally buys a brand will hold at least a moderately favourable attitude toward it. Even new category users may have formed some tentatively positive attitudes about a brand. For example, young mothers probably have begun to form brand attitudes for baby food some time before actually having their baby. In such cases, if we find our target audience has at least some positive brand attitude we will want to try to increase it.

If we find that the majority of our target audience already has a strong positive attitude toward a brand, the brand attitude communication objective will be to *maintain* that already favourable attitude. We often find this situation in more mature markets where a large proportion of a brand's users tend to be relatively loyal.

The alert reader may wonder here how this idea squares with that part of our brand attitude definition which points out that brand attitude is *relative*. In a sense it is true that one is probably always trying to increase brand attitude. But in a case where the competitive environment is stable and your brand has a generally loyal customer base and a dominant share, maintaining that strong brand attitude is a proper objective. However, the advertiser must always be alert to positive shifts in competitive brand attitude which could signal a shift in the brand attitude objective for your brand.

What we mean by *modifying* a brand attitude is basically to reposition a brand. In a sense, what you are trying to do is increase your potential target market by appealing to a different motivation or reason for seeking certain benefits in the brand. A good recent example of this is the way in which many diet control products have been repositioned from strictly 'diet-oriented' products to products that are good for 'watching' your weight, and then repositioned again as products that are more 'healthy' for you. This type of change in brand attitude was recognized when Findas introduced Lean Cuisine, and positioned it as a product for watching weight rather than dieting to lose weight.

While almost any target audience could potentially be seen as appropriate for a modified brand attitude if the advertiser sees changes in the marketplace that demand this sort of action, modifying brand attitude can also be useful as a communication objective when it doesn't appear feasible to increase brand attitude. Examples here are the way in which Arm & Hammer baking soda modified brand attitude in suggesting to consumers that they should use a box of Arm & Hammer in the refrigerator to absorb odours, and how Vaseline extended its usage through repositioning as a lip balm.

It is necessary to *change* brand attitude when a significant proportion of your target audience holds a negative attitude toward the brand. Regardless of the number of positive beliefs a consumer may hold toward a brand, if there is a significant negative belief it will in almost all cases 'overrule' the positive beliefs. Choosing to change brand attitude as a communication objective involves removing the negative link between the brand and the reason why a consumer purchases the product. If this link is not removed, regardless of what your advertising may say about a brand, the consumer will still be likely to think: 'Yes, that may be true, but . . . ' It is essential to remove the reasons for this 'but'.

Look at Advert 8.2 for the Volkswagen Polo L. In the mid-1990s Volkswagen significantly reduced their prices in the UK, yet the image of Volkswagen as unaffordable persisted. People felt Volkswagen made quality cars (positive belief), but also felt they were expensive (negative belief). The creative challenge was to change the negative aspect of brand attitude while retaining the positive. This is always a tricky job when you are dealing with a price–quality interaction, but it is well handled in this advert, which ran in London Underground stations as part of a larger campaign. The obvious humour in the association with Underground 'danger' warnings helps attract and hold attention as the eye is visually drawn to the price and then on to the tag line, 'surprisingly ordinary prices'. The advert deals with the negative belief in a humorous way, stimulating generally positive feelings, without challenging or jeopardizing the quality image.

We cannot minimize the potential danger to a message if negative attitudes remain with the target audience; nor can we minimize the difficulty in changing a negative brand attitude. In fact, it may come to the point where it is simply not feasible even to try to change the attitude, and we must eliminate those people from our target audience.

We should remember that different segments of the potential target audience may hold different initial attitudes toward a brand, and as a result the advertiser may need to isolate those segments that are most likely to respond to the brand. Some brand attitude objectives will be easier to achieve, and if you can match those objectives with segments in the market that offer a reasonable likelihood of responding to the brand's message, you will in effect be maximizing advertising and marketing objectives for the brand.

Characteristics of Brand Attitude

Earlier we mentioned that there are four important characteristics about brand attitude which we need to understand. They are: what the consumer wants now from the brand, what they know and feel about the brand, the beliefs that make up that knowledge, and the relativity of brand attitude (see Table 8.2).

Brand attitude depends upon what the potential buyer wants *now* from the brand. This is really the motivation that drives someone to behave in a certain way. We will spend more time talking about this later, but for now we need only realize that it is essential to know why someone is motivated to make a purchase or utilize a service in a brand's category. It also stands to reason that if the consumer's motivation changes, they may also re-evaluate the brands in the category. With a different motivation other things

8.2 This advert for the VW Polo L provides a good example of how humour can be used in helping change a negative perception without jeopardizing a quality image. Courtesy Volkswagen

Table 8.2 Important Characteristics of Brand Attitude

---

1. Brand attitude depends upon what the target audience wants **now** from the product
2. Brand attitude is made up of what someone 'knows' about a product and what they 'feel' about a brand
3. What someone 'knows' is usually made up of a number of different beliefs
4. Brand attitude is a **relative** concept

---

about a brand could become important, changing the consumer's evaluation of the brand.

Most people studying consumer behaviour see brand attitude as made up of two components: what someone knows about a brand and what they feel about a brand. Psychologists often refer to these two components as cognitions (beliefs) and affect (feelings). We will learn more about these two components below. While some psychologists also include a behavioural (conative) component when talking about attitudes, this is generally not considered a part of brand attitude in consumer behaviour, but a separate idea.

What someone knows about a brand, the cognitive component, could be made up of several different beliefs. As we relate these beliefs to advertising we will be concerned with the benefits associated with these beliefs. A person's brand attitude will be made up of these benefit beliefs, weighted by their importance (as we saw in the last chapter when we discussed the expectancy-value model of attitude).

Finally, brand attitude is a *relative* concept. In almost any product category, a number of brands will probably satisfy a consumer's motivation in purchasing or using a product. But given the associations the consumer draws between the brand and its supporting beliefs, one brand will usually end up being seen as relatively better than the others in meeting their motivation to buy.

We will now look at each of these points in more detail. As we mentioned above, once we begin to relate all this to specific examples, you will understand its importance to advertising and why a good understanding of brand attitude is necessary to a good understanding of how advertising works.

Brand Attitude and Motivation

We pointed out above that brand attitude is related to the underlying reasons behind why people behave—what we know as *motivation*. Also, we pointed out that brand attitude could change if the associated motivation changed. As a matter of fact, while this is certainly a straightforward and common-sense notion, you would be surprised at how many managers ignore these connections when setting communication strategy. Too often advertisers will rely upon brand information that is not linked to a motivation. For example, simply to ask someone why they think a particular brand is best may completely overlook situational motivations. What results is very general information about attitudes that may be practically meaningless.

Consider for a minute what goes through your own mind when you think about purchasing such diverse items as calculators and beer. All calculators have certain basic functions, but beyond that what you are looking for in a calculator might be related to a specific area of interest: e.g. financial functions or maths functions. From this simple example we can imagine a number of possible segments. (Think about how partitioning a market, as discussed in the last chapter, applies here.) Originally, all you may want is a basic calculator—you may be motivated simply to avoid the problem of doing all those arithmetic calculations by hand (like balancing your chequebook!). Later, you may be motivated by different reasons, and want a calculator more suited to your new role as an economics student. A brand that was fine originally no longer measures up. Brand attitude has changed. We need to know what motivation we are dealing with if we are to effectively advertise, in this case, a calculator.

Now let's consider beer. If you are out with your friends after playing a ball game, you are probably ordering a beer because you are thirsty. As we will learn later, this would be in response to a positive, sensory gratification motivation. But what if you were having lunch with a prospective employer and were asked if you would like a beer? The brand choice here would probably be motivated by a desire to 'look good', a different positive motivation: 'social approval'. Chances are that the brand you choose in these two situations would be different, because the motivation in each situation is different. In the first situation, perhaps almost any beer you like might be appropriate, but in the second situation, perhaps you would want a beer like Grolsch. If so, the advertising for these brands would need to reflect these different underlying motivations.

Cognitive and Affective Components of Brand Attitude
The cognitive and affective components of brand attitude reflect the beliefs and feelings associated with a brand. As mentioned earlier, some psychologists talk about behavioural intention or conation as part of a definition of attitude.[5] However, along with most people working in the area of consumer behaviour we believe that a two-component view is probably more useful. This does not mean we ignore behavioural intent (it is, after all, one of our communication effects), only that we do not find it critical to defining brand attitude. There is interesting support for this idea from the neuroscience literature, where we learn that the brain receives and handles cognitive and affective inputs in a parallel fashion.[6]

Let us now see how the cognitive and affective components of brand attitude fit together to form an *overall* brand attitude. Our definition of brand attitude is how someone evaluates a brand with respect to its perceived ability to satisfy what he or she is looking for in the product—in other words, the appropriate motivations. The cognitive and affective components of brand attitude relate to this perceived ability to satisfy and the underlying motivation to behave.

In the last chapter we looked at the expectancy-value model in determining overall attitude toward a brand for purposes of positioning. We were dealing with these same two components. Now we are taking this idea one step further and relating it to *motivation*. This next step is essential for brand attitude strategy.

The *cognitive or belief* component represents the existence and strength of the perceived linkage between the brand and the underlying motivation. In other words, it represents the perceived ability of the brand to satisfy the motivation. This belief or perception guides or directs the consumer toward a particular brand. The *affect or feeling* component is generated by the motivation itself. Whether this belief is or is not important depends upon the motivation to buy or use a product or service. Since the motivation must be relevant *at the time*, the motivation is experienced as an emotional or felt deviation from the consumer's current state. This feeling energizes the target audience to choose a brand.

Beliefs as Benefits in the Cognitive Component It would be very unusual indeed for an advertiser to try to directly build brand attitude by referring specifically to why the consumer wants a brand. In fact, most of the time people don't really know what motivations underlie their behaviour, or at any rate don't really give it much thought. If you are hungry for a snack, do you say to yourself 'I want something to remove my feeling of hunger' ? Not likely. This negative problem-removal motive is certainly what leads you to think about a snack, but that is a *category* decision. Once you have decided on a snack, if you are at home you are much more likely to say to yourself, 'What do I have around that's not too filling?' or 'What's in the house that tastes good?' These are the benefits that people think about when they are looking for *brands* in a category that can be related to their underlying motivations. In this case, the motivation will be *positive*: you are looking for something to enjoy.

Advertising especially, but other marketing communication as well, must communicate the benefits of the brand to the target audience. An advert must take specific attributes, benefits, or emotions and link them to a brand in such a way that it is seen as *uniquely* satisfying their motive.

Brand Attitude as a Relative Concept

While it is certainly possible to think about brand attitude in terms of the brand's perceived ability to meet absolutely what the potential buyer is looking for in a product, it makes a lot more sense to think about brand attitude as *relative*. There is rarely a brand that offers exactly what every individual buyer is looking for. Almost always there are other brands out there trying to beat you in meeting what potential buyers want. Even when a company has a virtual monopoly of a category, they should adopt a relative stance toward brand attitude. You never know when stronger competition may arrive. This makes sense when we remember that even in product categories where there is one dominant brand, the target audience will still have other brands to choose from. In almost all product categories, brand attitude communication effects will stimulate *relatively* more positive feeling about the brand.

Importance of Involvement and Motivation

We have talked off and on throughout this book about *involvement* and *motivation*. This is because they are the critical elements affecting purchase and usage behaviour, and as such must be taken into account when creating advertising and other marketing communication. In terms of involvement, we need to know whether or not the target audience sees any risk in the decision to buy or use a product or service. This perceived risk can be seen in either fiscal or psychological terms, and is dependent upon the target audience.

For most of us, the purchase of a new automobile carries with it a substantial financial risk. We don't want to make a mistake, so we will do a lot of work to be as certain as we can that we are making the right choice. But what about a rock star or seriously wealthy investment banker? They could see a new car on the road, perhaps a Ferrari, and simply call up a dealer and order one. If they don't like it after a month or so, they will just trade it in and buy something new.

So you can see that perceived risk must be determined *for the target audience*. While perceived risk in terms of money might be more or less correlated with financial circumstance, psychological risk is open to a much greater likelihood of individual differences. What is absolutely required dress for one group of teenagers may be completely different for another. What one cohort or culture sees as a status brand may not be seen as such for another.

The reason this idea of involvement is so important, as we shall see in Chapter 10, is that in processing a message, when involvement is low and there is little if any risk involved, you do not really need to believe the message is true. If the advert merely excites your curiosity or interest, something Maloney calls 'curious disbelief', that will be enough.[7] On the other hand, when the decision is high-involvement and fiscal or psychological risk is involved, you must accept the message as true before you will consider the brand.

A more detailed model of involvement and processing that has had a great deal of influence is the Elaborative Likelihood Model (ELM) developed by Petty and Cacioppo in the early 1980s.[8] In their model they look at involvement in terms of something they refer to as central vs. peripheral processing.

The central route deals with attention to the actual content of the message. Here the four-step sequence, as we have called it, is essential. To form a brand attitude via the central route of processing requires message comprehension, learning, and retention. The peripheral route, on the other hand, associates positive or negative cues with the brand as a result of the execution or message without engaging in any extensive benefit-related thinking. Here, a positive (or even negative) brand attitude can result simply from affective cues in the execution. This could include almost anything, such as liking the spokesperson or liking the actors used in the advert, or the humour; or even a more limbic-based response to some element in the execution.[9]

To summarize what we have been saying about the importance of motivation, if we do not know *why* someone wants to purchase a product or use a service, we will not be able to identify effectively the appropriate brand attitude and associated benefits. And if we cannot identify these, we will not be able to come up with tactically optimal creative executions. Fundamentally, motivation can be divided into negative vs. positive motives (although some psychologists argue that all motivation is negative). Please remember that when psychologists talk about 'negative' motives they do not mean 'bad'. What they mean is that the motivation is negatively originated. You have a headache (problem) and you want relief (solution); you don't want to worry about getting a flat tyre (problem avoidance). Negative motives generally concern solving or avoiding problems. Positive motives generally involve seeking more personal satisfaction.

A good way to illustrate why it is so important to understand whether the underlying motivation driving behaviour is positive or negative is to look at the calorie-controlled food category. What exactly motivates people to watch their weight? Research into this question has shown that women are positively motivated to watch their weight while men are negatively motivated. A woman will see an attractive woman and think 'I would like to look like that . . . I better watch my weight.' Men don't react that way at all. They are more likely to respond to seeing someone overweight and out of breath from climbing stairs and think 'I don't want to get like that . . . I'd better watch my weight.' You should certainly be able to see that you cannot use the same creative execution for both men and women. Their basic motivations to watch their weight require different appeals. Women are driven by the positive motive of 'looking good' (sensory gratification or social approval) while men are driven by the negative motive of problem avoidance.

The Rossiter-Percy Grid

Given the importance of involvement and motivation in understanding how and why purchase decisions are made, Rossiter and Percy have suggested integrating these two dimensions into a strategic grid.[10] Basically, when you are dealing with positive motives, you are creating a mood, and when dealing with negative motives you are providing information to help address a perceived (or potential) problem. In their model, they refer to brand attitude strategies when motives are positive as *transformational* (transforming your mood) and when motives are negative as *informational*.

Others in the past have attempted to deal with criteria they feel are important to communication strategy by proposing various grids to help identify types of marketing communication. Perhaps the best-known example is the so-called FCB grid introduced back in the 1960s.[11] Unfortunately, while many texts and even some practitioners continue to refer to it, the FCB grid has a number of problems.[12]

The Rossiter–Percy grid begins with the distinction between recall and recognition awareness, reminding the manager that whatever the brand attitude strategy, it must be associated with the correct brand awareness strategy. But the real strength of the Rossiter–Percy grid in planning is that it helps focus the manager's thinking about a product or service in terms of the *target audience's* involvement with the choice decision and the motivation that drives their behaviour. This in turn alerts the manager to specific *tactical* requirements for creative execution (see Fig. 8.1).

Looking specifically at the brand attitude strategy quadrants of the grid, when involvement is low and motivation is negative, a wide variety of creative options are open because the target audience does not need to be 'sold', only interested or curious. The target audience doesn't even need to like the advertising. This doesn't mean you should necessarily purposefully make the advertising unappealing, only that the key to this type of communication is the information provided, not how it is delivered. With high-involvement decisions where the motives are negative, unlike the low-involvement case, you cannot overclaim because the target audience must be convinced by the message.

However, when dealing with positive motives, regardless of whether involvement is low or high, the key to successful communication is the *emotional authenticity* of the execution for the target audience. This means the target audience must like the execution and they must see themselves in it. Often, the feeling conveyed by this type of advertising actually becomes the brand benefit. This is a very important point, and one that is often

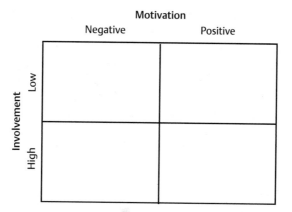

Fig. 8.1 Brand Attitude Strategy Quadrants from the Rossiter–Percy Grid

difficult for advertisers to accept. There is a strong temptation to include a more tangible benefit when advertising a low-involvement product purchased from positive motives, a kind of benefit more appropriate when dealing with negative motivations.

An example of what we are talking about is illustrated in a test conducted in Sweden of two Toblerone commercials using Åke Wissing & Co.'s Ad Box technique, a procedure for pre-testing advertising. Toblerone is a chocolate bar, a perfect example of a low-involvement product where you need to address a positive purchase motive, sensory gratification. A good commercial was produced creating a positive emotional experience, but there was some question as to whether the good feeling created by the commercial would be enough to drive purchase intent. A second version of the commercial was produced, identical to the first except for the ending, where an attribute was added: 'You can now buy Toblerone for the normal price, but you get 10 per cent more chocolate.' Frames from the commercial are shown in Advert 8.3, illustrating the different endings. Results of the test showed that the original version consistently out-performed the attribute-added version, including buying interest—65 per cent vs. 55 per cent (see Fig. 8.2).

Table 8.3 Tactical Creative Requirements Suggested by the Brand Attitude Strategy Quadrants of the Rossiter-Percy Grid

---

1. When involvement is low and motivation is negative:
   - A wide variety of options are open because the target audience does not need to be convinced, only interested
   - The key is the information provided

2. When involvement is high and motivation is negative:
   - The target audience must be convinced by the message

3. When motivation is positive:
   - 'Emotional authenticity' is the key
   - The target audience must like the advertising

8.3 The same commercial, but with two different endings, the first reflecting a positive emotional experience, the second a specific product attribute. The first version significantly out-performed the second, as we would expect for a low-involvement product where purchase is driven by positive motives. Courtesy Toblerone and Åke Wissing & Co.

Using the creative tactics appropriate for the purchase motivation involved is critical to ensuring the most effective advertising. As this case shows, even when the advert is only somewhat modified, if it is not appropriate it will lessen the effectiveness of the advertising. Appropriate creative tactics are summarized in Table 8.3 and will be dealt with in more detail in Chapter 11.

What we have in the Rossiter–Percy grid is a management tool that reminds us of the important distinction between recognition and recall awareness and helps relate the two fundamental characteristics of behaviour, involvement and motivation, in a way that helps direct brand attitude strategy.

Summary

In this chapter we have discussed the development of communication strategy, based on the four communication objectives of category need, brand awareness, brand attitude, and brand purchase intention. We have emphasized the important distinction between recognition brand awareness and recall brand awareness, and the implications for creative and media strategies. The critical importance of involvement and motivation was highlighted and related to the processing of messages.

Questions to consider

8.1   What are the four possible communication objectives?

8.2   Under what circumstances does category need become a communication objective?

8.3   Distinguish between recognition brand awareness and recall brand awareness.

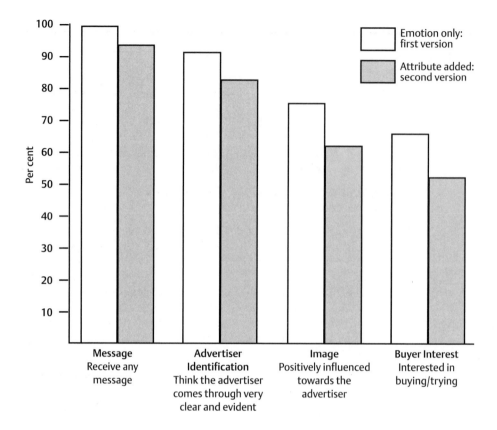

Fig. 8.2 Communication pre-test results from two versions of a Toblerone commercial
Source: Åke Wissing & Co.

8.4 What are the four characteristics of brand attitude?

8.5 When might brand purchase intention be a communication objective?

8.6 What is the primary reason for selecting recognition brand awareness as a communication objective?

8.7 Under what circumstances does recall brand awareness become a communication objective?

8.8 What are the five brand attitude strategic options?

8.9 Why is it important to think about brand attitude as a relative concept?

8.10 In what way is involvement and motivation important to setting brand attitude strategy?

8.11 When is emotional authenticity the key to successful communication?

Notes

1   The four communication effects discussed here, and their use as communication objectives, follow from the work of John Rossiter & Larry Percy, first introduced in their 1987 text *Advertising and Promotion Management*, (New York: McGraw-Hill). This book also talks about a fifth communication effect, something Rossiter and Percy call purchase facilitation, to account for situations where the advertiser may need to address issues arising from problems with other components of the marketing mix.

2   This very important distinction was first made in Rossiter and Percy, *Advertising and Promotion Management*.

3   Measures of *advertising* recall are not valid predictors of advertising effectiveness. The most that can be said of day-after recall (DAR) measures is that they *might* provide some indication of attention to an advert. What is important is that the *brand* is remembered. Even published studies by leading DAR companies have never shown advertising recall to be a valid measure of effectiveness. See, for example, M. H. Blair, 'An Empirical Investigation of Advertising Wearin and Wearout', *Journal of Advertising Research*, 28:6 (1988), 45–50 and P. R. Klein and M. Tainter, 'Copy Research Validation: The Advertiser's Perspective', *Journal of Advertising Research*, 23:5 (1983), 9–17.

4   To understand fully the attitudes of your target audience, it will be necessary to conduct *primary* research. There is really no alternative to measuring your target audience's perceptions of your brand and competitors, and general category attitudes.

5   See M. Fishbein and I. Ajzen, *Belief, Attitude, Intention, and Behavior: An Introduction to Theory and Research* (Reading, Mass.: Addison-Wesley, 1975).

6   See Steven P. R. Rose, *The Making of Memory* (London: Bantam Books, 1993).

7   See J. C. Maloney, 'Curiosity versus Disbelief in Advertising', *Journal of Advertising Research*, 2:2 (1962), 2–8.

8   See R. E. Petty and J. T. Cacioppo, 'Central and Peripheral Routes to Persuasion: Application to Advertising', in L. Percy and A. G. Woodside, *Advertising and Consumer Psychology* (Lexington, Mass.: Lexington Books, 1983), 3–24.

9   Limbic-based responses emanate from the palaeomammalian mind and are unconsciously stimulated. An example would be the warm feeling you have when you see a small baby. For a discussion of how such responses can influence advertising processing, see L. Percy, 'An Introduction to the Theory of Symbolism of Habitat and its Implication for Consumer Behavior and Marketing Communication', in Flemming Hansen (ed.), *European Advances in Consumer Research*, vol. 2 (Provo, Utah: Association for Consumer Research. For a more detailed medical discussion see Paul D. MacLean, *The Triune Brain in Evolution: Role in Paleocerebral Functions*) (New York: Plenum Press, 1990).

10 See J. R. Rossiter and L. Percy, *Advertising Communication and Promotion Management* 2nd edn. (New York: McGraw-Hill, 1997).

11 See R. Vaughn, 'How Advertising Works: A Planning Model', *Journal of Advertising Research*, 20:5 (1980), 27–33.

12 See J. R. Rossiter, L. Percy, and R. J. Donovan, 'A Better Advertising Planning Grid', *Journal of Advertising Research* 30:5 (1991), 11–21.

Chapter 9

Media Strategy

We have made the point at various stages of this book that the decisions relating to media are of major importance. In this chapter we review the strategic factors that affect decisions regarding media selection. To a large extent the decisions relating to media scheduling are at the tactical level and are now largely handled by specialist media-buying agencies who have each developed very sophisticated suites of computer programmes, such as Zenith Media's Zoom systems. They are therefore not dealt with here in any detail. Interested readers should consult the specialist media planning literature, such as Rossiter and Danaher or Sissors and Baumber.[1]

The Turbulent Media Environment

The last twenty years has seen an explosion in media channels that has been accompanied by a fragmentation and segmentation of audiences. In the UK in 1982 there was one commercial TV station; in 1999 there were more than a hundred. Over the same period commercial radio has grown from 28 stations to more than 200, consumer magazines from 1,300 to 2,600-plus, and business magazines from 2000 to 5,400-plus.[2] And, of course, there are the new media, including the Internet, CD-ROMs, and other screen-based channels, and the bewildering variety of ambient media such as petrol pump handles, postcards, shopping trolleys, litter bins, and bus tickets.

As a result, media selection decisions have become far more complex and have led to the growth of specialist media agencies which are used by many major advertisers instead of their advertising agency's media departments. In a parallel move, some of Europe's largest advertisers, including Procter and Gamble, BT, and Unilever, have put media planning at the heart of their communications strategy. For example, 'communication channel planning' has been made mandatory across all of Unilever's world-wide businesses, where after setting brand priorities and objectives, media channel recommendations are agreed before a communications plan and subsequent creative briefs.[3] It is against this turbulent and fast-changing background that we will examine how media strategy can be guided by the communications strategy concepts developed in previous chapters.

The Media Trade-off Trinity

Before we go any further it is important to define some of the specialist terminology used in relation to media (see Table 9.1). *Reach* is the percentage of the target audience that is exposed to an advertisement in a given time period, usually four weeks. *Frequency* is the number of times an individual member of the target audience is exposed to a particular media vehicle in a given time period. *Opportunities to see* (OTS) refers to the cumulative exposures achieved in a given time period and is usually used instead of frequency in media planning. *Gross Rating Points* (GRPs) is a summary statistic for the achievement of a media plan and is calculated by multiplying reach by frequency. The word 'gross' indicates the problems with this statistic, as a media plan that achieves, say, 180 GRPs could be achieved by reaching 90 per cent of the target audience with an OTS of 2, or by reaching 45 per cent of the audience with an OTS of 4.

Effective frequency is a hypothetical construct that attempts to estimate the number of OTS that are required to have an effect on the target audience. Despite extensive econometric modelling and some highly exaggerated claims, there is no general answer to this question. One obvious problem is the widespread assumption that all advertising executions are equal. This is of course nonsense. As Millward Brown have demonstrated through tracking studies of hundreds of brands around the world, a good advert can be at least three times as effective as the average for a category, and over ten times as effective as the worst.[4] Some media auditing studies have shown a variation in the effect of advertising on sales due solely to creative execution of 10 to 1.

There are also a few terms associated with how advertising is scheduled that it is good to know. One very popular way of scheduling media is to be in the market for two or three weeks, then out for a few weeks before returning. This is known as *flighting*. Another practice is where advertising appears heavily a few times a year between long periods of no advertising. This is referred to as *bursts*. When advertising runs more or less continuously, this is known as *continuity scheduling*.

Table 9.1 Key Media Concepts

Reach	The percentage of the target audience exposed to an advertisement in a given-time period
Frequency	The number of times an individual member of the target audience is exposed to an advertisement in a given time period
Opportunities to see (OTS)	The cumulative exposures achieved in a given time period, usually used in media planning in place of frequency
Gross Rating Points (GRPs)	A summary statistic for the achievement of a media plan, calculated by multiplying reach by frequency
Effective Frequency	A hypothetical construct that attempts to estimate the number of OTS required to have an effect in the target audience

Reach vs. Frequency

At the heart of media strategy is the fact that there is never enough money to achieve very high reach and very high frequency for a very long period of time. Hence media strategy involves decisions between three elements which trade off frequency for coverage or vice versa, and whether to have a heavy weight of advertising for a shorter time period or less weight for longer. A media plan must deal with these three basic variables: reach, frequency, and timing. The ideal media plan, of course, would enable you to reach everyone in your target audience as often as necessary to ensure a positive response to your message. But you never have this luxury because it would require an all-but-unlimited budget. The reality of set budgets requires careful trade-offs between how many members of your target audience you can successfully reach, how many times you reach them, and when. While the timing of a schedule is an important consideration, the key is the trade-off between reach and frequency. This is a critical strategic issue.

A strategic emphasis on reach means spending the advertising and marketing communication budget in a number of different media, and a number of different vehicles, in order to reach as many members of the target audience as possible. By utilizing a number of different media you help ensure that people who do not use certain media are none the less reached. Some people watch a lot of television, some very little; others read a lot of magazines, some none at all; many people do not read newspapers at all. If reaching as many members of the target audience as possible is your goal, it will require using many different media, and then for each medium, a number of different vehicles (e.g. different types of television and radio programmes, and several different magazines).

When you emphasize reach, frequency suffers. If your emphasis is on frequency, you want to make sure that members of the target audience are exposed to your message a number of times. As we shall see below, higher frequency is important for recall brand awareness and for brand attitude strategies that deal with positive motives.

So how do you optimize media strategy in terms of reach and frequency? The key is something known as *minimum effective frequency*. Minimum effective frequency is the point at which we can reasonably expect that our advertising will begin to work, the point where the target audience will have had enough opportunity to process the message successfully. If the frequency is below this minimum level, the likelihood is that the advertising will not work at all. Computing the minimum effective frequency needed for a particular campaign is not easy, but there are models available for estimating it.[5] A good point to remember is that it is better to ensure you successfully communicate with at least some of your target audience so they are disposed to buy than to reach a lot of your target audience without being able to communicate successfully. In the trade-off between reach and frequency, it is better to err on the side of frequency.

Selecting Media

Back in Chapter 4 we talked about three characteristics of media that must be considered when thinking about the two essential communication objectives of brand awareness and brand attitude: visual content, time to process, and frequency potential (see Table 4.4). Just as we have already noted for creative strategy, a media strategy depends upon your communication objectives. Because brand awareness and brand attitude are always communication objectives, they largely determine media selection. Table 9.2 details how a number of primary media rate on the three characteristics. We can now explore the implications for media selection decisions of brand awareness and brand attitude strategies discussed in the last chapter.

Brand Awareness Strategies

The difference between brand recognition and brand recall has important implications for media selection. Brand recognition requires an emphasis on the visual representation of the pack or logo, while brand recall puts the emphasis on frequency to build an association between the brand name and category need. This difference of emphasis, for example, would lead to the conclusion that radio is unsuitable for brand recognition, but offers cost-efficient high-frequency repetition. Let us look at what this means for other media.

Brand Recognition

When brand recognition is our communication objective, we are looking for good visual content, not much time should be required for processing, and low frequency will do. If we look at Table 9.2, we see that television, magazines, posters, the Internet, and direct mail could be considered. Radio is out because you cannot see the package, and while newspapers might be a possibility, we must be sure good that colour reproduction can be counted on.

Table 9.2 Primary Media Ratings on Essential Media Selection Characteristics

	Visual Content	Time to Process Message	Frequency
Television	Yes	Short	High
Radio	No	Short	High
Newspapers	Limitations	Long	High
Magazines	Yes	Long	Limitations
Posters	Yes	Long	Limitations
Internet	Yes	Long	High
Direct Mail	Yes	Long	Low

Source: Adapted from J. R. Rossiter and L. Percy, *Advertising Communication and Promotion Management* (New York: McGraw-Hill, 1997).

Brand Recall

If brand recall is our communication objective, our biggest concern is with frequency. Good repetition of the linkage of category need and brand name is necessary, and this requires high frequency. Looking again at Table 9.2, we see that television, radio, newspapers, and the Internet offer the potential for high frequency. Magazines and direct mail have obvious frequency limitations. Posters have a potential frequency limitation because they are stationary media (unless, of course, they are on a bus or train, which will have their own frequency limitations).

Brand Attitude Strategies

The importance for brand attitude strategy of media selection focus on the three characteristics of visual content, processing time, and frequency will be discussed in detail in the next chapter. What we want to do here is look at which media make sense for specific brand attitude communication objectives. Each of the four basic brand attitude strategies are reviewed next. You will recall from previous chapters that brand attitude strategies reflect low vs. high involvement in the purchase decision process and whether the underlying motivations driving the use of products or services in the category are positive or negative.

Low-involvement, Negative-Motivation Strategy

Brand attitude communication objectives that reflect a low-involvement brand decision coupled with negative motivation can be addressed by almost any medium. It is perhaps the easiest communication objective to deal with in terms of media selection. There is no strong visual requirement, only a brief processing time is needed, and high frequency is not necessary because the benefits used in adverts following this type of brand attitude strategy must be learned in one or two exposures if it is to be effective. This is why almost any medium can be selected. A possible exception would be if the benefit must be *demonstrated*, in which case the medium selected must be capable of presenting the demonstration.

Low-Involvement, Positive-Motivation Strategy

With a brand attitude strategy for a low-involvement brand decision when the underlying motivation is positive, *good visual content* is critical. Although only a brief processing time is required, a relatively high frequency is necessary because of a generally slower brand attitude development. Here television is the ideal medium. All of the other primary media, with the exception of the Internet, are a potential problem because of processing time or frequency limitations. The exception here is radio, but it must be excluded because it lacks visual content. We should point out, however, that highly creative radio can sometimes overcome this problem if it can really make you 'see' the product.

High-Involvement, Negative-Motivation Strategy

Because brand attitude strategies that involve high-involvement brand decisions and negative motives require a longer processing time for the more extensive information content necessary to convince the target audience, media selection emphasis is likely to be on print-oriented media. And since frequency is not an issue, again because the benefits must be accepted in one or two exposures, almost any print medium will do (including the Internet).

High-Involvement, Positive-Motivation Strategy

As with low-involvement strategies associated with positive motivations, visual content is critical. The key difference here is that there is no need for high frequency. You may think this strange since we pointed out that brand attitude builds slowly in the low-involvement choice situation. The reason for this seeming contradiction is that most low-involvement/positive-motivation brand attitude strategies involve fast-moving consumer goods with a relatively *short purchase cycle*. This means there is not a lot of time for the advertising to work. With high-involvement brand decisions we are usually dealing with brand decisions for products with much longer purchase cycles. This is what permits a relatively lower rate of frequency. Of the primary media we have been considering in Table 9.2, television and most print media could be selected. Newspapers have the potential colour limitation we discussed earlier. Radio would not be appropriate.

A caveat should be noted here. Even though we are dealing with positive motives, because the brand decision is high-involvement, eventually it might be necessary to provide a certain amount of detailed information. When that is the case, processing time will need to be considered in your media selection.

Brand Awareness and Brand Attitude Strategies

An important point to remember in media selection is that an attempt must be made to accommodate *all* of your communication objectives. This means that, at the very least, the media selected must meet *both* brand awareness and brand attitude strategies. When recognition is the brand awareness communication objective, because all of the primary media are acceptable, selection will be driven solely on the basis of the brand attitude strategy.

But, when brand recall is the communication objective, you must be careful to consider the requirements for both brand recall and the brand attitude strategy in your media selection. Selection options in this case are summarized in Table 9.3. As you can see, the only medium that works regardless of the strategy is the Internet. In every other case you must check for compatibility between the two communication objectives involved, and look carefully at potential limitations.

Even if a medium cannot achieve total compatibility between these two objectives, it might still be worth using; but it should not be the *primary* media selection. For example, television is a perfect medium for driving up awareness of any kind. Even though it is not really suitable for high-involvement brand decisions when the motivation is negative, it could certainly be used to generate recall brand awareness as long as another, more appropriate medium carries the primary informational message with sufficient time for processing.

Table 9.3 Primary Media Selection Options to Satisfy Brand Awareness and Brand Attitude Communication Objectives

	Brand Awareness		Brand Attitude			
	Recognition	Recall	Low-involved Negative Motive	Low-involved Positive Motive	High-involved Negative Motive	High-involved Positive Motive
Television	Yes	Yes	Yes	Yes	No	Yes
Radio	No	Yes	Yes	No	No	No
Newspapers	Yes	Yes	Yes	Limitations	Yes	Limitations
Magazines	Yes	Limitations	Yes	Limitations	Yes	Yes
Posters	Yes	Limitations	Yes	Limitations	Limitations	Yes
Internet	Yes	Yes	Yes	Yes	Yes	Yes
Direct Mail	Yes	Limitations	Yes	Limitations	Yes	Yes

Source: Adapted from J. R. Rossiter and L. Percy, *Advertising Communications and Promotion Management* (New York: McGraw-Hill, 1997).

Scheduling Media

One of the more vexing questions in developing effective media strategies is how to schedule media. Earlier we defined three basic types of scheduling: flighting, bursts, and continuity. While these basic types do indeed define the *structure* of most media scheduled, the actual scheduling itself is a much more difficult issue. There is seemingly an almost infinite number of circumstances that could have an effect upon how to optimize your media schedule. What is the purchase cycle for the category? Are sales seasonal? If so, do we want to break the pattern? How do competitors schedule their advertising? What creative units are to be used (e.g. 15-second vs. 30-second vs. 60-second commercials, or half-page vs. full-page vs. two-page spreads in magazines)? How many different creative executions are being used? How difficult is it to reach the target audience? Is the target audience segmented? If so, how? You should be getting the idea.

There are, of course, many models available to help the media planner put together a good media schedule. But most media models, by their very nature, make general assumptions and tend to average. It is virtually impossible for any one model to take into account all of the many variables involved. This has led to a number of rules of thumb among media planners. But again, because every brand's situation is different, and often changes from campaign to campaign, following well-known formulas may not lead to the most effective schedule.

Does this mean the task of developing an effective media schedule is all but hopeless? Not at all. What it means is that each schedule must be carefully assessed, and assessed for *each* media plan developed. How to go about this task is quite beyond the scope of this book, but there are a number of good books that deal with scheduling in depth. One book in particular offers a great deal of insight into this problem: Simon Broadbent's *When to*

Advertise.[6] Broadbent has had a significant influence on media issues over the last thirty years, especially in the UK. What we like about his approach is that he defines a *process* to determine when to advertise. He suggests that to schedule media effectively you must look at what you need to pay for the media, when you most want it to have an effect, and how you think the advertising will work. You can see how these points address the kind of issues raised by the many questions associated with trying to optimize a media schedule. There is nothing at all easy about how you go about implementing this process, but he offers a framework for addressing the problem. The important point is that it acknowledges the fact that effective media scheduling depends upon the 'particular circumstances, there is no single solution'.[7]

Target Audience Factors and Brand Ecology

In Chapter 5 we discussed at length the issues of target audience selection and suggested that brand loyalty segmentation based on attitude is the most effective method for developing communication strategy. Whilst the customer's relationship with the brand is an essential element in communication planning and usually has to be based on primary market research, a new approach to media selection also uses the customer's relationship with the media as an input into media selection. Syndicated audience research services provide a wealth of quantitative data about media use. The Target Group Index (TGI) in the UK also provides usage data on 4,000 brands in 500 product categories, cross-referenced to usage of print media and TV. In addition, it provides some basic attitudinal data as well as standard demographics. Major media also supply extensive syndicated audience data. In the UK the Broadcasters' Audience Research Board (BARB) provides TV viewing behaviour on a continuous basis, showing audience figures per programme on the major terrestrial and satellite channels. Rich data on over 250 newspaper and magazine titles in the UK are provided by the National Readership Survey (NRS), and similar data are provided for radio by Radio Joint Audience Research (RAJAR). Similar services are available in other countries. These syndicated audience data sources are the basis of all the major media planning systems, and are also utilized within the most sophisticated propriety media systems such as Zenith Media's ZOOM Excalibur, which models effective frequency levels against marketing and media factors.

However, the fragmentation of the media landscape over the last twenty years has led to the emergence of a new active media consumer, who can choose from a huge portfolio of media to construct a 'personal media network' using an increasing array of technology and information to actively edit their own media environment.[8] The opportunity in this fragmentation of audiences is that it offers the possibility of going beyond simple demographics to understand the relationship smaller audiences have with their chosen media, and to develop an understanding of consumer 'brand ecology'.

Brand ecology considers not just the attitudinal, emotional, and behavioural aspects of brand consumption, but explores how this brand-related behaviour integrates with wider social and cultural experience in the life-world of the active consumer. As we pointed out in Chapter 5, demographics and lifestyle analyses are not stable predictors of consumer behaviour across categories, and as media choice explodes, multi-TV households become the norm, and technological aids such as the Electronic Programme Guide (EPG) proliferate, the media are responding with ever more focused offerings that can be built into a consumer's personal media schedule.

The close relationship between consumers and their personal media architecture is at least as important as any brand–consumer relationship, because it is from our trusted media that we construct our view of the world, gain enjoyment, entertainment, stimulation, and information. A deep understanding of the consumer–media relationship can also be the prompt for great creative work as it informs the creative brief with a three-dimensional picture of the target audience. As Henny has put it: 'Find out what makes them laugh. What makes them cry. What they think about current affairs, what books they read, what music they prefer, and if there are any other cultural things they are into because then I can rip those off for the creative execution.'[9]

Understanding Brand–Consumer–Media Relationships

The starting point for exploring media aspects of brand ecology is the wealth of industry audience data described above. Interrogating these data can set out the parameters of media usage, related to attitudinal and lifestyle dimensions; but for developing really effective media strategy we require information on the emotional aspects of media consumption, its social and cultural context and the meaning it carries in consumers' lives. In an era of money-rich but time-poor people working ever-longer hours, media consumption often involves active choice behaviour between competing alternatives and this choice behaviour is itself driven by attitudes and emotions to the various media and how its consumption integrates with other individual and social activity.

Consumers have media imperatives, such as a 'must-view' appointment with an episode of a soap opera, or a 'must-read' appointment with a heavyweight Sunday newspaper. Increasingly the same consumer can consume a paradoxical range of media, often in a different mind-set at different times of the day or week. One TV consumer may switch from low-involvement consumption of US comedies, to high-involvement consumption of a high-brow arts programme, to high-involvement consumption of a football match, all on the same evening.

In order to match our brand attitude strategy with media consumption we need to know how and why they are consuming the media, not just that they are in the same room as the TV. The *who* question of media consumption has a very complex answer once we recognize the variety of consumption modes within the same person's media architecture. Some media are often consumed alone—print media for example—while some depend on company for satisfying experience, for example TV comedies. But consuming media in a social setting may itself vary greatly depending on the composition of the group and the social rules and expectations that apply. The relationship with a medium may involve high levels of trust, respect, affection, and personal and family history. Alternatively it may involve distrust, lack of respect, an absence of any emotional connection, and little history.

We need to be able to profile our target audience on these and other emotional, social, and cultural factors and be able to relate them to their brand relationships in order to maximize our ability to make appropriate media choices. This investment in researching our target group's media consumption is a vital step towards developing effective media strategy, as 'traditional data is simply too broad and too shallow to yield the detailed insights which can inspire imaginative media solutions'.[10]

Evaluating the Efficiency of Media Strategy

The demand for greater media accountability continues to grow,[11] and we now consider some important approaches to evaluating the efficiency of media strategy. As will be discussed in Chapter 14, continuous tracking studies make a major contribution to evaluating the effectiveness of creative strategies, and they also have an important role to play in assessing media strategy in combination with creative content against communication objectives. However, the method of choice for evaluating media efficiency is 'media auditing'. A major media auditing operator is the Media Audits Group, which operates in 60 countries and provides media audit services for over 300 clients on $3 billion adspend. Media auditing operates by comparing a specific advertiser's media expenditure with that of a very large data pool containing actual prices paid for media supplied by clients and then advising on buying efficiency. This comparison of price paid for media against the pool average gives powerful information to advertisers and allows them to put pressure on their media-buying agency to lower costs. Using econometric models, a number of media auditors offer advice on such issues as media weighting, frequency rates, weighting between media, and regional effects.

The New Media

Now we turn to a consideration of the new media, specifically the Internet, and its implications for media strategy. First, it has to be recognized that at the moment the Internet is a small-niche medium. In April 2000 the top 165 Internet sites in the UK delivered 952 million impressions, during the same period BARB-monitored commercial TV channels delivered 55,000 million impressions, i.e. the Internet audience share relative to TV is 1.73 per cent. However, forecasts for the Internet's growth as an advertising medium are very bullish, linked to predictions that the online population will reach at least 50 per cent of the UK population by 2003 via three key platforms: personal computer, interactive TV, and mobile phone.[12]

Consumer activity in relation to the Internet focuses on three functions: communication and communities, content, and commerce. Communication by e-mail and its associated chat rooms and news groups is the major use of the Internet, and this is expanding and developing into virtual communities coalescing around a myriad of different interests. Content in the UK is most often related to information about BBC entertainment programmes, especially soap operas, sport, news, and financial investment.[13] Commerce is at present the least popular use of the Internet but is predicted to grow enormously, extending beyond the current focus on computer goods, books, and travel. Current predictions for Internet advertising are that direct mail will be the most heavily affected traditional media channel. Companies that currently advertise online will do so increasingly, leading to a 33 per cent fall in direct mail expenditure by 2004. Over the next four years online will also increasingly take spend from outdoor and radio advertising, and will begin to dent press advertising, but is not expected to have much impact on TV advertising over the next four years.[14]

An important implication of the Internet for developing media strategy is the question of control of brand messages. Orthodox media strategy aims to control the different channels and methods through which the brand can target the consumer. However, with the rapid enabling of consumer networks of contacts and peers, brand messages are becoming increasingly uncontrollable, which means that official brand messages are becoming increasingly unimportant compared to the unsanctioned 'word of mouse' within a particular brand or anti-brand community.[15] The interactive and uncontrollable nature of the Internet raises serious issues for media strategy, and suggests that in the future we will have to engage consumers in dialogue rather than monologue format and attempt to invite customers to participate in 'conversations' rather than being passive targets for messages. So once again we return to the need for in-depth understanding of consumer behaviour as the driver for all strategy, and in the next chapter we turn to examining how consumers process messages.

Summary

This chapter has introduced some of the specific concepts and terminology used in relation to media. We began by pointing out some of the key issues of reach vs. frequency. We then related media selection decisions to communication objectives, especially the brand attitude objectives based on involvement and motivation. We considered media scheduling decisions and then went on to discuss the concept of brand ecology and the importance of understanding the consumer's emotional relationship with various media. Lastly, we discussed the new media and the implications for media strategy of the interactivity and uncontrollability factors related to brand messages.

Questions to consider

9.1 What is 'communication channel planning'?

9.2 What is the media trade-off trinity?

9.3 What is meant by flighting?

9.4 What is meant by minimum effective frequency?

9.5 What are the media selection implications of brand recognition strategy vs. brand recall strategy?

9.6 Give some examples of ambient media.

9.7 What are the media selection implications when low involvement and positive motivation drives strategy?

9.8 What are the media selection implications when high involvement and positive motivation drives strategy?

9.9 What is meant by brand ecology and how does it affect media strategy?

9.10 What implications do the interactivity and uncontrollability associated with the new media have for media strategy?

Notes

1   Perhaps the best book available for anyone really interested in media strategy is John R. Rossiter and Peter J. Danaher, *Advanced Media Planning* (Norwell, Mass.: Kluwer Academic Publishers, 1998), which comes with its own disc containing all of the models discussed. Another good book is the latest edition of J. Sissors and L. Baumber: *Advertising Media Planning*, 5th edn. (Lincolnwood: NTC Business Press, 1987).

2   A. Tillery, 'The Strategic Importance of Media', in L. Butterfield (ed.), *Excellence in Advertising* (Oxford: Butterworth Heinemann, 1999).

3   A. Rutherford, 'Managing the Media', *Uniview Magazine* (1999).

4   *The Millward Brown Link Tests* (London: Millward Brown, Ltd, 1997).

5   This issue of minimum effective frequency is discussed in some depth in J. R. Rossiter and L. Percy, *Advertising Communication and Promotion Management*, (New York: McGraw-Hill, 1997).

6   Simon Broadbent *When to Advertise* (Henley-on-Thames, Oxon.: Admap Publications, 1999). See also the books cited in n. 1.

7   Broadbent, *When to Advertise*, 102.

8   See Tillery, 'The Strategic Importance of Media'.

9   G. Henny, 'Creative Briefing: The Creative Perspective', in Butterfield (ed.), *Excellence in Advertising*, Oxford.

10 G. Michaelides, 'Street Wise', *Admap*, May 2000, 27.

11 J. Billet and I. Fermoi, 'The Agenda of Media Accountability', *Admap*, June 2000, 33–5.

12 S. Foster, 'The Evolution of the New Media Species', *Admap*, Sept. 2000, 22–95.

13 Fletcher Research website, http//:www.fletch.co.uk

14 Fletcher Research website, http//:www.fletch.co.uk

15 Happy Dog website, http//:happydog.co.uk

Part Four

Making it Work

Chapter 10

Processing the Message

Processing a message is clearly critical to successful advertising communication, as we discussed in Chapter 3 when we introduced the idea of a communication response sequence. Processing is much more than an abstraction. While it does reflect what must go on in a person's head as they are exposed to advertising and other marketing communication, at the same time it also suggests what we must include in the execution if it is to be correctly processed. Once we understand what goes into processing, we will be in a better position to understand why and how various creative strategies and tactics are used in order to satisfy particular communication objectives.

What do we Mean by Processing?

For our purposes, we define processing as that which goes on in a person's mind when they are exposed to an advert or any form of marketing communication *in response to it*. This would include all of their reactions when they are actively *or passively* looking at or listening to it, as well as after the exposure if they are still thinking about it. These reactions can quite literally be anything, as long as they are in response to the communication itself. For example, look at Advert 10.1, which appeared in a British women's magazine.

What are you now thinking about as you look at this advert? Whatever it may be, it reflects your processing of the advertising. You may be thinking 'That looks interesting' or 'I wish I could float like that.' Perhaps you are thinking 'I didn't think any washing machine was easy to unload.' You may even be thinking 'I don't need a washing machine.' All of these responses represent processing of the advertising.

When psychologists talk about processing, they are generally referring to what occurs in something they call active, or short-term, memory. Many psychologists like to classify the way a person handles information, or more accurately their response to any stimuli, by saying it is first processed in short-term memory, then stored in long-term memory. Because short-term memory is always busy, some things may not be correctly processed; and many things that are processed in short-term memory never make it into long-term memory. While we needn't be too concerned with this now, we will be returning to this notion later on in the chapter when we make a distinction between full and partial processing.

10.1 Whatever you are thinking about as you look at this advert reflects what and how you are processing the advert. Courtesy Whirlpool Corp.

We should point out that there is another way of looking at processing, advanced by Craik and Lockart,[1] which eliminates the short- vs. long-term distinction and considers something they call depth of processing. In their formulation, shallow processing corresponds to short-term memory and deeper processing to long-term memory. We might think of this as a continuum of processing vs. the more traditional two-step formulation.

There are four main processing responses that can occur when you are exposed to advertising and other marketing communication:

- *attention* to the advertising itself;
- *learning* something from the advertising;
- *accepting* or believing what the advertising says;
- *emotion* that is stimulated by the advertising.

We shall briefly introduce each of these processing responses, and then delve much further into them.

Attention. Before anything else can occur, you must first pay attention to the advertising. In Chapter 3 when we introduced exposure, the first step in our communication response sequence, we pointed out that exposure was an opportunity to see the advertising. But until you pay attention to the advertising, you have not begun to process it. Exposure is necessary or you do not have the opportunity to process the message. Once you are aware of the advertising, you have paid attention to it and begun processing. This is true even if you go no further than identify it as, say, an advert and not part of the programme you are watching, at which point you leave the room to get a snack.

Learning. Once you have paid attention to the advertising you are in a position to learn something as a result of what is presented in the execution. In a sense, all you are doing is acquainting yourself with the content of the advertising. Returning to the Whirlpool advert, assuming you have looked at it in the magazine (and therefore paid attention to it) you probably learned that it is an advert for a washing machine. You may have even gone further and found that it also talks about how easy it is to unload.

The advert also says 'it's not magic, it's Whirlpool'. If you read that, in terms of processing this would also be something you learn. Yet an important point must be made here. You will have learned that the advert claims it is easy to unload, but you may not necessarily believe it. Believing what the advertising says constitutes acceptance, and that is a separate processing response.

Acceptance. If you have learned something from advertising, you are then in a position to accept or reject it. The entire thrust of the various elements in advertising, both words and pictures, is to present the brand in the most positive way possible. Whirlpool quite literally wants you to believe their machines are easy to unload. Interestingly, while the claim is made in the copy, the major impact comes from the visual. So, if your reaction when first seeing the advert was 'That looks easy', you have personally accepted the message as true. In terms of processing you paid attention to the advert, learned from the pictures, copy, or both, and, from what you learned, accepted the fact that their machines must be easy to unload. In other words, if this was your reaction to this advert, this was how you processed the advertising. When we discuss this in more detail below, we will see that it is not always necessary to accept the message for advertising to be effective.

Emotion. Beyond everything we have just talked about, there is a fourth response to advertising that mediates both learning and acceptance. This is the emotional response you have to advertising once you have paid attention. Emotional responses are something that just happen, actually a response of the autonomic nervous system. You like something or you don't. For example, if your reaction to the Whirlpool advert was a positive sense of 'floating', or simply a pleasant response to the flowing illustration, you were reacting emotionally to the visual elements in the execution. These emotional responses will help energize or stimulate learning and acceptance responses.

An important point to understand here is that when we talk about processing advertising, we are not referring to some general or overall process. What in fact goes on is that each of the elements in the advertising has the ability to communicate, and therefore has the opportunity to be processed. Depending upon the medium, everything from the pictures to the spoken word, from the written word to music, can contribute to the overall communication of the message. Each of these components may be processed, and if they are successfully processed, they will follow the sequence described above: attention followed by learning and, if necessary, acceptance; and all of this will be facilitated by emotion.

If an advert is to be truly effective, the processing of each important component of the advert must be successful if the overall communication objective is to be reached. If recognition is the brand awareness communication objective, then the *package* must be processed, or, for verbal recognition awareness, the brand name. For recall awareness, we will want to see the brand name repeated and *linked* to the category need. In terms of awareness, whether recognition or recall, the brand name should be clearly communicated.

Brand attitude in many cases relies heavily upon visual components, and this is almost always the case in television adverts. While the copy can and does contribute to brand awareness, the real communication potential is more often conveyed by the visual representations. An interesting test of this for television commercials is to view it with the sound off and see what the visuals alone communicate. Emotion too is almost wholly contained within the visual component. As a result, to be truly effective, separate processing of both the visual and verbal components of an advert must occur in order to realize effective brand awareness and brand attitude communication effects. And it should go without saying that the visual and verbal component should reinforce each other in what they communicate.

Now that we have a feeling for what we mean by processing in advertising, it is time to take a closer look at each of the four main processing responses and how they facilitate achieving our communication objectives (see Table 10.1). First, we will address attention, learning, and acceptance.

Attention

As we have already mentioned, attention is a necessary processing response before any other processing can occur. This should be obvious. If you haven't paid any attention to something, how can you learn or accept what has been said? But there is a subtle, and

Table 10.1 Processing Necessary for Achieving Communication Objectives

	Attention	Learning	Acceptance	Emotion
Category Need	Yes	Yes	Yes	No
Brand Awareness	Yes	Yes	No	No
Brand Attitude:				
Low involvement	Yes	Yes	No	Yes
High involvement	Yes	Yes	Yes	Yes
Brand Purchase Intention	Yes	Yes	Yes	Yes

very important, point we must consider when thinking about attention. Yes, you must pay attention, but you may not do it conscientiously. So while you may think you have not 'paid attention' to an advert, if you were within earshot of the message, or if your eyes even glanced at the TV or magazine, you will have attended to the advertising. This is something we call *reflexive attention*.

Reflexive attention is initiated every time there is a change in your stimulus environment, and it is a wholly involuntary reaction. For example, when a commercial comes on TV, even if you were only half attending to the programme, the switch in programming from the show to the commercial will cause you to notice the commercial. If you then jumped up to run to the kitchen in order to get something to eat because of the commercial break, it is because the change in the stimulus (in this case the TV programming) involuntarily attracted your attention. The same thing occurs each time you turn a page in a magazine. Even if you are only skimming the magazine, each time the page turns your attention will involuntarily be drawn to the page. If there is an advert on the page, you will process it at least far enough to identify it as such, and in most cases choose not to spend time actually reading it.

Unfortunately, this reflexive attention doesn't last very long. If the stimulus is visual, such as the beginning of a TV commercial or a page turned in a magazine, reflexive attention only lasts about one-tenth of a second[2] and if the stimulus is a word that your eye fixates upon or that you hear spoken, the reflexive attention will be only about three-tenths of a second.[3] Only if something in that brief period of attention *holds* your attention will you actually spend time with the advert.

This might be a good place to answer a question that may have come to mind as you read this material on reflexive attention: the question of subliminal perception. We do not intend to spend any time on this issue because, quite frankly, it is not a significant consideration in either the execution or processing of advertising. Much has frequently been made of subliminal additions to adverts. The fact is that even if some advertisers were to include subliminal cues in their advertising (and there really is no evidence that they do), it would have little if any influence. In some studies conducted by Moore,[4] it was shown that even when such cues were purposely included in an advert, it had no significant effect on the advertising's ability to communicate or persuade.[5]

Returning to our discussion of attention, there is a second type of attention that we must be aware of: *selective attention*. Selective attention occurs when you voluntarily pay attention to advertising. This could occur, for example, if you see an advert for a laptop computer when you are actively thinking about buying one. You would first reflexively attend to the advertising, and assuming there is enough there to link the advert to your category need for a new laptop you will likely pay further attention to the advertising. This is no guarantee that you will read or listen to the entire advert, but you will certainly spend more than a fraction of a second with the advertising. In such cases, attention must be maintained with a good execution.

How do we Maintain Attention?

The key to maintaining attention to an advert lies in the elements used in the execution, as we shall see in Chapter 11. While these can vary, depending upon the communication effects involved, let us take a brief look at the manner in which they relate to our two primary communication effects: brand awareness and brand attitude. Remember that all advertising must achieve these two responses, and in fact, they are always communication objectives.

Brand Awareness

As you might suspect, it doesn't require a great deal of processing to effect positive brand awareness. In fact, once we have achieved exposure to the advertising and at least reflexive attention, one strategy that can be used to continue stimulating reflexive attention is to utilize something a bit different either visually or verbally within the execution itself. Another way of maintaining reflexive interest is with unexpectedly positioned ads. For example, you could use the equivalent of a full-page advert in a magazine horizontally run as two consecutive half-page spaces. Because we are so used to seeing advertising as same-page executions, reflexive attention should be maintained here as the mind tries to figure out what is going on. The same principle is sometimes used with broadcast advertising when a commercial is continued after a station break or other commercials. Specific creative tactics to help maintain awareness are discussed in the next chapter.

Brand Attitude

In our discussion of brand attitude as a communication objective in Chapter 8, we learned that brand attitude must be associated with the motivation that drives target audience behaviour in the category. Since attention is the first, and necessary, step in processing an advertising message, it is especially important in initiating the desired brand attitude. However, this is much more complex than the attention response associated with brand awareness. What we find with attention and brand attitude is that target audiences will be likely to attend *selectively* to advertising *only* if the message in the advert relates to their *current* motivation in the category.

Here are a few examples to help clarify what we mean. At the extreme, if you are a man there is probably very little likelihood that you would selectively attend to a cosmetic advert for a new eye shadow. You would have no motivation to respond in this category. On the other hand, women could be motivated to respond to an advert for men's cosmetics, because they may want to encourage a friend or spouse to purchase or use the product. At a more general level, if you do not have a baby, you are unlikely to attend selectively to advertising for baby food, or if you do not have a problem with athlete's foot, you will not attend to advertising for an athlete's foot remedy.

In each of these examples, you would pay reflexive attention, enough to let you know you were not interested in the category, and hence have no interest in further processing the advert. However, if you were actively seeking information in this category, once reflexive attention has oriented you to the content of the advertising, your selective attention would be activated as you related the subject of the advertising to your current category motivation.

The underlying motivation to respond here has a great deal of significance for how likely you are to attend selectively to the advertising. If the underlying motivation is *negative*, unless the problem involved is current or likely to recur, there really isn't much likelihood that you will attend to the attitudinal content of the advertising. On the other hand, if the motivation is *positive* there is a greater likelihood that you will. After all, who doesn't like to see a really sensuous dessert or a 'glamorous' image? It simply makes you feel good. Now this doesn't mean you will necessarily respond positively to the advert's message, only that you will be more likely to selectively attend to the message because of its positive reinforcement.

Of course, a well-executed advert will have the ability not only to attract attention, but to hold it as well. What we want to happen is for *something* to be learned, even if only at a sub-cognitive level. Reflexive attention alone provides enough time at least to impress the brand name and a positive association with the brand *if* the execution embodies this in a clear fashion. Then, the more unique the execution, the greater the selective attention. Advertising cannot assume the target audience will pay attention. We must assume they will probably not, and so ensure we communicate something, if only during the reflexive attention span.

In an advert for London Transport (Advert 10.2) we have a really good example of how a unique execution not only can attract and hold attention, but also facilitate the processing of the message itself. London Transport had a problem because people were confused about zone boundaries and fares for buses in London. They decided to reduce the fare structure to a simple two-zone division for all of the city: zone 1 for the inner city and zone 2 for everything else. Utilizing the simple device of a fried egg to symbolize the new two-zone structure helps communicate the desired benefit of 'making London simple'. This is a concrete image (which we will discuss in the next chapter) that easily and quickly facilitates processing the message. Both the visual imagery and the written message reinforce each other. After only three weeks, the campaign had generated a 73 per cent awareness of the new two-fare system.

You should now have a pretty clear understanding of what we mean by paying attention to advertising. It is the first step in the processing sequence, but in and of itself is not sufficient to effect the desired communication response. For advertising to be effective it must also stimulate a learning *or* acceptance response, depending upon the particular communication objective involved. As we have just seen, London Transport did a good job in gaining attention *and* stimulating learning. In the next two sections we will explore the processing responses of learning and acceptance.

Learning

The second processing response necessary for effective communication is *learning*. When we talk about learning as a processing response, we are really referring only to a very

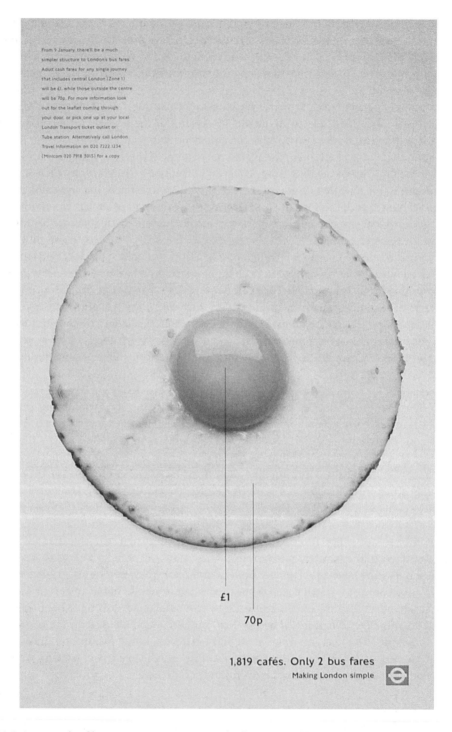

From 9 January there'll be a much
simpler structure to London's bus fares.
Adult cash fares for any single journey
that includes central London (Zone 1)
will be £1, while those outside the centre
will be 70p. For more information look
out for the leaflet coming through
your door, or pick one up at your local
London Transport ticket outlet or
Tube station. Alternatively call London
Travel Information on 020 7222 1234
(Minicom 020 7918 3015) for a copy

£1

70p

1,819 cafés. Only 2 bus fares
Making London simple

10.2 An example of how a unique execution can both attract *and* hold attention to help you process the message of the advert. Courtesy London Transport

simple response. And unlike your academic studies, where you are always expected not only to learn but also to understand, when the decision associated with purchase is low-involvement the learning process need be nothing more than a rote response. If all we achieve is a passive response, one that occurs whether or not the perceiver is consciously trying to learn, the advertising will have had some effect. Of course, we are aiming for understanding as well, but that is really only essential for high-involvement decisions. Next we will take a look at how this learning response facilitates brand awareness, and then low-involvement brand attitude.

Brand Awareness and Learning

If you stop to think of it, learning a brand name is very much like learning new words in a foreign language. Suppose you were studying German and were introduced to the word 'schwarz'. Your attention is drawn to the word, and you form a verbal and visual image of the word in your mind. If this is all you did, you should at least be able to recognize the word if you saw or heard it again, and identify it as a German word. In this case you are associating the word with the category 'German words'. As we all know, this will not get you very far on a German test. You will also need to learn the meaning of the word.

In order to become aware of a brand such that you are able either to recognize it or recall it when it comes time to make a decision to buy, you must learn the association between the category and the brand. You will remember that we spent a great deal of time on this point in Chapter 8. The category cue is critical, and will actually determine how likely it is that your brand will be chosen in various purchase situations.

Brand Recognition

When the brand awareness objective is recognition, what is the learning process involved? From what we already know about brand recognition, when it is an objective the advertising should feature the package as it will be seen at the point of purchase. What happens is that the consumer recognizes the package on the shelf, or perhaps sees a fast-food chain while driving, and thinks: 'I need that' or 'I'm hungry, so let's stop.' This is precisely what the learning response is for a brand recognition communication objective. You recognize the brand and associate it with the correct category need.

Brand Recall

Brand recall is a more difficult communication objective to achieve than brand recognition, because the learning process is more involved. If a family decides to go out for dinner, they are not very likely simply to go out and drive around until they recognize some place where they would like to stop. They are going to make their destination decision before they start out. For a restaurant to be considered, it must be recalled at the time the category need occurs, which in this case would be when a decision is made to go out for dinner. Here the learned awareness response is the link between the category need and some brand as the best, or one of the best, ways to satisfy that need.

Consider Advert 10.3. Here we have a very good example of linking a brand to category need for brand recall awareness. The advert itself helps attract attention with the unique, almost sub-cognitive image of an airplane, which reinforces category identification. The actual 'need' is travel between London and Chicago, and the brand that meets this need is American Airlines, four times a day. You learn that American has frequent flights to

10.3 The link necessary for recall brand awareness between a need (a flight to Chicago) and the brand is clearly made in this advert for American Airlines. Courtesy American Airlines

Chicago, the link necessary to associate the brand with the need in a flyer's mind when a choice decision must be made.

Brand Attitude and Learning

You will recall from our earlier discussions that brand attitude responses are a function of the type of decision involved and whether the underlying motive to behave is positive or negative. The type of decision has important implications for brand attitude learning.

Low Involvement

With low-involvement decisions, really all that is required is rather simple rote learning of the benefit associated with the brand. The target audience is aware of what the product is because they have just associated the brand with the category. Now the question is: So what? The benefit expressed in the advertising should answer that question. In effect what is going on here is that while the target audience is processing the message, they will learn the connection between the brand and the benefit claimed for the brand, along with the *degree* of that connection.

High Involvement

This will not be the case with high-involvement decisions. The key to high-involvement decisions is *acceptance*, which we will be discussing next. But high-involvement learning is tied into acceptance. With low-involvement learning you can be effective if the target audience only tentatively learns a positive benefit, but with high-involvement learning there is usually more than one simple benefit involved.

Acceptance

Acceptance in processing is when the target audience *personally agrees* with something they have learned from one of the components in the advertising. Acceptance is only required for *high-involvement* decisions. With low-involvement decisions, learning is sufficient processing to generate purchase because there is little if any risk involved. But with high-involvement decisions, because of the need to be sure of your decision prior to purchase, the message (or at least a significant part of it) must be accepted as true.

To understand better what we mean by acceptance, consider Advert 10.4 which is for PlayStation, Sony's videogames system. This would be a high-involvement purchase decision, so in processing the message, it must be accepted. The illustration here does an excellent job relating to the target audience. Something off-beat and different is suggested, and this should be consistent with the positive motives likely to be driving a post-teen target audience for videogames. Right away you realize this is not being positioned as an ordinary videogame. The copy then reinforces this:

The mind gets more powerful the more you feed it. So gorge it on the most widely varied and most technologically advanced mental assault course in the world. Stretch it with greater and more demanding tests of speed and agility. Expand it with dazzling depth and detail. At the same time, distort it with the built in sounds of The Prodigy or The Chemical Brothers. After that, do with it what you will.

This copy does more than hint at possible enjoyment, which is all that would be

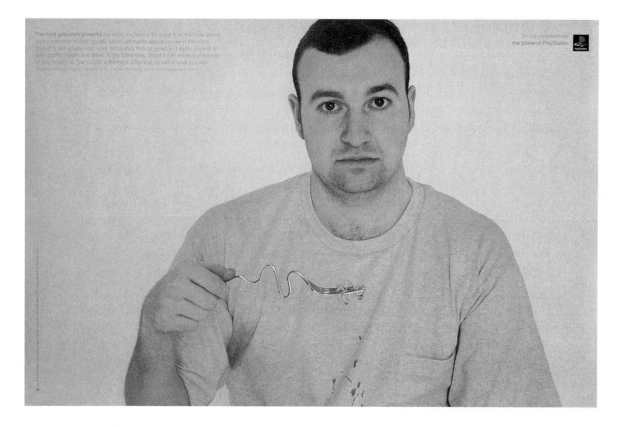

10.4 By doing a good job reflecting the target audience in an off-beat way this advert encourages the acceptance of the message which is necessary for the high-involvement purchase decision involved. Courtesy Sony

needed for a low-involvement decision. The benefit claim is solidly supported with specific attributes: 'the most widely varied and most technologically advanced', 'more demanding tests of speed and agility', 'dazzling depth and detail'. All this is then underscored by the tagline, 'Do not underestimate the power of PlayStation.' From the information provided in this advert, the target audience has what they need to 'accept' the message, and consider spending £129.99 for the PlayStation console and £19.99 to £59.99 for the games (prices included at the end of the message).

In fact, in all but brand awareness and low-involvement brand attitude communication responses, acceptance will be required. Think about each of the other communication responses:

- *Category Need.* When making a decision, it is necessary that you accept that a need does in fact exist. Advertising that addresses category need either tries to stimulate interest on your part in the category, or to remind you of a latent need.

- *Brand Attitude (high involvement).* Because of the risk involved, it is necessary for you to accept what the advertiser is saying about the brand before a decision to buy can be made because of the risk involved.

- *Brand Purchase Intentions.* In advertising that is more directly seeking an intention to buy now, you must *accept* the call for action.

Cognitive Responses in Processing

Now that we have a general idea of what we mean by acceptance in the processing of advertising, we need to take a closer look at what is involved when the target audience actually does accept the message of an advert. The key to this explanation is something psychologists call *cognitive responses*. In its simplest form, a cognitive response is the activity that occurs in your mind when you are confronted with something new.

Think of what occurs to you when you are introduced to someone for the first time. Before that person says a word, your mind is already forming opinions. The way the person looks or is dressed provides visual impressions that you associate with various images. You may or may not like what you see, given previous experiences. If you are at a formal party, and this new person is dressed very casually, you may think: 'What a slob.' This would be a cognitive response that occurrs because in your mind you expect people to dress according to circumstance, and those who don't, at least in your experience, leave something to be desired. Because of your existing beliefs, the contrast of what you expect and what you see generates negative images of this person.

The same thing occurs when you look at advertising. You bring to the advertising a certain set of beliefs and expectations related to the product category or brand, and you process the images and information in the advertising within that context. As you think about what you see or read, you will be generating a number of thoughts or feelings stimulated by the advertising. To the extent that these thoughts or images, these cognitive responses, are generally positive they will help generate a positive brand attitude. If the cognitive responses tend to be more negative, a negative brand attitude will result.

Cognitive response theory assumes that you will generally try to make sense out of what is going on around you. As you are exposed to new information, from advertising or any other source, you will tend to compare it with what you already know and feel. Thinking specifically about advertising, this suggests that if you are really paying attention to the advertising, and the advertising is for something you might be highly involved with, you are going to be very interested in what the advertising is saying. On the other hand, if the advertising is for something that does not require much consideration on your part during the purchase decision, you may or may not become actively involved with the message.

What this tells us is that when you are *highly involved* with a purchase decision, for advertising to be effective you *must generate* positive cognitive responses toward the brand. If your purchase decision is *low-involvement*, active cognitive responses, while desirable, are *not necessary*. You should now see that active cognitive responses are necessary for acceptance when processing advertising. This is the process that goes on in your mind as it deals with the images and claims generated by advertising, and is essential for products with high-involvement purchase decisions.

Emotion

Up to this point we have talked about processing in a rather straightforward, analytical manner. Some element within an advert—the picture or illustration, headline, copy-points (ideally *all* of the elements working together)—must first of all be attended to and something must be learned from it. Then, unless you are dealing only with brand awareness or low-involvement brand attitude effects, if that learning is to communicate anything, it must be accepted as true. But the context within which this processing is occurring will also stimulate a response: an *emotional* response. The advertising itself will trigger certain emotional responses, and in certain cases this emotional response will mediate what is learned and whether or how a particular point is accepted.[6]

Elements that Affect Emotion in Processing

An interesting aspect of emotional responses is that they generally occur quite naturally. For example, most people get a warm feeling when they see puppies playing together, jump when they hear a loud noise, or relax in a room decorated in soft tones. Psychologists and anthropologists may argue about which emotional responses are triggered by hereditary traits and which from earlier experiences, but there is no doubt that various sights and sounds can elicit very definite emotional responses.

Good creative people in advertising have a solid understanding of how to use the many devices available to them in order to generate particular emotional responses. There are basically six categories of elements available to creatives in preparing advertising, but not all of them are available in every medium—for example, sound cannot be used in print advertising. Table 10.2 reviews which elements are available for the primary media of television, radio, magazines, newspapers, and outdoor. These six basic elements for eliciting emotion in advertising are discussed below.

Sound

In broadcast advertising, spoken words or sound effects can be used to evoke a variety of emotional responses. With words, we are not so much concerned with their literal meanings, but the manner in which they are spoken. For example, a speaker can sound excited or sober; and certain voices have the ability to stimulate trust, others amusement.

Music

Like spoken words or sound effects, music is restricted to broadcast advertising. Music has the ability to elicit an entire range of emotional responses from up-beat and happy to solemn or relaxed.

Table 10.2 Basic Elements Affecting Emotion in Message Processing

	Appropriate Media				
	Television	Radio	Magazines	Newspaper	Outdoor
Sound	Yes	Yes	No	No	No
Music	Yes	Yes	No	No	No
Written word	Yes	No	Yes	Yes	Yes
Pictures	Yes	No	Yes	Yes	Yes
Colour	Yes	No	Yes	Yes [1]	Yes
Movement	Yes	No	No	No	No

[1] Colour is appropriate in newspaper only where colour reproduction is of high quality

Written Words

Here we are concerned not only with sentences, which can clearly be written to elicit particular emotions, but also with the selected use of words that the mind immediately associates with emotions. Some examples of these emotionally laden words are *free, great, awful*, and *help*. These are words that are almost universally associated with a particular emotion when the eye sees or reads them. They can be used in all advertising except advertising that will run on radio.

Pictures

We are all familiar with the powerful effect which pictures can have on our emotions. Think of the photography you have seen of starving children in Third World countries, paintings by artistic masters, or pictures of a really delicious-looking dessert. Each of these clearly has the ability to elicit emotions, and often quite strong emotions. Again, pictures may be used in all but radio advertising.

Colour

Colour itself has the ability to elicit emotional responses independent of the illustration or photograph. Certain colours, like reds and yellows, in certain circumstances can excite us; others, like blues and greens, relax us. But beyond that, think of the difference between a colour picture and a black-and-white copy of the same thing. The use of colour has the ability to stimulate emotion, but the colour reproduction must be good. This is why colour in newspapers is not always satisfactory. And, of course, colour does not apply to radio advertising.

Movement

The last of the six elements available to creatives for eliciting emotion from advertising is motion or movement. Watching people eating and enjoying themselves is often more compelling than a static shot of the food. Motion or speed and corresponding feelings of excitement can only really be communicated well through the use of motion. Movement, of course, can only be found in television advertising.

It should now be clear that the ways in which various elements are used in the creation of advertising will determine the extent to which specific emotions will be elicited in the processing of that advertising. Emotion plays a mediating role in what we learn from advertising and our likelihood of accepting the message. Just exactly how emotion accomplishes this task is beyond the scope of this text, but we will return to this subject in the next chapter.

Processing Internet Advertising

Back in the first chapter when we talked briefly about Internet advertising, we pointed out that basically it is processed like any other advert, with one difference. That difference was occasioned by the structure of Internet adverts. If we look at an example of a banner advert for homestore.com (Advert 10.5), everything we have been talking about in this chapter regarding how print advertising is processed will apply to this advert.

First of all, someone must pay attention to the advert, then learn that you can find everything for the home at homestore.com. Because this is a banner advert on the Internet, you do not really need to *accept* that in fact you will find everything for the home at homestore.com *to look further*. Clicking on the banner is a low-involvement decision, unlike actually visiting a retail furniture outlet. Finally, the colour and copy headline will stimulate an emotional response that the advertiser hopes will facilitate the processing of the message. Specifically, the word 'everything' should stimulate curiosity or even excitement, encouraging the viewer to click on the banner.

But because there is more to this advert's structure, there must be additional processing. Rossiter and Bellman have introduced the idea of a micro- and macro-structure of advertising.[7] They suggest that while all advertising shares a common micro-structure, which they define as the links between content variables, the real difference between Internet adverts and other forms of advertising is caused by macro-structure if you click on the banner. They mean by this, roughly speaking, the association and link within the advertising's content between pages in the Internet advert. In other words, because of the macro-structure of Internet advertising, a person must 'navigate through the Web ad' (in their words), and they are free to navigate in any way they choose. Their path will reflect what Rossiter and Bellman call a self-constructed Web ad schema, and this may *not* be the path the advertiser would prefer they follow.

10.5 Everything we have discussed about how print advertising is processed applies to Internet banner adverts like this one for homestore.com.

As they go on to point out, the macro-structure of a television or radio commercial is usually automatic, and it is obvious with collateral advertising such as brochures and direct response adverts. But with Internet advertising the (advertiser's) preferred processing route is neither automatic nor evident. What this means is a potential loss of control for the advertiser. This would be particularly true for the emotional responses associated with processing. Perhaps the most obvious example would be the result of any difficulty or frustration encountered in trying to navigate successfully through a site.

Overall, the creative tactics we have talked about in this chapter, as well as what we will discuss in the next chapter, apply to Internet advertising, especially its micro-structure. What you need to be concerned about, however, is facilitating and controlling (if possible) the processing of the macro-structure. This will be very difficult because individual users of the Internet will be developing their own Web ad schema, or ways of navigating Internet adverts.

Summary

In this chapter we have focused on the ways that consumers process messages, and how knowledge about this can be used to develop creative strategy and tactics. We introduced the four basic processing responses of attention, learning, acceptance, and emotion, and then discussed in detail how each response can be used to facilitate the achievement of communication objectives. We explored the different levels of processing associated with different levels of involvement, and the key role of acceptance in high-involvement decisions and its link with cognitive responses. We then considered the vital role of emotion in relation to advertising and how emotion mediates processing. Then we saw how all this applies to processing Internet adverts.

Questions to consider

10.1 What are the four processing responses to an advertisement?

10.2 What is meant by reflexive attention?

10.3 How can reflexive attention be maintained?

10.4 What is the relationship between selective attention and motivation?

10.5 What is meant by learning as a response to advertising?

10.6 When is acceptance required as a response to an advertisement?

10.7 What are cognitive responses to advertising?

10.8 What are the six basic elements for eliciting emotional responses to advertising?

10.9 How are Internet adverts processed?

Notes

1   See F. I. M. Craik and R. S. Lockhart, 'Levels of Processing: A Framework for Memory Research' *Journal of Verbal Learning and Verbal Behaviour*, 11 (1972), 671–84.

2   See I. Bredeman, J. C. Rabinowitz, A. L. Glass, and E. W. Stacy, 'On the Information Extracted from a Glance at a Scene', *Journal of Experimental Psychology*, 103 (1974), 597–600.

3   See G. R. Loftus, 'Tachistoscopic Simulations of Exposure Fixation on Pictures', *Journal of Experimental Psychology: Human Learning and Memory*, 7 (1981), 369–76.

4   Although the idea of 'subliminal persuasion' has been widely sensationalized, especially by Wilson Key in his book *Subliminal Seduction* (Englewood Cliffs, NJ: Prentice-Hall, 1974), Timothy Moore has convincingly demonstrated that even if advertisers utilized subliminal cues in creative executions, they would not affect brand choice. See T. E. Moore, 'Subliminal Advertising: What You See is What You Get,'*Journal of Marketing*, 46 (Spring 1982), 38–47.

5   For a review of how subliminal sexual imagery may in fact stimulate *sexual* arousal, see W. J. Roth and H. S. Mosatche, 'A Projective Assessment of the Effects of Freudian Sexual Symbolism in Liquor Advertisements', *Psychological Report*, 56: 1 (1985), 183–8. While Moore's work (see n. 4) shows that subliminal cues generally are not effective in advertising, what the Roth and Mosatche study suggests is that subliminal sexual imagery might have an effect in the specific case where a purely emotion-laden benefit focus is appropriate.

6   Emotion in advertising is not only misunderstood, but often ignored. K. Fletcher, in his book *A Glittering Haze* (Henley-on-Thames, Oxon.: NTC, 1992) points out that when practitioners talk about advertising, they are more likely to talk in terms of information than any emotional contribution.

7   John R. Rossiter and Steven Bellman, 'A Proposed Model for Explaining and Measuring Web Ad Effectiveness' *Journal of Current Issues and Research in Advertising*, 21:1 (Spring 1999), 13–31.

Chapter 11
Creative Tactics

Up to this point we have been concerned with communication strategy, and our focus has been on '*what* to say' in advertising and other forms of marketing communication. In this chapter we will turn our attention to '*how* to say it'. Creative tactics deal with the ways in which words and pictures are used in marketing communication to deliver the message. As we shall see, this is a much more involved issue than it might appear on the surface, because meaning in communication is dependent upon many things beyond the obvious content of the message. For example, the semantic and grammatical structure of copy can have a significant effect upon how well a message will be understood, as well as the way in which visual illustrations are presented.

The reason it is so important to understand this sort of thing is that the easier we make it for our target audience to process and understand our message, the more likely we are to achieve the desired communication effect. You will remember that in Chapter 3 we talked about a communication response sequence and McGuire's notion of compound probabilities. After exposure, the next step in the response sequence is *processing*. The more people who *correctly* process the message, the greater the number of people likely to make a positive response to the message.

We talked more about processing in the last chapter. After someone pays attention to an advert or other marketing communication, it is then necessary for them to *learn* what we wish to communicate, and when dealing with high-involvement decisions, to *accept* the message as well (what McGuire calls 'yielding'). In this chapter we will be discussing a number of general principles concerning how to use words and pictures to optimize attention and learning. Then we will be looking more specifically at the creative tactics needed to effect the correct brand awareness and brand attitude communication objectives.

Tactics for Attention

When we consider what creative tactics can help maximize attention, particularly *initial* attention, we must be concerned not only with how the advertising or other marketing communication is put together, but also the effect of the creative unit chosen. Creative units are such things as the size of a print advert (e.g. full-page, half-page, two-page spread) or the length of a radio or television commercial (e.g. 15, 30, or 60 seconds). In many ways the creative unit is important in media planning, but first and foremost it is a *tactical creative* decision. The creative unit must be considered in terms of the best way to deliver the message, not satisfy a media plan.

Creative Units and Attention

The most important factor in terms of creative units for generating attention in radio and television advertising is the length of the commercial. Attention to both radio and television commercials is directly related to length. Longer commercials stimulate greater attention than shorter ones, but the relationship is not proportional. For example, while a 60-second commercial will gain more attention than a 30-second commercial, the increase in attention is only about 20 per cent, not double; and while a 15-second commercial attracts less attention than a 30-second commercial, it will generate about 80 per cent of the attention of a 30-second commercial, not merely half.[1]

This same rule of thumb also applies to print advertising. Larger ads tend to attract more attention than smaller ads, but not proportionately. Table 11.1 demonstrates this general rule for newspaper and magazine adverts.[2]

Word and Picture Influence on Attention

The key to attention in print-based marketing communication is the words chosen and the illustration; with broadcast communication it is the initial audio (words or music); and with television or the Internet, the visuals. The reality of advertising and most other marketing communication is that people simply are not inclined to pay attention. Why should they? It is the job of good advertising to draw attention to itself, and in so doing communicate quickly at minimum a good positive brand attitude, and *resonate* with the target audience. Good strategy helps increase the likelihood of resonance, but the appropriate creative tactics help ensure it.

What we mean by resonance is a recognition by the target audience that a particular advert is talking to them about something with which they are concerned. If you are not

Table 11.1 Advert Size and Attention

Advert Size	Attention Index	
	Consumer and Business Magazine Adverts	Newspaper Adverts
2 Pages	1.3	1.2
1 Page	1.0	1.0
½ Page	0.7	0.7
¼ Page	—	0.5

Source: Adapted from J. R. Rossiter and L. Percy, *Advertising Communication and Promotion Management* (New York: McGraw-Hill, 1997).

in the target audience the advertising is unlikely to resonate, but it should leave a positive feeling for the brand. All of this must occur during the attentional response.

In order to maximize the likelihood of gaining attention, marketing communication must pay careful attention to the ways in which the words in a headline or sub-head and in the initial audio of broadcast advertising is used, and how the visuals and video are presented. In this section we will review some of the things we know about how words and pictures can help attract attention (see Table 11.2).

Attention and Words

In a very insightful analysis of words in advertising, Greg Myers has pointed out that 'when there are many ads competing for the audience's attention, there is an enormous pressure on finding patterns of language that are unusual or memorable'.[3] He goes on to suggest that one of the simplest ways to call attention to words in marketing communication, at least with the printed word, is to use unexpected letters. This can be accomplished, for example, by using infrequently encountered letters, such as *q*, *x*, or *z* (think of brands like Exxon or Oxo), or by deliberately altering the spelling of words (Smooooth!).

Let us consider the following slogan used by Heinz:

Beanz Meanz Heinz

Not only does this slogan attract the reader's attention by using the letter *z* in place of *s* in the words *beans* and *means*, creating a new spelling, but it has also managed to do this with a rarely used letter, *z*. Additionally, the change from *s* to *z* tends to draw attention to the repetition of the consonant sound. The repetition of consonant sound or vowel sounds helps make the slogan easier to remember. While unexpected spellings are obviously difficult to use effectively in broadcast advertising, the repetition of individual sounds is even more effective in the spoken word.

Another way to draw attention to advertising is to vary the emphasis or stress of certain words in a headline or in the audio content of commercials, or to use them in unexpected ways. Our ear is accustomed to hearing things in a particular way, and when it confronts something unexpected, we pay attention. For example, in normal conversation we are not likely to emphasize conjunctions such as *or* and *and*. But if the emphasis is placed on a conjunction, it is likely to attract your attention because you are not used to hearing this. Consider this line from a cosmetic advert:

Table 11.2 How to Use Words and Pictures to Gain Attention

Words	Use unexpected words or infrequently used letters such as Q, X, or Z
	Vary emphasis or stress of certain words in headlines or audio content, or use them in unexpected ways
	Keep headlines to less than 7–8 words
Pictures	Use larger pictures
	Use colour
	Keep visual cuts in commercials to fewer than 20 per : 30 second advert
	Use pictures that **hold** attention at least 2 seconds

> Diminish undereye circles and discourage their reappearance.

Now, suppose you heard the line as follows (or even saw it printed this way as a headline):

> Diminish undereye circles AND discourage their reappearance.

The unexpected emphasis on *and* draws attention not only to the line, but also to the *relationship* between 'Diminish undereye circles' and 'discourage their reappearance'.

Headline Length

Another aspect of how words can influence attention to printed marketing communication is the *length* of the headline. Psychologists have found that when the number of words in a sentence or phrase is less than seven or eight, all that is required to understand what is there is mere exposure.[4] You do not really need to *read* the words to know what they say, only to *see* them. Look at this headline:

> A solution to problem dry skin
> you can count on.

If you only glance at this headline, all you really 'see' is a block of words, perhaps picking out one or two. Most people looking at this briefly will only 'see' the words *solution*, *problem*, and *can count*. To get any meaning from this headline you must *read* it. Now, look at this headline:

> Quick start, Cool finish

Just glancing at this conveys the full content. It is not necessary to 'read' it to understand what it says. This is because the mind does not process text one word at a time, but in sets as you read.

This means that when you turn the page of a newspaper or magazine, the reflexive attention you automatically pay briefly to the new page to decide whether or not there is anything there worth paying particular attention to is sufficient to comprehend a headline if it is short enough. This is especially important for poster and outdoor adverts. To work, they must be able to communicate at a glance.

Attention and Pictures

As you might imagine, pictures play a more important role in gaining attention than words. This is especially true of print advertising. In fact, the average time spent looking at a magazine advert is about 1.65 seconds, and 70 per cent of that time is spent with the picture.[5] Without an effective picture to attract the reader's attention and draw them to the text it is unlikely the advertising will work. The size of the picture and the use of colour can significantly affect the ability of a print advert to attract attention. In terms of picture size, the larger the image, the more effective it will be. There is an old rule of thumb in advertising that recognition of print adverts increases roughly with the square root of the size of the picture. In other words, if you increase the size of the picture in an advert four times, attention will double.

Regarding the use of colour, in both magazines and newspapers full colour draws more attention than two-colour, and two-colour more attention than black and white. While it is sometimes argued that using black and white adverts in a magazine where all the other advertising is in colour will attract more attention because it will stand out, there is no real proof that this is the case. Table 11.3 summarizes the likely difference in attention to an advert in both magazines and newspapers in terms of colour. For magazine adverts, attention to a black and white advert is likely to be about 30 per cent less than to a standard four-colour advert, and 20 per cent less than to a two-colour advert. With newspapers, the use of two colours tends to increase attention 50 per cent over a standard black-and-white advert; and the use of four colours 80 per cent. While these estimates may be somewhat overstated for all-colour newspapers such as *USA Today*, there is still no question that colour will be significantly more effective. Again, this argues against the notion that using a black-and-white advert to stand out in an otherwise all-colour newspaper format.

Pictures, of course, dominate almost all television commercials. In terms of attention, an important consideration is the pacing of the scenes in the commercial. There has been a great deal of talk in recent years about the so-called MTV generation, and how young audiences are used to, and demand, rather frantic, fast-cut editing of visual content. Unfortunately, when the average scene time drops, so too does attention. In fact, at an 'MTV rate' of twenty or more cuts per 30-second commercial, the attention loss is about 17 per cent. And even more interestingly, the loss of attention is an even *greater* 25 per cent among that very 18- to 34-year-old MTV generation.[6]

Before leaving the subject of pictures and attention, it is important to understand that it is not enough to look for pictures that will attract attention; pictures must *hold* attention. A number of psychological experiments have shown that pictures are recognized and remembered best if they can hold the reader's attention for at least two seconds.[7] This helps explain why attention to television commercials drops when cuts in the visual come too rapidly.

Remember too that attention is only the first step in the processing of marketing communication. Attention means very little in and of itself if it does not lead to fuller processing of the message *for the target audience*. Attention simply to the brand name and an associated positive feeling is fine for non-members of the target audience, but those in the target audience are meant to complete the full communication response sequence. Attention to the picture leads to attention to the copy in the headline, and as this resonates

Table 11.3 Colour and Attention

Colour	Atttention Index	
	Consumer and Business Magazine Adverts	**Newspaper Adverts**
4-Colour	1.0	1.8
2-Colour	0.8	1.5
Black & white	0.7	1.0

Source: Adapted from J. R. Rossiter and L. Percy, *Advertising Communication and Promotion Management* (New York: McGraw-Hill, 1997).

with the target audience it arouses interest in paying additional attention to the complete message. The ability to hold attention facilitates the brand attitude response.

Unfortunately, in creating advertising, too often people are more concerned with just getting attention rather than getting and *holding* attention. When you think about it, looking at a picture in a print advert for two seconds is actually quite a long time, especially when we know that the average reader doesn't spend that much time in *total* looking at an advert. We mentioned earlier that research has shown that the average time spent looking at a magazine advert is only 1.65 seconds.

Frequently an advertisement will use some kind of novelty picture or situation in order to attract attention. In a recent corporate advert, a large picture of five long-stemmed red roses was used to attract attention to the advert, which discussed the company's successful fiscal record. This rather novel approach did manage to attract the attention of half those reading the magazine in which it appeared, but only 8 per cent read most of the copy. What did this obviously attention-getting device do for the company? Very little, because the roses communicated nothing about the company, and it did not hold the reader's attention long enough or effectively enough to interest people in reading the headline (which was about a dozen words), let alone the body copy.

Look at the advert for Anthisan PLUS (Advert 11.1, see colour plates section). This is a really excellent example of much of what we have been talking about. The picture is large, and uses the novelty of the spray container as a flying insect to *attract* attention, and the obvious link to the product category to *hold* attention. The headline 'Flying Doctor' uses words in a unique and unexpected way, tied directly to the picture. It is short, and easily processed with the picture and brand name at a glance. The sub-head, 'FAST, ANAESTHETIC STING RELIEF', is also easily understood without reading as the eye moves down the page. A brief exposure to this ad, even if simply flipping through the pages of a magazine, will attract attention and communicate the intended benefit of sting relief with Anthisan PLUS. A *very* good example of using words and pictures to attract and hold attention.

Tactics for Learning

We know that for any marketing communication to be successful, once someone has been exposed to it and has paid attention, they must fully process the message if you are to achieve the desired communication effect. William J. McGuire, perhaps the foremost expert on attitude change theory, who we talked about when we discussed the communication response sequence in Chapter 3, once remarked about communicating with advertising that it is not enough to lead a horse to water, you must push his head under to get him to drink.[8] Anything we can do to help make it easier for our target audience to process our message makes it more likely it will be correctly understood, and more likely we will achieve the desired communication effect.

The words and pictures we use obviously play the most important role in delivering the message, but *how* we use them can provide a real plus. A great deal of research has been done in this area, especially by psycho-linguists and psychologists working in visual imagery, providing insight into the ways in which words and pictures can be used to facilitate learning. As we know, learning is essential for all marketing communication. In this section we will review a number of specific ways in which to use words and pictures to increase the likelihood that our target audience will learn what we want them to from our advertising or other marketing communication.

Words and Learning

It may seem almost too obvious to suggest that you must pay attention to what you say in advertising copy if it is to be understood. While this is certainly true, less obvious is the effect the way in which words are used may have on how they are understood. The often complex relationship between the linguistic construction of copy and the way the mind deals with it in processing the message is known as psycho-linguistics.

While there are a number of studies in psycho-linguistics that can be applied to creating more effective marketing communication, one of the real difficulties in applying psycho-linguistic principles is the large number of interactions which we deal with, especially in advertising. Advertising is made up of a good deal more than a single word, phrase, or sentence (the units which psycho-linguists work with). There is a full context for the headline and copy, which almost always includes pictures or other visuals. Nevertheless, we do know that if we use words (and pictures, as we shall see later in this chapter) in ways known to facilitate learning and avoid using them in ways that tend to make learning more difficult, our marketing communication will be more effective.

We talked in a previous section about using words in unexpected ways to help attract attention. While this will certainly help gain attention, unfortunately the use of unfamiliar words in copy can get in the way of learning There are literally dozens of studies which have shown that using familiar words in familiar ways helps learning.[9] This illustrates a problem McGuire identified long ago. Often the things that help attract attention in communication are the very things that get in the way of comprehension or acceptance of the message.[10] What this means for us is that while we may want to use an unfamiliar word or use words in an unexpected way as a part of a headline to gain attention, we do not want this in the sub-heads or copy, where learning is the objective.

Concrete, High-Imagery Words

One interesting concept in psycho-linguistics that has a direct bearing upon copy in marketing communication, especially in advertising, is the notion of the 'concreteness' of the words used. Concrete words are generally described as those that refer to objects, persons, places, or things that can be experienced by the senses; those that do not are called abstract. Concrete words are more effective than abstract words in communicating ideas, and are better remembered. Think back to the headline of the Anthisan PLUS advert: 'Flying Doctor'. This is a good example of a concrete headline.

The reason concrete words help with learning is that they tend to arouse mental images quickly and easily.[11] While it is certainly not impossible, strictly speaking, for more abstract words to evoke visual images, it is a lot less likely. Consider the following headlines taken from adverts in a UK women's magazine:

Because it really matters

For skin this soft

Some days matter

Which of these headlines bring a visual image to mind? Most likely only 'For skin this soft'. This is concrete, while the others are more abstract. You can 'see' or imagine soft skin, but it is more difficult to focus upon a specific image for 'Because it really matters' or 'Some days matter'. Imagery value is important in facilitating easier communication and learning.[12]

Using Negatives

Overall, people are much more likely to make favourable rather than unfavourable judgements. As a result, in every language, for example, there are far more favourable than unfavourable adjectives. Additionally, a lot of research has shown that negative words or constructs are difficult to process, and should be avoided in communication. To understand the meaning of negative words or constructions requires a two-step process. You must recognize the negative for what it is, then 'reverse' the meaning. As a result, there is a chance someone may misunderstand or overlook the negative while processing the message.

Consider this headline from a cruise line advert: 'This is not a normal day'. What the mind must do is consider first what is a 'normal day', then negate it—assuming the eye picked up *not*, and didn't skim over it. You may be thinking to yourself that this is making a lot out of very little. After all, who is likely to misunderstand? Not many, we would hope, but some will. It depends upon the focus.

In an interesting study dealing with just this issue it was found that when two claims are made and one is stated in the negative, misunderstanding is greater when the negative claim is second.[13] People were asked to read one of the following headlines, and decide if taste or calories was the main emphasis (and to the advertiser, the answer was taste):

It's the taste that counts, not just the calories

It's not just the calories, it's the taste that counts

The number of people correctly saying 'taste' was only 77 per cent in the first example vs. 85 per cent in the second. This is because the negative claim in the second example is not necessary to correctly process the claim, but it must be processed in the first example. Again, you may be thinking this isn't much of a difference, but remember we need to ensure that the maximum number of people make it through the communication response sequence.

What do you make of this sub-head from a deodorant advert?

No, not the twit pressing the nozzle

Here we have an odd example of two negatives where one is *not* meant to negate the other. The juxtaposition of the two makes it quite easy to misunderstand the sentence as 'Yes, the twit pressing the nozzle,' if you are just glancing at the copy and not reading it.

In fact, negative constructions are not often used in marketing communication, and for good reason. Why ask your target audience to go to the extra effort and time of dealing with the two steps needed to correctly process negative constructions?

Using Puns

Puns are a way of playing with meaning, and puns are often found in advertising. This is especially true of advertising in the UK, where both visual and verbal puns are often found in abundance. Look at these advert headlines from a single issue of a UK women's magazine:

> For a healthy diet—this Paper needs Fibre too!
>
> Anything less simply won't wash
>
> Have a shower with everything on
>
> Big cheeses on the board watch out
>
> When soap and water are out of reach

Without knowing the product being advertised, what do these headlines tell you? Even with the full advert in front of you, they require a lot of work, and that is the problem. Does it help you to know that these headlines advertise, respectively, the use of raw material in the paper industry, bathroom accessories, showers, cream cheese, and hand-cleaning gel? Perhaps a little, but not much.

Puns do require more work to process,[14] and as we have said over and over in this chapter, our job is to make it *easier*, not harder, for the target audience to process our message. This is what facilitates learning. At the root of most puns are homonyms, words that have the same spelling or sound, but different meanings. (Did you know that the word 'taste' has some thirty-two meanings in *Webster's Unabridged Dictionary*?) The important thing to remember when homonyms are being used is to be certain that your intended meaning is the most familiar one for that market.

Sentence Structure

The issue of how sentences are put together has a real impact upon how easy it will be to process marketing communication, and the likelihood that correct learning will occur. Unfortunately, it is beyond the scope of this book to go very deeply into this, because it is a very complex area. In fact, many of those who have studied it find it a very complicated subject with which to deal.[15]

It is important that we understand that there can be difficulties when sentence structure becomes more complicated, even with such a seemingly simple thing as where a clause is placed. To avoid potential problems, keep things *simple*. For example, we know that it is much easier to process and understand active than passive sentences. Researchers have found that passive sentences take longer to process correctly, and the likelihood of understanding passive sentences tends to be lower.

Let's look at this sub-headline:

A fluoride supplement should be taken by children living in non-fluoride water areas

This is written in the passive voice. The grammatical subject is actually the psychological object. In effect, the passive construction has reversed the order in which words are usually encountered. We know that human memory is affected greatly by the order in which words are encountered. What if this were written in the active voice?

> Children living in non-fluoride water areas should take a fluoride supplement

While the meaning of both sentences is the same, the active construction will be easier to process. In addition, the main focus of the sentence, 'children living in non-fluoride water areas', is encountered first, and that will provide the desired cue in memory for fluoride supplements. If you were living in a non-fluoride water area and had children, which of these sentences would most likely catch your eye if you were flipping through a magazine containing this advert? You are much more likely to pay attention to something about your children than something about fluoride supplements, and that is how we want learning and memory to occur. We want the parent to learn 'my children need a fluoride supplement', *not* 'fluoride supplements are for my children'.

The form of a sentence itself can also aid message processing. Myers provides the example of the following Mars bar slogan:

> A Mars® a Day Helps You Work Rest and Play

He points out that this slogan will be memorable primarily because it draws attention to its *focus*. It establishes a rhythm, and it rhymes 'play' with 'day'. Also, of course, it echoes the old saying that 'An apple a day keeps the doctor away.'[16]

Another possible way sentences can help facilitate processing of a message is by suggesting a personal, face-to-face interaction between the reader or viewer and the advertising. When you use such things as questions or strong declarative statements you imply a certain sense of one person talking to another.[17] Look at the following headlines:

> Which anti-ageing cream makes you look this radiant?

> You can't eat our new wrapper

> What do you wear to talk to your bank manager?

> Do you resist change or embrace it?

> Take the test. Get the answers.

Each of these headlines engages you in an almost personal conversation because of their use of a personal question or declarative statement. This sense of personal address will help facilitate processing (even though several of these headlines have more words in them than one would like).

Pictures and Learning

While the old adage of a picture being worth a thousand words may not be literally true, there is certainly a well-understood superiority of pictures over words in learning.[18] In fact, with most print advertising some 70 per cent of the looking at the advert is directed to the picture. One of the reasons for this superiority of pictures over words is the way in which people interact with pictures. As we have just noted, one of the ways words can be used to help facilitate learning is by using strong declarative sentences or questions because this tends to engage the reader. Pictures automatically engage the reader or viewer, but in a different way.

When we read a sentence or listen to dialogue our mind tends to provide an answer or response in words. Pictures, on the other hand, have the ability to provoke a much more elaborate response. Myers offers a good example of this. You would no doubt be very sceptical if you read or heard a claim that a particular brand of soap could make anyone beautiful. But if this same claim was *implied* by a picture of a beautiful woman holding the soap, you would be a lot less sceptical.[19] Additional support for the superiority of pictures over words comes from work by Bryce and Yalch.[20] They showed that information conveyed visually is significantly better learned than the same information content conveyed in the audio. A good way to test the ability of visuals to communicate is to look at a TV commercial with the sound off.

There is another important aspect of pictures to be considered. While words may be used to suggest you are in the 'presence' of what is being said, as when copy directs a question to the reader or viewer, visuals offer a much greater potential for 'including' the reader or viewer. As we look at any picture, a relationship is established between the viewer and the image. This goes for any visual image, from adverts to great works of art. There will be something about the picture that draws us to it. Depending upon the image itself, we will imagine ourselves as either *part* of what is shown in the picture, or *outside* observing what is there. The space between the viewer and the actual picture is something Shearman has called *liminal space*, and it becomes in many ways an extension of the picture itself.[21] Why should we be concerned with such a seemingly abstract notion as the space in front of a picture? Because in certain cases we will want our target audience to feel they are present and a part of the situation depicted in the advertising, while in other cases we will want them to feel they are outside of the situation. The execution of the illustration or visuals in the advertising will dictate how the viewer will feel, and this applies not only to print advertising, but also to television.[22]

If you look at the advert for Umbro (Advert 11.2), there is no doubt you feel a part of what is going on. The grass field almost literally carries beyond the constraints of the page to 'fill' the space between you and this image. The sense of connectedness with the viewer is strong, and helps ensure the emotional authenticity of the experience of the advertising. As we shall see later in this chapter, this is essential for advertising dealing with positive motives.

Contrast this feeling with what you experience looking at the Pirelli advert (Advert 11.3). It is quite clear that as you look at this advert, you are an outside viewer. You are not meant to be participating in the action depicted, but rather to be drawing the analogy between the physical control implied by a well-conditioned athlete and the control afforded by the new P6000 Pirelli tyre. Because the advertising is high-involvement informational, you need to be convinced of the benefit, and your position outside the action permits an objective consideration.[23]

These adverts provide an excellent example of how understanding what goes on in the liminal space directly in front of a picture can help maximize the power of the illustration in facilitating learning. The viewer's relationship with the picture in these adverts is consistent with the tactics necessary to deliver the brand attitude objective (as we shall see later in this chapter).

Myers offers an interesting observation along these lines. He reminds us that pictures provide a point of view in much the same way as pronouns do in language. When there are people in advertising, their positions and where they are looking is important to how we respond. Pictures can also suggest prior or future action, as well as context for evaluation.[24] Getting all of this consistent with the message is critical to effective processing. Myers also makes an interesting point about the gaze of principal figures in advertising. He suggests that more often you will find women in advertising looking out at the reader or viewer while male figures are more likely to 'keep to their own business'.[25] This observation may be anecdotal, but it is interestingly consistent with the pop-psychology idea that women are more concerned with bonding when communicating with people while men are more concerned with establishing dominance.

Next, we will turn our attention to five areas where we know there are direct relationships between the picture and learning: the size of the picture, the use of colour, showing the product with users or in use, high-imagery pictures, and word–picture interaction.

Picture size

We have already talked about how larger pictures tend to attract more attention. It also seems that the larger the picture the more visual images the mind will generate, and this, in turn, leads to better learning.[26] Research has shown that picture size has a positive impact on beliefs and brand attitude. In fact, it would seem that the larger the picture, the more favourable your attitude toward the advertised product.[27]

There is only one print advertising situation where picture size is not important: direct-response advertising with long copy. With direct-response advertising, memory is not a significant factor because the target audience is expected to respond immediately. Also, since a lot of direct-response advertising involves high-involvement product decisions, a great deal of information is needed to convince the reader to make a decision 'right now'. Consequently, there is a necessary trade-off between the space needed for a larger picture and that needed for more detailed copy. But in all other cases, the larger the picture, the better.

Colour vs. Black and White

Just as with picture size, we saw earlier that colour positively influences the gaining of attention. But colour also has a significant effect upon processing generally. Some years ago two psychologists in the research laboratories of Xerox Corporation demonstrated that the principal effect of colour in communication is motivation.[28] If all you need to do is communicate information, black-and-white pictures could be enough. This means you should *never* use black-and-white pictures with advertising addressing positive motives. However, with informational advertising, such as the UK advert for the Army (Advert 11.4), black and white can be quite effective.

Product and User

People are more likely to learn something from advertising if they can make a familiar association with its content. This is known as *associative learning*, and is aided by pictures that show the product being used in some way rather than leaving it up to the reader or viewer to infer interaction between the product and the user or how the product is used.[29] The importance of interactive pictures or visuals is underscored when we consider the motivation underlying behaviour. People often buy status goods or other products because they suggest a particular image with which they wish to be associated, as we saw when we discussed positive motives and transformational advertising. On the other hand, when dealing with negative motives and informational advertising, a product or brand must be seen as suitable for solving or avoiding a problem. Showing users interacting with a product, or seeing a product in use, helps connect the product with the motive to purchase or use.

While it is quite common to find these types of interactions in television advertising, they are much less common in print. Too often we see a picture of a user or endorser next to, but not using, the product, or the context for usage is discussed in the copy, but not shown visually. It is important in print adverts as well as television to show the brand being used. The Ford Puma UK advert (Advert 11.5) provides a very good example of how a series of pictures within a print advert provides a real sense of the car being used by the driver.

High Imagery Pictures

We saw earlier that concrete, high-imagery words help facilitate learning. The same is true of concrete or high-imagery pictures. More concrete, higher-imagery pictures are those that tend to arouse *other* mental images quickly and easily. They are more realistic than abstract, low-imagery pictures. These realistic pictures are probably superior for learning for at least two reasons. First of all, people can relate more to concrete representations than to abstract ones. This in turn is probably a function of their *imagery* value, regardless of their specific content. Secondly, because of something psychologists call *dual coding* people can more easily attach a verbal label to realistic visuals.

Older children and adults automatically assign verbal labels to all but the most complex and novel pictures, and thus 'double-code' them in their minds as both picture *and* words.[30] For example, if you were to see a picture of an apple, you would encode not only the image of the apple in your mind, but also the label 'apple'. Look at Advert 11.6. As the image registers in your mind, it is labelled as the Eiffel Tower. This is an excellent example of a high-imagery visual. Not only does the image of the Eiffel Tower register, but you no doubt quickly and easily imagined things about Paris. And as you look at the picture, the very creative integration of the railway bed into the tower's structural support immediately connects with the advertiser, eurostar.

Many television ads use animation, and often you see cartoons or drawings in print adverts. This can in fact be very realistic because of its simplified rendering of its subject. Using this technique can basically 'strip' its subject to its essential denotative characters, making them very concrete.[31]

Word–Picture Interaction

In a very interesting study it was found that learning is significantly increased if the eye confronts a *picture–word* rather than a word–picture sequence.[32] This may seem to imply that you should always place the headline in an advert toward the bottom of the page so that the picture will be easily seen first, but this is not necessary. The eye is generally drawn initially to an illustration, so an effective use of the picture relative to the headline will ensure that it is seen first, regardless of where the headline is placed. Look at the advert for Fairy non-biological detergent (Advert 11.7). There is no question that the eye goes first to the picture, then to the headline at the top of the page. Even though the headline is positioned first, its size relative to the picture means the eye is drawn first to the picture.

What happens is that when the picture is seen first it tends to draw the reader into the advert to maximize communication, and as a result, facilitates learning. This same point also applies to television. Important spoken copy-points or printed 'supers' should either be *preceded* by an appropriate visual introduction or introduced simultaneously.

Consistent with this idea is the notion of the 'rhythm' established between the words and pictures in television commercials. Rossiter and Percy have speculated that an overall picture–word pattern, based upon traditional learning theory, should enhance learning from television commercials.[33] The pattern they suggest for informational commercials is to introduce the 'problem' visually at the beginning of the commercial, followed by a break in the story for a visual introduction of the brand while the benefit is delivered in the audio words. Then the 'solution' to the problem is presented in the visual, followed by visual and audio brand identification and a reinforcing tagline in words for closure. The 'rhythm' established here is built around two pauses in the story or action in order to facilitate brand awareness and learning, allowing the 'problem' to be recognized by the target audience, and then the 'solution' with the brand to register.

The 'rhythm' when dealing with positive motives and transformational strategies will be different. The brand should be introduced verbally, then a positive reinforcement builds throughout the commercial through the visual presentation, culminating with the brand name spoken and shown so that the brand is linked to the positive experience of the advert, with a verbal reinforcement through the tagline. Remember that with positively motivated behaviour, you begin at equilibrium and *build*, unlike negatively motivated behaviour, which begins with a 'problem' that must be 'solved' before you can return to equilibrium. The 'rhythms' between words and pictures in television advertising should reflect this.

Overview of Tactics for Attention and Learning

Tables 11.2 and 11.4 summarize how words and pictures are used to maximize attention to and the learning of marketing communication. Before leaving this subject, it would be a good idea to turn from the general discussion we have been having and look at how these creative tactics apply to the five traditional advertising media and the Internet.

Table 11.4 How to Use Words and Pictures to Help Learning

Words	Use familiar words
	Use concrete, high-imagery words
	Avoid negatives
	Be careful with puns
	Keep sentences simple
	Avoid passive sentences
	Suggest a personal interaction with the advertising
Pictures	Be certain picture is consistent with intention for viewer to be included as observer
	Colour unless you only need to provide information
	Show product being used or with user
	Use high imagery, concrete pictures or illustrations
	Use pictures so they are seen before words

Remember that we are looking specifically at creative tactics, always understanding that the *creative idea* must be consistent with the overall strategy, interesting to the target audience, and unique to the brand.

Television. The key tactics needed for facilitating attention to television commercials are to vary the emphasis in the audio copy in unexpected ways, and to keep the visual cuts to less than twenty in a 30-second commercial. These tactics will help ensure attention to the advertising. To facilitate learning, be sure the words 'fit' the visuals, and be certain the 'rhythm' of the commercial is consistent with the overall brand attitude strategy (i.e. the problem–pause–solution–brand summary rhythm of informational strategies vs. the brand introduction–reinforcement build–brand situation summary link rhythm of transformational strategies). Be sure that the main benefit claims are preceded by or heard simultaneously with an appropriate visual, and that the visual content *on its own* has the ability to convey the message.

Radio. As with television, vary the emphasis in the audio in unexpected ways to help attract attention, and consider using unexpected words. Use high-imagery words and sentences to enhance *visual* imagery in the target audience. Suggest a personal interaction with the target audience, and above all, keep the copy simple.

Magazine. Headlines should be short (less than eight words), and unexpected words or letters can help attract attention. Colour is essential, and larger pictures that *hold* attention should be used. To help learning, be sure the pictures are seen before the headline, personalize copy, and use concrete, high-imagery words.

Newspaper. Tactics for newspaper advertising are generally the same as for magazines, with allowance for the heavily retail orientation of much newspaper advertising. Newspaper adverts ideally will be in colour unless all that is needed is to convey information. *Never* use black and white in transformational advertising. Even with purely informational adverts, colour will enhance attention. Use as large a picture as possible. Often the picture is just as important here as in magazine advertising, even for retail adverts. High-imagery, concrete words in *short*, positive headlines should be used.

Poster and outdoor. The key to most poster and outdoor advertising is that it attracts attention and can be processed with *minimal* attention to the advert. This means very large pictures that embody or suggest the benefit, *short* headlines which communicate the benefit (either directly or indirectly) because the headline is the copy, and strong brand identification.

Internet. Banner adverts on the Internet follow the same general rules as poster and outdoor. You want to attract attention, and communicate quickly. This means a short copy-line in the nature of a headline, and a compatible illustration that communicates a positive brand attitude. And like a headline in a print advert, the message communicated by the banner advert should encourage further enquiry, usually clicking to a website. Once into the website, the principles for print advertising continue to hold, but attention must also be paid to facilitating the way readers navigate the site.

These general guidelines for applying appropriate creative tactics for specific advertising media are summarized in Table 11.5.

Table 11.5 General Creative Tactic Guidelines

Television	Words must 'fit' the visual content
	Consider the rhythm in terms of brand attitude strategy
	Adequate time to process the benefit claim
	The visual should work on its own
Radio	Vary emphasis in unexpected ways
	High imagery words and sentences
	Personal interaction
	Keep copy simple
Magazines	Short headlines, under 7–8 words
	Unexpected use of words or letters
	Colour is preferred
	Larger pictures or illustration
	Pictures that hold attention
	Pictures seen before words
	Personalized copy
	Concrete, high-imagery copy
Newspapers	Use colour where appropriate
	Use as large a picture as possible
	Use appropriate, involving pictures
	High-imagery, short, positive headlines
	Keep copy simple
Poster and Outdoor	Very large pictures that embody or suggest the benefit
	Short headlines that communicate the benefit
	Story brand identification

Brand Awareness and Brand Attitude Creative Tactics

Throughout this book we have discussed the importance of brand awareness and brand attitude as communication objectives for all marketing communication. In the last chapter we specifically addressed this issue. Because of the nature of recognition vs. recall brand awareness and the differences in the four strategic brand attitude quadrants of the Rossiter–Percy grid, certain specific creative tactics are needed to ensure you will achieve these communication objectives.

Brand Awareness Creative Tactics

The number one task of brand awareness is to associate the *brand* with category need in the target audience's mind. As we have seen, brand awareness as a communication objective is more than simply being aware of the brand. The brand must be linked to the appropriate need in the target audience's mind when that need occurs. But before that can happen, marketing communication, and advertising in particular, must first be seen as 'belonging' to your brand. This is the only way the message can be associated with the brand. This may seem almost childishly obvious, but how often have you thought about a particular advert, perhaps because it was entertaining or unique in some way, but you couldn't correctly remember the brand being advertised?

Only after you are sure the message is firmly linked with the brand are you ready to address the issue of recognition vs. recall brand awareness. You will remember from the previous chapter that the appropriate brand awareness objective is dependent upon the *choice situation*. When and how the brand choice is made dictates a recognition or recall brand awareness strategy, and the creative tactics differ for each (see Table 11.6).

Table 11.6 Brand Awareness Creative Tactics

Recognition	Package must be shown as seen at the point of purchase
	Category need must be obvious
Recall	Category need must be clearly linked to the brand, and in that order
	Repeat the association
	Personalize the association between the need and the brand

Source: Adapted from J. R. Rossiter and L. Percy, *Advertising Communications and Promotion Management* (New York: McGraw-Hill, 1997).

Recognition Brand Awareness

When the brand choice is activated at the point of purchase, such as when shopping at a supermarket or pharmacy, recognizing the brand in the store will remind the shopper of a need. This means that in advertising the package must be shown as it will be seen at the point of purchase, and the category need must be obvious. Look at the Entenmann's advert (Advert 11.8). This is a very creative presentation of the package for brand recognition. The advert itself quite literally represents the Entenmann's package as you see it in the store—a white box with the logo in the upper left-hand corner, and the product clearly visible through the see-through top of the package. There is also no doubt of the category need. You see the package in the store and you are reminded you would like a sweet roll.

Recall Brand Awareness

When the target audience must think of the brand prior to the point of purchase, the brand awareness objective is recall. A need occurs, and you must think of brands that might possibly meet that need. This means the advertising must *clearly* link the need to the brand, *in that order*, and *repeat* the association. It also helps to personalize the association between the need and the brand. This is very easy to accomplish in radio and television advertising, but it is also needed in print when recall brand awareness is necessary. The advert for Kilroy Travels (Advert 11.9) is a good example of how these tactics should be used. The need comes first—holiday fun—then the link to the brand, Kilroy Travels. The association is repeated, and the copy personalizes the need.

Brand Attitude Creative Tactics

The creative tactics needed for brand awareness help link the brand to the need. The creative tactics for brand attitude help *persuade* the target audience that your brand is the best alternative for satisfying the need.[34] In our discussions of brand attitude we referred to the expectancy-value model of attitude, where attitude toward an object (a brand in our case) is made up of what you believe about it weighted by the emotional importance attached to those beliefs, combined to form your overall attitude toward the brand. These same two considerations, beliefs and emotions, structure the creative tactics to be used to maximize brand attitude. When dealing with informational brand attitude strategies we must be primarily concerned with the benefit claim being made; when dealing with transformational brand strategies we must be primarily concerned with the emotion portrayed in the advertising (see Table 11.7).

Informational Brand Attitude

With informational brand attitude strategies, the key is the *benefit claim support*. When the decision is low-involvement, you want to use a simple problem–solution presentation of one or possibly two benefits. Since the decision is low-involvement you can use *extreme* benefit claims, such as:

Instant hygiene without soap and water

Swap tired heavy legs for a fresh pair

Table 11.7 Brand Attitude Creative Tactics

Informational	**Key is Benefit Claim Support**
	Use only one or possibly two benefit claims for **low involvement** decisions
	Use extreme benefit claims for **low involvement** decisions
	Keep benefit claim at an upper level but do not overclaim for **high involvement** decisions
	Be certain benefit claim falls within the target audience's acceptable level of attitude toward the brand for **high involvement** decisions
Transformational	**Key is the Emotional Portrayal**
	Creative execution must be unique to brand
	Target audience must like the advertising
	Emotional portrayal must seem authentic
	Target audience must personally identify with the emotional portrayal with **high involvement** decisions
	Some information may need to be provided by **high involvement** decision

Source: Adapted from J. R. Rossiter and L. Percy, *Advertising Communications and Promotion Management* (New York: McGraw-Hill, 1997).

Why? Because the message does not need to be accepted as literally true. All that is necessary is what Maloney years ago called 'curious disbelief'.[35] There is little risk involved in the choice decision, so you can exaggerate the benefit in order to tempt the audience to purchase. It is not necessary that you really believe a hand-cleansing gel will provide 'instant hygiene without soap and water' or that a herbal gel will really give you a 'fresh pair' of legs. You need only feel the products might do a good job. If they don't meet your expectations, you simply do not repurchase.

But when you are dealing with a high-involvement decision, you should *not* overclaim, but keep the claim at an acceptable upper level. The benefit claims must be believable because the message must be accepted. The following benefit claims appeared in an advert for a cooker:

it's 100% reliable

it has plenty of room for a family sized joint

the practical electronic controls make setting accurate 'wok times' child's play

To be successful, the target audience must accept these claims as basically true. They are certainly pitched at an upper level of believability, especially the '100% reliable' claim. Because a cooker is a high-risk purchase, for someone to consider this brand, they must believe the substance of these claims.

This means that to ensure a *convincing* presentation of the benefit claims, it is essential to understand what the target audience's attitudes are toward the category and the brands within the category. Following our example, does the target audience believe it is possible for a cooker to be 100 per cent reliable? What about this brand? What is its reputation for reliability? For the benefit claims to be effective with high-involvement informational advertising they must be within an acceptable range of believability among the target audience.

Transformational Brand Attitude

The key creative tactic for transformational brand attitude strategies is the emotional portrayal. With transformational strategies, the feelings evoked by the advertising are often the only brand benefit. As a result, it is absolutely essential that the creative execution be *unique* to the brand. Additionally, the target audience must like the advertising. Unlike advertising for informational strategies, where it isn't really necessary to actually like the advertising per se because the execution embodies the benefit, with transformational advertising you must like the advertising to like the brand.[36]

Interestingly, the actual identity and taste of beer in the US is created quite literally by the advertising! In a very interesting study, beer drinkers were asked to taste and evaluate a number of beers ranging from lower-calorie Miller Lite to premium beers like Budweiser, all the way through malt liquors and Guinness Stout. When the results of these taste evaluations were analysed, the 'lighter' beers were separated from the 'heavier' beers like malt liquor and stout. Also, the 'regular' beers were distinguished from the more 'premium' beers. The tastes of these beers were positioned just as their advertising presented them. However, a matched set of beer drinkers went through the same exercise, but tasted the beers blind, not knowing what brands they were tasting. When their taste evaluations were analysed, with the exception of the stout, *all of the beers* were seen as tasting alike. Clearly, the 'taste' of these beers was defined by the emotional portrayal of the brands in their advertising.[37]

Because this idea of a correct emotional portrayal is so important to transformational advertising, we will take a closer look as just what this means. When you look at a good advert for perfume or fashion, you want to *imagine yourself* as being similar to the person in the advert. If you can see yourself (or your imagined self) in the advertising, the emotional portrayal is authentic and that feeling you get becomes the benefit for the brand.

A very good example of what we are talking about here is illustrated in an Imeeden advert (Advert 11.10). It would not be unusual for a product like Imeeden to be aimed at a negative purchase motivation. But like fashion and cosmetics the benefit here addresses a positive purchase motive. Imeeden will help you *feel* beautiful. The wonderful serenity implied by the visual, and the imagery congruence with nature as exemplified by the foliage, contribute to a strong emotional authenticity. This is not the sort of product where the benefit clearly follows from use, as is the case when you take something for pain and it goes away (a problem-driven, negative motive). The benefit is indirect, a sense of well-being. Imeeden has been able to embody this benefit directly in the advert. You 'see' yourself feeling like this. The visual and headline quickly and easily link the benefit to the brand.

But how would this work for something more generic, like so-called 'instant' or dehydrated packaged side dishes for meals? Too often advertisers for products like this, which require a transformational strategy, tend to focus on a benefit like convenience. Convenience is a *category benefit*. You purchase 'instant' packaged side dishes for convenience. They are quick and easy to prepare. That is *not* why a brand is selected. In this case

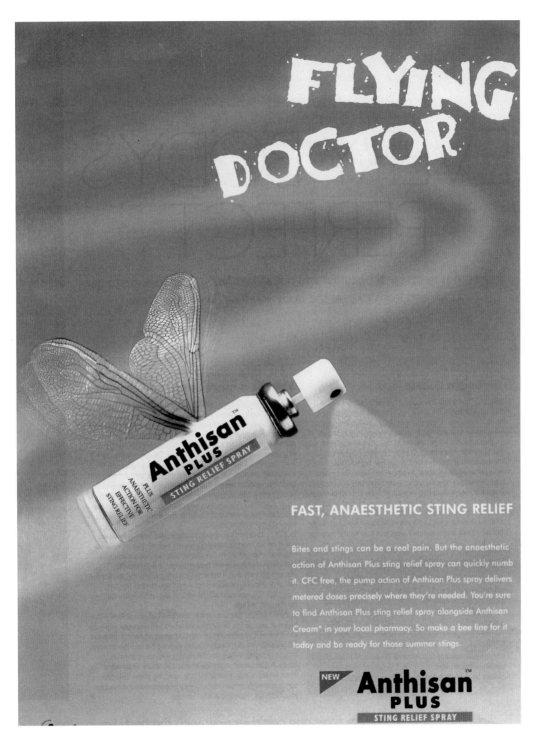

11.1 This advert for Anthisan Plus is a very good example of using words and pictures to attract and hold attention. Courtesy Anthisan Plus

11.2 There is no doubt when you look at this advert that you feel a part of what is going on. Courtesy Umbro

11.3 In this advert you are not meant to be a part of the action, but outside of it. This permits an objective consideration of the message. Courtesy Pirelli

11.4 Here we can see that colour is not necessary for this advert to be effective because it is basically providing only information.
Courtesy Army UK

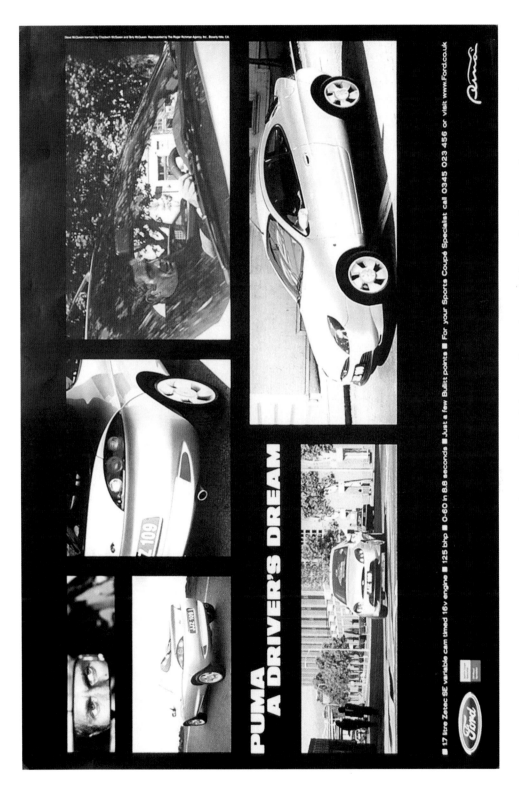

11.5 Here is an example of how a series of pictures within a print advert helps provide a real sense of the product being used. Courtesy Ford Motor Corp.

11.6 This is an excellent example of high visual imagery in an advert. It quickly arouses images of Paris and connects these images positively to the brand. Courtesy Eurostar.*

* This advert was initially conceived in 1995. At the time this book went to press, Eurostar were running 21 trips per day from London to Paris.

11.7 Even though the headline in this advert comes first, the eye is still drawn initially to the picture ensuring the desired picture–word sequence for optimum processing. Courtesy Fairy

A Slice of America.
The Raspberry Danish Twist.

11.8 For recognition brand awareness it is important to see the package as it appears at the point of purchase, and this very creative execution quite literally turns the advert into the package. Courtesy Entenmann's

11.9 For recall brand awareness a link between the need and brand is necessary, something not easily done in print. But Kilroy does a good job setting up the need, then linking it to the brand, and repeating the link. Courtesy Kilroy Travel

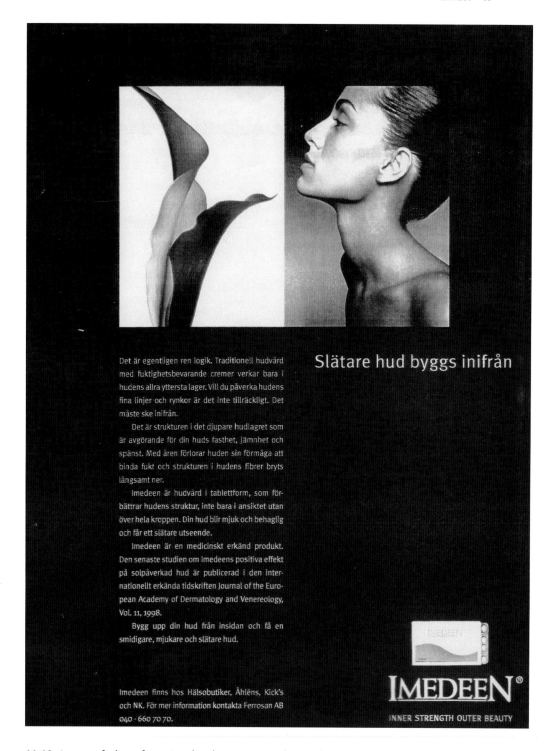

11.10 A strong feeling of emotional authenticity is evident in this advert where the benefit, 'well-being', is believably associated with the brand via the illustrations. Courtesy Imedeen

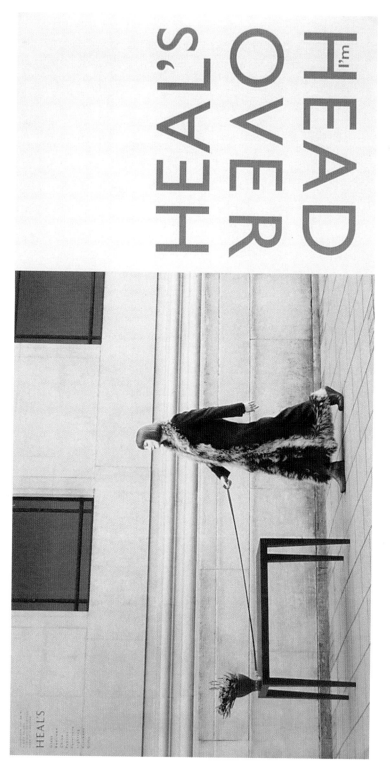

11.11 This advert for Heal's provides a good example of creative tactics facilitating both the processing and acceptance of the message. Courtesy Heal's

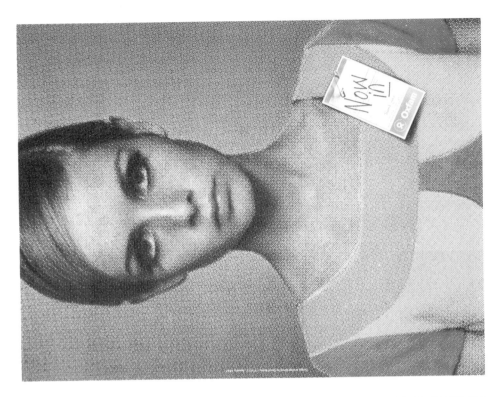

11.12 The high fashion models used in these adverts for Oxfam provide a good example of how an attractive, highly visible source is correctly used with a transformational brand attitude strategy. Courtesy Oxfam

the category decision is based upon a negatively originated motive (problem-solving) while brand choices are driven by positively originated motives (sensory gratification). More often than not with food products, brand choices are driven by taste. But in a generic category like this, how can you deal *originally* with taste as a benefit? One way is to move up the emotional scale, linking the brand to how the consumer uses the product in an emotionally compelling way.

Continuing with our example, 'instant' packaged side dishes are part of a meal. This would mean positioning the brand as part of an ideal meal. Research has shown that for most women the ideal meal is when everyone is present around the table and the family has an opportunity to talk. It may not happen often, but that is what they want. Given this, advertising could be created around this idea of everyone enjoying a meal together. The key is that the images and action are *realistically* portrayed. The family must be seen as behaving in a natural, not exaggerated manner, at a meal where our brand is part of the menu served. If the execution is seen as real (even if the 'reality' is an imagined ideal meal), a warm emotional response to the advertising *and* brand results.

This response to the meal, where our brand is served, becomes the brand's benefit. When the homemaker is shopping and sees the brand on the shelf it will remind her of the warm feeling experienced when she saw the advertising, and this becomes the reason for purchase. This is not to suggest that she actually feels there is a cause and effect, that serving our brand will ensure a lovely family meal. It only means that our brand will be a catalyst, occasioning a positive feeling, and this can be reason enough to buy in an otherwise very generic product category. Perhaps one of the very best examples of the effective use of this tactic was the long-running series of commercials in England for Oxo.[38]

Emotional authenticity is required for both low- and high-involvement transformational brand attitude strategies. With high-involvement transformational strategies, because of the risk involved it may be necessary to provide some more tangible information to help facilitate acceptance of the message. Additionally, in the high-involvement case the target audience must *personally* identify with the emotional portrayal, again because of the risk involved.[39]

An advert for Heal's (Advert 11.11) in many ways provides a good summary of what we have been talking about in this chapter. The creative tactics all work together, and facilitate both the processing and acceptance of the message. The visual and verbal elements work together, reflecting the appropriate use of words and pictures we talked about early in the chapter. Both the surprisingly inverted headlines, and the congruence between the brand, Heal's, and the visual imagery of a 'dog' at heel, helps attract and hold attention. The advert illustrates the tactics needed for a successful high-involvement, transformational brand attitude strategy. It is emotionally authentic and the target audience can personally identify with the imagery. The 'attitude' portrayed is real. You can imagine yourself in the picture (if you see yourself as part of the target audience). Everything here works well toward building a positive brand attitude.

VisCAP

Psychologists have long studied what it is about a person who presents a message (what they call a 'source') that influences how well it is received. For example, someone dressed in a white lab coat will be more convincing when talking about health problems than the same person dressed more casually. The first attempt to synthesize this work and apply it to advertising and other marketing communication was the VisCAP model of source effectiveness, introduced by Percy and Rossiter in 1980.[40] VisCAP is an acronym for visibility, credibility, attractiveness, and power, the main source characteristics in communication.

The source of a message in marketing communication can be anything from a person delivering a message, such as a friend, doctor, or salesperson (word-of-mouth marketing communication), to the medium through which the message is delivered. Think about an advert in a magazine. The type of magazine, the environment in which the reader finds the advert, can affect how you respond to the advertising. An advert for running shoes in *Runner's World* could be received much differently from the same advert in a general magazine. A source here is the magazine itself. The brand being advertised is itself a source of information, based upon the image it has in the mind of the target audience. But what we are concerned with here are the source effects communicated by people or characters that appear in advertising to present the benefit claim.

People or characters in advertising span a range from celebrity endorsers to experts to cartoon characters to actors playing (or actual) ordinary people. What you must consider in the selection of the people or characters to be used in advertising is how a particular person or character will affect the processing of the message. To facilitate processing, they should be selected in such a way that their personal characteristics are consistent with the communication objective. There are specific source characteristics that are best suited to specific communication objectives, and these are described by the VisCAP model.

The four components of the model are defined as follows:

Visibility: *how well known or recognizable* the person or character is from public exposure.

Credibility: *there are two components to credibility: expertise*, perceived knowledge of the source concerning what is being advertised, and *objectivity*, the perceived sincerity or trustworthiness in communicating what the source knows.

Attractiveness: *there are also two components to attractiveness: likeability* of the source, and the perceived *similarity* of the source to the target audience.

Power: *the source's perceived ability to instil compliance* on the part of the target audience.

The way these source characteristics match up with communication objectives is rather straightforward. *Visibility* helps facilitate brand awareness, especially if a celebrity is used. But with a celebrity you must be very careful that attention to the celebrity does not overpower the brand. Awareness of the celebrity must be *transferred* to the brand. Also, when using a celebrity you must remember that you are always subject to possible changes in their popularity. This is especially true for sports celebrities. Certain long-running characters or cartoons can achieve high levels of visibility, and this will continually be associated with the brand.

The source characteristic that helps facilitate informational brand attitude communication objectives is *credibility*. You need to have perceived expertise in a source for both low- and high-involvement informational strategies, but objectivity in the source is only needed for high-involvement informational strategies. Why? Remember, you do not really need to accept a benefit claim as literally true with low-involvement informational advertising, but it must be believed and accepted as true with high-involvement informational advertising.

With transformational advertising, you want the source to be *attractive*. Here, likeability is the important source characteristic for low-involvement transformational advertising and *similarity* for high-involvement transformational advertising. Remember that one of the differences in creative tactics for low- vs. high-involvement transformational advertising is the need for the target audience to identify personally with the high-involvement advertising. That is why perceived similarity to the source is important. This does not mean that the sourse must be seen as acting like the target audience, but it should be seen as similar to what they imagine or want themselves to be.

A really good example of what we are talking about can be seen in two adverts for Oxfam (see Advert 11.12). Oxfam is a charity that resells a variety of items, including clothing, in their shops in the UK. In an effort to help raise funds for Oxfam by attracting younger, more upscale patrons to their shops, they have reprinted actual fashion photography from Vogue magazine archives that features styles now back in fashion and available at Oxfam shops: hence the headline 'Now In'. Not only do we have well-known or recognized fashion models to help attract attention and build brand awareness, but we also have very attractive people consistent with what we want in the source for positively motivated purchases like clothing.

Power is not often a factor in advertising or marketing communication, because it is not easy to imagine how someone in an advert can reward or punish the target audience. One possible exception is with certain fear appeals. Another might be when '9 out of 10 doctors' recommend a certain behaviour for a particular problem. If you feel you might have that problem and do not follow the recommendation of the advertising, you might feel your doctor could 'punish' you if you must see him. To the extent that power might operate, it will help facilitate the communication objective of brand purchase intention.

The VisCAP model is summarized in Table 11.8.

Summary

This chapter first considered general principles of how to use words and pictures to optimise attention and message processing. We then went on to focus on specific creative tactics related to brand awareness and brand attitude communication objectives. We introduced the concept of the creative unit, and explained its use in generating and

Table 11.8 VisCAP Model of Characteristics to Look for in Matching People or Characters to Communication Objectives

Communication objective	Characteristic to Look For	
Brand Awareness	Visability	How recognizable is the person or character
Informational Brand Attitude	Credibility	
Low and high involvement	Expertise	Person or character's perceived knowledge of the product category
High involvement	Objectivity	Sincerity or trustworthiness of person or character in talking about the product category
Transformational Brand Attitude	Attractiveness	
Low involvement	Likeability	Person or character is seen as personable or attractive
High involvement	Similarity	Target audience sees person or character as similar to them
Brand Purchase Intention	Power	Perceived ability of the person or character to instill compliance with the message

Source: Adapted from J. R. Rossiter and L. Percy, *Advertising Communications and Promotion Management* (New York: McGraw-Hill, 1997).

holding attention in various media. We considered various ways of using words and pictures to enhance processing, especially the role of high levels of imagery. We emphasised the different creative tactics required for informational vs. transformational brand attitude strategies, and particularly the role of emotional authenticity in transformational strategies. Lastly, the VisCAP model was introduced to understand the effectiveness of the source of a message.

Questions to consider

11.1 What is meant by advertising having resonance?

11.2 How long should a headline be if it is to be understood without fully reading it?

11.3 What proportion of the average time spent looking at a magazine advertisement is spent with the picture?

11.4 What are concrete words and what is their effect on the processing of advertisements?

11.5 Why should negative claims be used very rarely in advertisements?

11.6 Why should black-and-white pictures not be used in transformational advertising?

11.7 Why can extreme benefit claims be used in low-involvement advertising?

11.8 How does the VisCAP acronym help to explain source effectiveness in advertising?

Notes

1   These attention estimates are suggested in J. R. Rossiter and L. Percy, *Advertising Communication and Promotion Management* (New York: McGraw-Hill, 1997). They are based upon a review of a number of empirical studies, including one conducted in South Africa utilizing 9,430 commercials, reported by E. DuPlessis in 'An Advertising Burst as Just a Lot of Drops', *Admap*, July/Aug. 1996, 51–5.

2   Again, Rossiter and Percy, *Advertising Communication and Promotion Management*, summarizes a number of studies that support this rule for print adverts (see esp. ch. 10).

3   Greg Myers, *Words in Ads* (London: Arnold, 1994), 3.

4   See A. J. Wearing, 'The Recall of Sentences of Varying Length', *Australian Journal of Psychology*, 25 (1973), 155–61.

5   See J. R. Rossiter, 'The Increase in Magazine Ad Readership', *Journal of Advertising Research*, 28:5 (1988), 35–9.

6   These results are reported in a rather extensive study of over 500 MTV-type commercials with over 20 cuts vs. 600 commercials with fewer than 20 cuts by J. MacLachlan and M. Logan, 'Commercial Shot Length in TV Commercials and their Memorability and Persuasiveness', *Journal of Advertising Research*, 33:2 (1993), 7–16.

7   This has been reported by, among others, B. E. Avons and W. A. Phillips, 'Visualization and Memorization as a Function of Display Time and Poststimulus Processing Time', *Journal of Experimental Psychology: Human Learning and Memory*, 6 (1980), 407–42.

8   Because of his work with attitude change, McGuire was frequently asked about the implications of his thinking for advertising. His seminal work is found in G. Lindsey and E. Aronson, (eds.), *Handbook of Social Psychology*, vol. 3, (Reading, Mass.: Addison-Wesley, 1969), 136–314.

9   A. Paivio, in his well-known book *Images and Verbal Processing* (New York: Holt, Rinehart and Winston, 1971), discusses research which found that more frequently used and more familiar words are heard, read, and repeated faster and with fewer errors. Lowenthal in 'Semantic Features and Communicability of Words of Different Classes', *Psychonomic Science*, 17 (1969), 79–80, found that meaning is easier to grasp with more familiar words.

10 McGuire introduced something he called a two-factor analysis, where low *or* high levels of arousal are less likely to lead to persuasion than some intermediate level. This so-called inverted U-shaped relationship is especially evident when fear appeals are used. A certain level of shock- or anxiety-causing copy or visuals will attract attention, but that very anxiety will inhibit processing of the message. See W. J. McGuire, 'Personality and Attitude Change: An Information-Processing Theory', A. G. Greenwald *et al.* (eds.), *Psychological Foundations of Attitudes* (New York: Academic Press, 1968).

11 See M. P. Toglia and W. F. Battig, *Handbook of Semantic Word Norms* (Hillsdale, NJ: Lawrence E. Erlbaum and Associates, 1978).

12 C. C. Jorgensen and W. Kintsch, in 'The Role of Imagery in the Evaluation of

Sentences', *Cognitive Psychology*, 4 (1973), 110–16, have shown that high-imagery sentences can be evaluated significantly faster as true or false than can low-imagery sentences. K. Holyoak, in 'The Role of Imagery in the Evaluation of Sentences: Imagery or Semantic Relatedness?', *Journal of Verbal Learning and Verbal Behaviour*, 13 (1974), 163–166 found that sentences rated high in imagery value are significantly easier to understand.

13 See L. Percy, 'Exploring Grammatical Structure and Non-verbal Communication', in S. Hecker and D. W. Stewart (eds.), *Nonverbal Communication in Advertising* (Lexington, Mass.: Lexington Books, 1988), 147–58.

14 See Myers, *Words in Ads*.

15 See, for example, T. Lowrey, 'The Relation between Syntactic Complexity and Advertising Persuasiveness', in J. Sherry and B. Sternthal (eds.) *Advances in Consumer Research*, vol. 19 (Provo, Utah: Association for Consumer Research, 1991), 270–4.

16 See Myers, *Words in Ads*, 30.

17 Ibid. 47–51.

18 See M. W. Eyesenk, *Human Memory: Theory, Research and Individual Difference* (Oxford: Pergamon, 1977).

19 See Myers, *Words in Ads*.

20 W. J. Bryce and R. F. Yalch, 'Hearing versus Seeing: A Comparison of Learning of Spoken and Pictorial Information in Television Advertising,' *Journal of Current Issues and Research in Advertising*, 15:1 (1993), 1–20. They make the point that because of language differences it obviously makes sense for commercials to be reasonably understandable from only the visual content.

21 John Shearman discusses this idea in a very interesting book, *Only Connect . . . Art and the Spectator in the Italian Renaissance* (Princeton, NJ: Princeton University Press, 1992). It may seem odd to be citing an art history book, but the art history literature can provide important insight into visual communication.

22 The implication of what this means, not only for marketing communication but also for cross-cultural communication, is discussed in a paper by L. Percy, 'Moving Beyond Culturally Dependent Responses to Visual Images' presented to the 2nd Conference on the Cultural Dimensions of International Marketing, Odense University, Denmark (1995).

23 A case history that discusses the origins of this campaign and how it had a significant impact upon Pirelli tyre sales, entitled *'Guida da Razza' : How Carl Lewis Helped Restore Pirelli's Fortunes*, is available from the Institute of Practitioners in Advertising (IPA), London.

24 See Myers, *Words in Ads*.

25 Ibid.

26 See S. M. Kosslyn, *Images and Mind* (Cambridge, Mass.: Harvard University Press, 1980)

27 Studies by both Rossiter and Percy and Mitchell and Olson have demonstrated the positive impact of larger picture size on evaluative responses and not just memory response. See J. R. Rossiter and L. Percy, 'Visual Communication in Advertising', in R. J. Harris (ed., *Information Processing Research in Advertising*) (Hillsdale, NJ:

Lawrence Erlbaum Associates, 1983), 83–126, and A. A. Mitchell and J. C. Olson, 'Are Product Attribute Beliefs the Only Mediator of Advertising Effects on Brand Attitude?', *Journal of Marketing Research*, 18 (1981), 318–32.

28　See R. P. Dooley and L. E. Harkins, 'Functional and Attention-getting Effects of Colour on Graphic Communications', *Perceptual and Motor Skills*, 31 (1970), 851–4.

29　See G. H. Bower, 'Imagery as a Relational Organizer in Associative Learning', *Journal of Verbal Learning and Verbal Behavior*, 4 (1970), 529–33.

30　This idea of double-coding was originally introduced by Paivio, and is well discussed in A. Paivio, 'A Dual Coding Approach to Perception and Cognition', in H. I. Pick and E. Saltzman, (eds.) *Modes of Perceiving and Processing Information* (Hillsdale, NJ: Lawrence Erlbaum Associates, 1978).

31　See J. R. Rossiter, 'Visual Imagery: An Application to Advertising', in A. Mitchell (ed.) *Advances in Consumer Research*, vol. 9 (Provo, Utah: Association for Consumer Research, 1981), 101–6.

32　See C. J. Brainerd, A. Desrochers, and M. L. Howe, 'Stages of Learning Analysis of Picture-Word Effects in Associative Memory', *Journal of Experimental Psychology: Human Learning and Memory*, 7 (1987), 1–14.

33　Rossiter and Percy review this in *Advertising and Communication Management*, where they discuss their own work and that of C. E. Young and M. Robinson: 'Video Rhythms and Recall', *Journal of Advertising Research*, 29:3, (1989), 22–5 and 'Visual Connectedness and Persuasion', *Journal of Advertising Research*, 32:2 (1992), 51–9.

34　This idea is explored in more detail in Rossiter and Percy, *Advertising and Communication Management*.

35　See J. C. Maloney, 'Curiosity versus Disbelief in Advertising', *Journal of Advertising Research*, 2:2 (1962), 2–8.

36　This idea of 'liking' an advert can be troubling. On the one hand there is research that shows the influence on brand preference from ad-liking is not strong, for example Jan Stapel's 'Viva Recall, Viva Persuasion', *European Research*, 15 (Nov. 1987), 222–5. On the other hand, Gordon Brown, in 'Monitoring Advertising: Big Stable Brands and Ad Effects. Fresh Thoughts about Why: Perhaps Consistent Promotion Keeps them Big', *Admap*, 27 (May 1981), 32–7, has suggested that ad-liking has a long term effect. You must look *carefully* at the adverts used in any research on attitude toward the advert. We should only expect a positive effect when dealing with advertising addressing positive motives. This important point has been underscored by Larry Percy in his paper 'Understanding the Mediating Effect of Motivation and Emotion in Advertising Measurement', in *Copy Research: The New Evidence*, Proceedings of the 8th Annual ARF Copy Research Workshop (1991).

37　This study was conducted for a major US brewer by one of the authors.

38　In the casebook edited by C. Baker, *Advertising Works 7* (London: NTC Publications, 1992) there is a detailed discussion of how this type of advertising helped revitalize the Oxo brand. This issue is addressed generally by Marc Weinberger and Harlan Spotts in their paper 'A Situational View of Information Content in TV Advertising in the U.S. and UK', *Journal of Marketing*, 53 (Jan. 1989), 89–94. They show that advertising need not provide information to be effective.

39 A much more detailed discussion of the creative tactics associated with the brand attitude strategy quadrants from the Rossiter–Percy Grid may be found in their *Advertising Communication and Promotion Management*.

40 Larry Percy and John R. Rossiter, *Advertising Strategy: A Communication Theory Approach* (New York: Praeger, 1980).

Chapter 12

Promotion Tactics

Up to this point we have spent most of our time discussing traditional advertising. Now we turn our attention to traditional notions of promotion. Most marketing texts are likely to refer to McCarthy's 'Four P's' concept of the marketing mix which we introduced in the first chapter: Product, Place, Price, and Promotion. In this formulation of the marketing mix, you will remember that 'promotion' is used to cover *all aspects* of marketing communication. Within marketing communication, of course, the term 'promotion' is used to describe what has historically been called 'sales promotion' techniques. As Simmons has put it, 'in a general sense everything that is done to sell a product is sales promotion'.[1] More practically, 'sales promotion', or what we call traditional promotion, is usually defined as any direct purchasing incentive, reward, or promise that is offered for making a specific purchase or taking a specific purchase-related action.[2]

While this is certainly a useful definition, there is more to consider. One important consideration is time. When consumer decision-making models were introduced in Chapter 6, we saw how important it is to understand the timing of various stages in the decision process. Just as with advertising, you need to integrate the use of promotional techniques in relation to the target audience's decision process. Some promotions may be more helpful early in the decision process, prior to purchase or use of a service, others more appropriate at the point of purchase, still others after purchase or even during usage.

Advertising, as we have seen, serves a longer-term strategic purpose in marketing communication. Promotion is used for more short-term, tactical objectives. But when you think of traditional promotion tactics, it must be considered as part of your overall marketing communication. Promotion techniques are generally used when you want to speed up the decision process, and should never be considered in isolation. Always, when promotions are considered, the manager should be thinking about whether and how a particular type of promotion can be an effective part of the *whole* marketing communication effort. Simmons puts this very well when he refers to the 'two great commandments of sales promotion—it must relate directly to the objective, and it must be compatible with the total brand proposition'.[3]

In Chapter 14 we will look specifically at how promotion works with advertising to generate a more synergistic whole. Here we will be looking at basic promotion techniques.

Basic Promotion Types

Promotions may be broadly classified as either *immediate* or *delayed*.[4] Those that offer an immediate reward tend to be more effective because of their immediacy, which is consistent with the short-term tactical nature of promotions. Immediate reward promotions include such things as price reductions, bonus packs, and coupons. Delayed promotion techniques delay the reward, usually until after the target audience takes some action. Delayed reward promotions include such things as sweepstakes, rebate offers, and frequent flyer programmes. This idea of immediate vs. delayed promotions is closely associated with our two target audience behavioural objectives, trial and repeat purchase.

Promotions are usually thought of as aimed at consumers, but in fact much more money is invested in promotions to the trade than to the consumer. There are three fundamental types of promotion: trade promotion, retail promotion, and consumer promotion.[5] We may think of a *trade promotion* as a programme of discounts or incentives aimed at increasing distribution or merchandising collateral aimed at moving more product; *retail promotion* is generally independent of the manufacturer and initiated by either the retailer or distributor; and a *consumer promotion* is a promotion directed toward the target audience to accelerate or reinforce the decision process.

Trade Promotion

As we have already mentioned, trade promotion takes up a significant proportion of most marketing communication budgets. Whether the promotion directly affects pricing or indirectly affects volume through merchandising material, the trade views trade promotions from the manufacturer as a way to move more money to their bottom line. Most trade promotions do this directly through a price-related promotion of one kind or another. These can include such things as direct price-off reductions from invoices, agreement to buy back any unsold product, and slotting allowances. Slotting fees are relatively new, but are fast becoming a cost of doing business rather than a promotion. With their new-found power, the trade now demands a fee to stock an item. Their reasoning is that with an ever-increasing demand to handle new products and line extensions, and given their high failure rate, they feel they need help in dealing with the cash flow and overhead involved. While there is certainly some truth to this, it is nevertheless estimated that as much as 70 per cent of slotting fees go directly to the bottom line and not to defraying costs.

If a marketer is offering a discount on its price to the trade, the trade has the option of retaining all or part of the discount, sending it to their bottom line. To the extent that any of the trade discount is passed on to the retailer or directly to the consumer, these trade promotions are still expected to increase volume, also leading to larger profits for the trade. This is also the reasoning behind the trade's interest in merchandising promotion. Here the marketer will supply collateral material such as in-store banners, special end-aisle displays, or sales incentive premiums for target sales goals. Of course, the marketer is looking for something in return: such things as better stocking and shelf positioning (e.g.

more package 'facings' and at a more desirable height on the shelf[6]), counter displays, and other opportunities for better exposure.

Unfortunately, in many markets the distribution channels, especially mass retailers, have become so powerful that even when trade promotions are given there is no guarantee the trade will offer anything in return. It is important to remember that the marketer's goals and the trade's goals are not necessarily the same. The trade profits from *category* sales. They do not particularly care which brands are stocked as long as they maintain or increase their margins. The marketer, of course, is vitally interested in their *brand*.

This underscores a very important point. Too often trade promotions (and retail and consumer promotions as well) are seen only as a way to buy share or sales in order to satisfy an immediate, short-term sales goal. True, promotion is a short-term *tactic*, but it must be seen within a larger marketing communication *strategy* for the brand. As we shall see in Chapter 14, this means integrating trade promotions with all other promotion and advertising activity.

To go beyond the obvious, trade promotions should be designed to improve relations with the trade in order to gain and hold new distribution, build inventory with the trade, or to obtain trade cooperation and merchandising support. There are three basic categories of trade promotion that we will consider: allowance promotions, display material promotions, and trade premiums and incentives.

Allowance promotions provide the trade a monetary allowance of some kind in return for buying or promoting a specific quantity of a brand, or for meeting specific purchase or performance requirements. *Display material promotions* are when the manufacturer actually provides special display material to be used in featuring the brand, often in conjunction with a trade allowance. *Trade incentives* are special gifts or opportunities to earn or win valuable trips or prizes in return for purchasing specified quantities of the brand or meeting specific sales quotas.

We will now take a closer look at these three types of trade promotions.

Allowances

The type of allowance offered to the trade can take many forms: everything from reduced prices across the board, to reduced prices according to purchase volume, to free goods. It is important to point out here that most governments keep a close eye on price allowances to the trade in order to ensure they are equitably applied regardless of the size or type of distributor.

Just as we mentioned with slotting fees, which could be considered an 'allowance' of sorts, the potential weakness with trade allowances is that there is no real guarantee they will have a positive effect on your customer base. You are hoping to secure a more positive position with the trade. Offering purchase allowances or free goods with certain order levels helps build inventories, which is essential support for customer-based marketing programmes. If you are heavily advertising or promoting a brand, you want it to be available. Performance allowances, you hope, will at least in part go to merchandising or retail advertising by the trade in support of the brand. Even though there is no guarantee the trade will cooperate, at least to the extent you might wish, consumer, retail, and trade support *must* be integrated in order to maximize your efforts regardless of the cooperation given by the trade in response to your trade promotion.

One way to help improve the likelihood of trade cooperation is to use trade coupons. Although trade coupons are offered to the trade, they are actually to be redeemed by consumers. The difference between a trade coupon and a retail coupon is that with trade coupons the marketer controls the conditions and value of the coupon, not the trade. Retail coupons, as we shall see later in this chapter, are generally under trade control, and as a result more difficult to integrate with your overall marketing communication programme.

Trade coupons are a delayed promotion where the trade pays for distributing the coupons to their customers, and are then reimbursed by the marketer after the promotion. The reason the trade likes these coupons is that they help stretch their own marketing budgets. But they must be carefully considered and included as a part of a brand's overall marketing communication programme. The brand's advertising and consumer promotions must be integrated with any trade coupons to ensure a seamless message to the target audience.

Displays

Display promotions can be in the form of either a display allowance or actual merchandising material. Perhaps the primary use of display promotions is to help reinforce consumer promotions, although they also play an important role in the introduction of new products and line extensions. Given that many purchase decisions are made at the point of purchase, especially with fmcg (fast-moving consumer good) brands,[7] display promotions can be an important part of an integrated marketing communication programme. Good display material leads to better attention, especially important for brands driven by recognition awareness. Here you can appreciate the need for a fully integrated programme. The display material must be consistent with consumer promotion and advertising, with the same 'look and feel', in order to heighten recognition at the point of purchase.

Good in-store merchandising material can also be a good way to effect cross-merchandising, where two different brands are being promoted together. An interesting new application of display promotion is the use of interactive computers. Interactive computers are placed in a kiosk or other display to help provide information or support for a brand. This has many applications for high-involvement product decisions, and has become quite popular with automobile dealers.

The use of display promotions has the advantage of generally being implemented quickly when needed, and the ability to support consumer promotion and advertising at the point of purchase. The disadvantage, as with all trade promotions, but especially here, is the need for trade cooperation. Unlike trade allowances or trade premiums and incentives, which we address next, in the case of display promotion if it does not receive widespread trade support it will not be effective.

Trade Incentives

This last area of trade promotion is more concerned with individual distribution sources such as wholesale or retail outlets, distributors, brokers, and trade personnel. Incentives can be offered to almost any level of trade, and tend to be very popular. They can be given for reaching specific sales goals, to individuals, departments, or stores. Awards or gifts might be offered to counter personnel for recommending or highlighting your brand, or to staff members who create new or innovative ways to promote your brand. Such incentive programmes can be a big help when introducing a new product or brand extension. They are also an effective way to help move slow products off the shelf.

One of the advantages of incentives as a trade promotion is that they are relatively inexpensive. Additionally, they are implemented quickly and easily. However, a disadvantage is that segments of the trade, especially mass merchandisers, have policies against them or regulations that severely limit the type of incentive promotion they will accept.

Retail Promotion

You may be wondering why we are treating retail promotions separately from trade promotions when retailers are a major part of the trade. In fact, everything we have just discussed in terms of trade promotion applies to retailers. But retailers form a very specific sub-set of the trade, one that has direct contact with the end consumer. Other aspects of the trade, such as brokers or wholesale distributors, do not as a rule deal directly with consumers. As a result, the effects of promotions to non-retail trade may or may not be passed on to the consumer through retailers.

We pointed out earlier in this chapter that it is largely up to the trade, and especially retailers, how they will use a particular promotion. A very interesting study has shown that the objective for many retail promotions is not simply to attract shoppers to their store, but to move product off the shelf, in effect reducing their inventory costs.[8] This strategy may not always be consistent with the strategy behind a trade or retail promotion offered to retailers. This can be a real problem for a marketer. In trying to integrate all of the elements of a brand's marketing communication, retail promotion can be a wild card. Later in this chapter we will be discussing channels marketing, which is a relatively recent attempt by marketers to gain better control over retail promotion, and better integration with advertising and other brand marketing communication.

We will be looking at three general areas of retail promotion, but must remember that the trade promotions just reviewed are also used by retailers. Retail promotions are almost always price-related. While they tend to be categorized in terms of specific *price-off* promotions, *point-of-purchase display* promotions, and *retail adverts*, the promotion itself almost always includes a price reduction.

An important consideration with retail promotions is that they are independent of a brand's marketing strategy. While the brand would like to coordinate retail promotions with their own marketing and communication strategy (as we will see when we discuss channels marketing), the reality is that retail promotions are offered *independently* of the pricing policy or other trade or consumer promotions offered by the brand. Often a retailer's promotion strategy is geared more to competitive activity than anything else.

Price-off Promotion

There are many pricing strategies that retailers use in price-off promotions. They must consider concurrent or recent consumer price promotions, inventory balance, and competitive activity. Remember, a retailer is interested in *category* sales. Suppose L' Oréal Paris is running a major price-off promotion in leading French women's magazines like *marie france* and *Biba* for Kerastase Aqua-Oleun. The cosmetic manager of a major retailer may decide to offer a similar retail promotion for Jacques Dessange or other hair-styling products in order to drive business in the entire category.

Price-off promotions are almost always a part of retail adverts, and frequently a part of retail point-of-purchase displays. But there are also many other ways of implementing a price-off promotion: everything from in-store flyers to 'shelf-talkers', where the price reduction is highlighted at the shelf on a small poster. There is actually some evidence to suggest that different consumers pay attention to different means of presenting price-off promotions, so it is in the retailer's best interest to use several means of conveying a price-off promotion.[9]

Point-of-Purchase Display Promotion

In-store displays are a significant part of trade promotion. But just as a brand offers display or other merchandising material to the retailer for a promotion, retailers on their own may use special point-of-purchase displays. Retailers like point-of-purchase display promotions because they are effective. They are effective for two reasons. First of all, point-of-purchase displays draw attention to themselves. Shoppers are attracted by newly introduced contrasts or changes to their shopping environment, and will pay attention to discover what it is all about. This can be done with such things as store banners, end-aisle displays, or other stand-alone features. Secondly, point-of-purchase displays are perceived by consumers to be offering a price reduction on the featured product *even if it is not discounted*.[10]

Retail Advert Promotion

When you think of retail adverts, the first thing that probably comes to mind are newspaper, food, or pharmacy adverts. But, of course, almost any retailer can use retail adverts as promotion, and automotive dealers, mass merchandisers, shoe stores, and even banks frequently do. Retail advert promotions are also found in local magazines and even on local radio and television. Retailers may do traditional advertising as well, and we must not confuse the two. If a retailer is talking about something related to the store or image, even if they are attempting to build their brand equity, this is *not* retail promotion. Adverts are retail promotions when they feature products and prices, whether discounted or not. Adverts 12.1 and 12.2 illustrate two typical retail advert promotions.

The retail advert for PC World is probably what comes to mind when you think about retail promotions. Within the advert we see price advertising and price promotions for a number of different products and brands available at PC World. The promoted products may or may not be linked to a brand promotion (which we discuss later in this chapter), but they are all a part of this PC World retail promotion. Contrast this with the Debenhams promotion advert. It is promoting a single brand, Jasper Conran's new collection of children's wear, 'one of eleven international designer brands in children's wear available at Debenhams'. Again, we do not know if this represents a brand-supported promotion or if it was created and paid for solely by Debenhams. Be that as it may, the advert is a very good example of how retail promotions can also help reinforce a positive store-brand attitude.

12.1 A retail promotion advert featuring both price advertising and price promotion.
Courtesy PC World

Boys' denim dungarees £18
Girls' striped dress
with apron pinny £25

GREAT NAMES.
GREAT BRANDS.
GREAT PRICES.

JASPER CONRAN'S
NEW COLLECTION.
IT'S UP TO
EIGHT YEARS OLD.

ONE OF ELEVEN INTERNATIONAL AND DESIGNER
BRANDS IN CHILDRENSWEAR AVAILABLE AT DEBENHAMS.
Clothing featured for children up to 3 years.

DEBENHAMS
BRITAIN'S FAVOURITE DEPARTMENT STORE
www.debenhams.com

12.2 A retail promotion advert featuring a single-brand promotion. Courtesy Debenhams

What is being featured in retail advert promotions is what the *retailer* is interested in promoting, which as we have been pointing out may or may not be consistent with a brand's marketing communication strategy. The retailer will be looking to draw add-itional customers to the store because of the featured items, especially if discounted, or may be primarily concerned with using the promotion for inventory control or adjustment.

Channels Marketing

'Channels marketing' is a relatively recent term used to describe all levels of marketing communication to the retail trade. It has come into being as a result of the increasing importance of trade promotion, coupled with the increasing power of retailers. Basically, it combines co-op advertising with tactical marketing. Co-op advertising has existed for a very long time, and is essentially an agreement between a retailer and brand to cooperate in part of the brand's marketing communication. The brand offers to produce advertising or promotions that include the retailer's name, and the retailer agrees to participate in funding the advertising or promotion along with the brand. Tactical marketing is a rela-tively new channel—(i.e. distribution)—oriented marketing communication system designed to return more control over promotion to the brand and to leverage incremental support for the trade, especially the retailer.

Traditional co-op advertising is generally broad in scope and *passive* in nature. Typic-ally, it is open to a brand's entire retail base, conditioned on sales volume: the more of the brand sold, the more money available for co-op advertising. The adverts and other mer-chandising material are provided by the brand, but used by the retailer as they wish. Then, on a periodic basis the retailer is reimbursed for their expenditures according to the co-op agreement.

With their expanding power, many retailers were treating traditional co-op as a profit centre, diverting funds to offset operating costs. Retailers were also beginning to force brands, as a condition of stocking, to participate in retailer-initiated promotions that often were not consistent or integrated with the brand's overall marketing communica-tion. *Tactical marketing* grew out of the desire on the part of brands to assume more control over the use of their co-op monies.

Tactical marketing, unlike traditional co-op, is always *pro-active*. Programmes are designed for particular retailers, tailored to their specific needs. With the cooperation of the retailer, the brand funds the programme, in accordance with the retailer meeting specific sales goals, and *implements* the programme. The benefit for the brand is *control*. Tactical marketing offers the retailer complete coordination of the programme and pro-duction of the materials used, while maintaining control over the content and timing of the advertising and promotions. The payoff for the retailer is the ability to go beyond the basic print orientation of most traditional co-op programmes (or at best very simple broadcast executions), and the ability to utilize the full marketing communication range of the brand within a plan optimized for each retailer.

Consumer Promotions

Consumers will not make a distinction between trade promotions delivered at retail outlets, retail promotions, and consumer promotions. If they see a special display in the store or have a coupon or see a price special, they are not concerned with whether it was the brand or the retailer that was responsible. But from the brand's perspective, there is a world of difference. Consumer promotions are initiated by the brand, not the retailer, and the brand controls the content.

As it happens, consumers tend to have a pretty good idea about how often brands are promoted.[11] This is important to the brand, because it will affect consumer buying strategy for the brand in light of the perception of the brand's availability on promotion. So even if you do not have control over retail promotions that include your brand, it is essential that you have knowledge of them and include that knowledge in your promotion strategy.

There are six fundamental types of consumer promotion that we will want to consider: coupons, rebates and refunds, sampling, loyalty and loading devices, sweepstakes, and premiums (see Table 12.1). While there are many other possibilities for consumer promotion—everything from the product itself to unique applications of distribution channels—generally speaking we may think about consumer promotions in terms of these six basic techniques.

Coupons

Because of its relatively low cost, the coupon is the most common form of consumer promotion. Basically, however, coupons are largely used for fmcg's. This is because of the nature of the discounts associated with coupons and the frequency with which most fmcg's are purchased. Generally, the face value of a coupon is not large because the retail price of the product is not high. There is no reason you could not offer higher-value coupons for less frequently purchased products, but directly discounting the price offers more control with higher-priced, less frequently purchased products.

One of the considerations that must be factored into using coupons as part of a consumer promotion strategy is the fact that very few people will actually redeem a coupon. The redemption rate for coupons can be expected to run between 2 and 5 per cent. The actual redemption rate will be a function of the face value of the coupon relative to the price of the brand, as well as the expiration period. The greater the value of the coupon and the longer the time available for redemption, the greater the redemption rate.

Table 12.1 Six Basic Consumer Promotions

Coupons	Low cost, most common form of promotion
Refunds and Rebates	Large price discounts, usually with more expensive products
Sampling	Opportunity to try or use brand at little or no cost
Loyalty and Loading Devices	Encourages repeat purchase or use (loyalty) or changes normal purchasing patterns (loading device)
Sweepstakes	Helps create excitement and reinforces brand image at a relatively low cost
Premiums	Helps facilitate purchase by offering a reward or bonus

It is absolutely essential that the expected redemption rate be carefully calculated. Remember that coupons represent a *budgeted* cost, and if the redemption rate is seriously underestimated the overall cost of the promotion will exceed the budget. Some of the other cost considerations in budgeting a coupon promotion, beyond the face value of the discount, are such things as additional manufacturing and distribution costs, lost profit, and the resources needed to administer the programme.

Traditionally, coupons are distributed to consumers via print media or direct mail. In magazines or newspapers, coupons may be a part of an advert, as we see in Advert 12.3. This advert for Weight Watchers from Heinz Fat Free Fromage Frais does a good job of integrating a 10p-off coupon within the execution without interfering with the advert's message. But most coupons, especially in newspapers, are delivered as FSIs, those often annoying 'free-standing inserts' of cards, single pages, or booklets, each with a coupon. In fact, the Weight Watchers from Heinz Fat Free Fromage Frais advert could easily have been an FSI. The only differences are that it would not have been bound into the magazine where it ran, and the coupon itself would likely have been perforated for easier removal. Sometimes a coupon may be included in or on a package, either good for future purchase of that brand (often called a 'bounce-back coupon') or a sister brand from the same manufacturer, called 'cross-couponing' or 'cross-ruff couponing'. Occasionally, a brand will run a joint promotion with a company in another product category, using a coupon. Joint promotions are useful for products that 'go together', such as ice cream and topping or swim gear and sunscreen. For example, a swimsuit manufacturer might offer a coupon on its package good for a certain amount off the purchase of a particular brand of sunscreen.

Technology is providing innovative new ways to deliver coupons. With today's sophisticated scanner capabilities, companies (and retailers) have the ability to monitor customer behaviour, and offer coupons to consumers at the till. For example, someone purchasing Flash anti-bacterial cleaner might be given a coupon for Domestos Germguard to be used the next time they are buying an anti-bacterial cleaner. Asda (acquired by WalMart in 1999) was one of the first grocery retailers in the UK to use this system. Research into redemption rates suggests a significant increase from the typical 2–5 per cent up to 6–8 per cent.[12] Additionally, this type of 'checkout' couponing offers the ability to target consumers much more tightly. Another application of technology for delivering coupons uses the Internet. Individual companies and services offering coupons from many companies provide on-line computer-generated coupons. The consumer need only log on, select the coupons they want, and print them out.

Refunds and Rebates

The pendant to coupons for more expensive consumer durable products is refunds and rebates. The primary difference is that with refunds and rebates the price discount is not offered at the point of purchase, but after sending in some proof of purchase to the manufacturer. The face value of a refund or rebate can be either a specific amount or some proportion of the retail price. As you might guess, the redemption rate is somewhat higher than it is for coupons, but still not high. Again, as with coupons, the request for a refund or rebate will be directly related to its relative value, and must be carefully planned to estimate likely use.

12.3 A coupon integrated within an advert without interfering with the advert's message.
Courtesy Yoplait Dairy Crest (McCann Erickson)

Most refunds and rebates are paid directly to the consumer by the manufacturer, but in some areas with very high ticket items a manufacturer's rebate can be assigned to the retailer at the time of purchase. This is not unusual, for example, when automobile manufacturers offer rebates. Their dealers will apply the rebate directly to the purchase price.

Refunds and rebates are used most often as a temporary sales stimulus or sometimes as a defensive response to competitive activity. The primary strengths of refunds and rebates include the ability to generate interest in high-involvement products, especially those with high price points, and an ability to control price discounts *without* trade interference. The weakness of refunds and rebates is that the reward is delayed, and consumers may not think the effort is worth the discount. To be effective, refunds and rebates must be seen as simple and easy to receive.

Sampling

Sampling provides your target audience an opportunity to actually try or use a brand at little or no cost. While most samples are free, specially-sized samples are sometimes offered at a significantly reduced price to encourage purchase. The ideal candidates for sampling are products with low trial or products with a demonstrable difference (especially if the advantage is difficult to convey convincingly with advertising), but many fmcg's include sampling in their consumer promotion strategy.

There are many ways of delivering samples to the target audience, and they come in a variety of forms. There are in-store use or taste tests, distribution of full-size packages of the product or specially-sized smaller packages, and even in-house or in-business use of a product for a limited period of time (a good way to 'sample' high-priced, high-involvement products).

Passing out samples in specific locations or offering in-store sampling has the advantage of low distribution cost, but little control over who receives the sample. Direct mail offers more control, but there are obvious limits to what can be sampled (e.g. not frozen or other perishable food items). Door-to-door distribution permits sampling almost anything, but while offering tight control is inefficient and expensive. Certain products such as fragrances can be sampled with 'scratch and sniff' folds in magazines, and as we see in Advert 12.4, it is even possible to offer small packs of cosmetics in magazines. This sampling promotion is part of a very clever advert that visually underscores the benefit of using Retinol Concentré Pur. In Advert 12.4*a* we see the promotion as it appeared in women's magazines; in Advert 12.4*b* we see the result when the sachet is lifted from the page.

Loyalty and Loading Devices

As the name implies, loyalty promotions are designed to offer a reward to those consumers who are loyal to a brand. The goal is to energize repeat purchase of the brand, and has the advantage of providing an excellent opportunity for developing a strong database of a brand's best customers. The best loyalty promotions utilize *continuity programmes*, where the consumer is required to engage in a continuing behaviour (e.g. saving stamps or accumulating some proof of purchase or use) over time in order to qualify for a reward. Perhaps the best-known loyalty promotions are airline frequent flyer programmes and hotel frequent 'stayer' programmes where customers earn points for

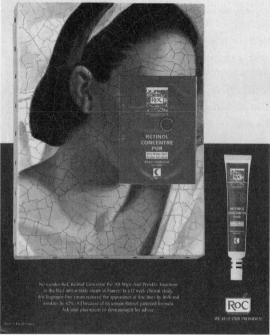

(a)   (b)

12.4a A clever advert that includes a sample promotion. Courtesy Retinol Concentré Pur
12.4b Advert 12.4a after the sample has been removed, underscoring the benefit of using the brand. Courtesy Retinol Concentré Pur

staying at a particular hotel chain. The more miles or points accumulated, the greater the reward. This idea has been copied in recent years by a number of different retailers and marketers; it has been used in everything from shopping points for money spent at a retailer to reward programmes for using a specific credit card or telecommunication company. The more you spend, charge, or call, the better the rewards available. Certainly programmes like this encourage loyalty to a single brand. But in addition, fmcg companies are increasingly using databases to identify heavy brand users in order to offer them special programmes or rewards.

Consumer loading devices differ from loyalty programmes in that they do not seek continuity, but rather seek to change a consumer's normal purchasing pattern. These promotions are designed to encourage customers to 'load up' on the brand by purchasing more than they normally do at one time. This is done by using special bonus packs, price packs, and price-offs. *Bonus packs* offer more of the product at the same price, either with a special larger size or an additional package bound to the original. *Price packs* are where a reduced price is printed on the package as part of the label, and *price-offs* are announced at the point of purchase. This can be a very effective and efficient way to encourage brand switching and as a defensive tactic. For example, if you know a competitor is about to introduce a 'new and improved' version of their brand, offering a loading promotion will in effect reduce the potential market for the competitor's initiative.

Of course, as always there are strengths and weaknesses to loyalty and loading promotions. Bonus packs do create an immediate incentive to buy, but the trade does not like them because they disrupt normal inventory stocking, and take up additional shelf space without necessarily providing additional profit for the retailer. Price packs and price-offs also offer an immediate inducement to buy, but unless coupled with advertising or other marketing communications, tend to subsidize regular users more than attracting new tryers or switchers.

Continuity programmes certainly energize loyal usage of a brand, but require a long–term commitment by both the consumer and the brand. Because of the long term nature of loyalty promotions, costs may end up being greater than expected. This has certainly been the case with frequent flyer programmes. Early competition among airlines led to 'sweetening' of the programmes, making it easier to reach threshold levels for free flights. This led to increased demand for free flights, which in turn made it more difficult for frequent flyers actually to redeem their miles for the free flights they wanted. This naturally upset the most loyal customers, and while the airlines feel they have invested too much in the frequent flyer programmes to change, they would certainly like to.

This is a good example of the frustrated target audience group we talked about when discussing the loyalty model groupings in Chapter 5. They continue to stay with the airline because of the high cost of switching. They could lose all of their frequent flyer miles, or at the very least would need to begin building miles with another airline. What began as an attempt on the part of airlines to build loyalty via a loyalty promotion, while it has generated repeat flying, has *not* helped build a positive brand attitude.

Sweepstakes, Games, and Contests

Sweepstakes are a consumer promotion where the winners are chosen by chance and proof of purchase is not required. On the other hand, with games and contests there is some chance or skill involved, or a demonstration of knowledge, but almost always proof of purchase is required. With contests someone may be asked to answer certain questions or identify pictures related in some way to the brand. Not surprisingly, sweepstakes are more popular than games or contests, being much easier to enter since no purchase is necessary. Soft drink bottlers and fast-food chains frequently use games as a consumer promotion. You scratch off a square or a card given to you when you purchase food or you look under the cap of a soft drink bottle to see if you have won.

If you are not careful, things can go very wrong with these types of promotions. Smith[13] relates the story of a disastrous game promotion sponsored by Pepsi in the Philippines where the equivalent of £26,000 was offered to anyone finding a bottle top with a specific number. Pepsi paid out £8 *million* before they realized that thousands of winning bottle tops had inadvertently been distributed, and then abruptly stopped paying. According to a report in the trade press, when Pepsi stopped paying there were public demonstrations, their bottling plants were attacked with grenades, their lorries were burned, and their executives hired bodyguards before fleeing the country.[14]

The important thing to remember when using sweepstakes, games, or contests is that they must be *fully integrated* with the brand's other marketing communications, and consistent with the brand's image. A sweepstakes where the prize is a trip to an exotic island would be great for a brand like Mars' Bounty chocolate bar because Bounty has a history of using exotic island imagery in its marketing communication. It would not be appropriate for a skiware brand, where a better prize would be a ski holiday.

Legal requirements are a real concern with sweepstakes, games, and contests. Unlike other consumer promotions, there are usually a number of legal restrictions concerning the wording, rules of compliance, and odds of winning; and these can differ among countries. As one lawyer specializing in these promotions has put it, after you have set your objective and outlined the sweepstake, game, or contest, your next step should be to involve a legal expert. From a legal standpoint, it is the rules of the promotion that are most critical. Even if you have run the same promotion in the past, it is best to check because even a seemingly insignificant change may mean that a new law applies. This is even more the case as the European Union adds a new level of regulation to the market.

Sweepstakes, games, and contests have the ability to help create excitement about a brand, and this can help reinforce the image of the brand, all at a relatively low cost. But the reward is limited to a small number of people and is delayed.

Premiums

There are many types of premiums, as well as any number of ways of delivering them to the consumer. Using premiums as a consumer promotion helps facilitate purchase, by offering the premium as a reward. Premiums may be free, or require a small payment from the consumer beyond the purchase price of the brand. When the consumer pays something, this is known as a self-liquidating premium because the price asked of the consumer is set to cover the cost of the premium to the brand. Because of the volume-buying power of the company offering the premium, coupled with potential discounts for joint merchandising (after all, the product offered as a premium is being promoted as well), the price to the consumer will be significantly less than they would otherwise be required to pay (usually 30 to 50 per cent of the retail price). Obviously a self-liquidating premium is not as attractive as a free premium. But if the premium is well matched to the promoted brand there should be interest among the target audience. The important thing, whether the premium is free or self-liquidating, is that the target audience perceives a real *value* in the offer.

Premium promotions have the advantage of creating excitement for a brand, especially if the premium is available at the point of purchase. This, however, can be complicated by the need for more retail space to accommodate the premiums, with no direct return on that space to the retailer. Mail-in requests for premiums with proof of purchase has the advantage of rewarding customers without the need for extra retail space, but the reward is delayed. Regardless of the type of premium, it should be supported by advertising and in-store merchandising, as well as being integrated into the brand's overall marketing communication.

As with all promotions, you must carefully plan any premium offer. The now classic case of Hoover's 1992 promotion illustrates just what can happen if you do not plan well. In the UK they offered '2 free flights to the US'—airline tickets worth £400, as a premium for buying any Hoover vacuum cleaner costing more than £100. The promotion was budgeted at £500,000. What the consumer quickly did was redefine the promotion as '2 tickets to the U.S. for £100' and set off to buy a new Hoover whether they needed one or not. Demand quickly strained supply and dealers began to increase the price of Hoover models originally priced at less than £100 so they would qualify for the promotions.

It is estimated that over 200,000 people tried to take advantage of this offer. One story has it that a man whose ticket had not arrived in the mail as promised telephoned Hoover customer service for a repairman. When the repairman turned up the man impounded his van until his tickets were sent. What was to have been a £500,000 promotion ended up costing £48 *million*, and, you can bet, a number of marketing jobs at Hoover. Add to this the bad publicity and the fact that the promotion was *totally unrelated* to Hoover or vacuum cleaners, and this stands as a real marketing disaster.[15] You can (and should) purchase insurance against potential problems and monetary losses associated with promotions, but the best insurance is careful planning and testing.

Trial and Repeat Purchase Objectives for Consumer Promotions

Back when we were discussing target audience buyer groups in Chapter 5, we introduced the idea of trial vs. repeat purchase objectives. New category users, other brand switchers, and other-brand loyals must try the brand, a *trial* objective; brand switchers and brand loyals must continue to buy the brand, a *repeat purchase* objective. Consumer promotion strategy must address these objectives, because certain consumer promotions are more applicable than others to stimulating trial or repeat purchase.

Actually, almost any consumer promotion should help generate trial or encourage repeat purchase. For example, while loyalty programmes are clearly designed to encourage and promote repeat purchase of and loyalty to a brand, if the loyalty programme is seen by non-users as particularly attractive, it could also encourage trial. Equally, while coupons are effective in attracting trial, they also encourage repeat purchase by existing customers by effectively reducing the price. All marketing communication should be encouraging a more positive brand attitude leading to continued purchase, but a repeat purchase promotion is a *tactical* tool to energize immediate repurchase. Yet in a marketing sense we must look at promotions for repeat purchase to generate *additional* purchases *beyond* what the brand's customers would normally buy as a result of their favourable brand attitude.

When we speak of a type of promotion being more oriented toward trial or repeat purchase, what we are talking about are general strengths. If we look at the six basic types of consumer promotions, coupons, sampling, and refunds are strong candidates for trial, while sweepstakes and loyalty promotions are best suited to repeat purchase. Premiums are a little more difficult to place because they can really be effective for either objective. An appropriately chosen premium could have a strong appeal to Other-brand Switchers, providing just the incentive to get them to try our brand along with the others they use. On the other hand, especially for more durable products with longer purchase cycles, a well-targeted premium could indeed get previous buyers to purchase again now. The

Table 12.2 Strengths of the Six Basic Consumer Promotions in Terms of Trial and Repeat Purchase

Trial Strength	Repeat Purchase Strength
Coupons	Sweepstakes
Refunds and Rebates	Loyalty and loading devices
Sampling	Premiums
Premiums	

strengths of the six basic types of consumer promotion relative to trial and repeat purchase objectives are summarized in Table 12.2.

Consumer Promotion for Trial

Of the three traditional consumer promotions, *sampling* is probably the most effective, for trial closely followed by *coupons*. When trial is low, sampling can be particularly effective, especially when, as noted earlier, a brand has a demonstrable and easily discernible benefit that will be apparent when sampled. Does your brand of deodorant really last longer? Are your pickled cucumbers actually crisper? Does your cleanser brand dissolve grease spots effectively? In cases like these, sampling makes the benefit claim believable. While coupons are somewhat less effective than sampling at generating trial, they do have the advantage of being much less expensive to implement, and, because of the price-off incentive, are especially effective when introducing new products.

Because of the delayed nature of *refunds* and *rebates* they do not provide as strong an inducement for trial of fmcg's, but they can be very helpful in encouraging trial of high-involvement product categories. Refunds and rebates are also extremely effective as a defensive tactic against strong competition when the category purchase cycle is long, as it is with consumer durables.

Consumer Promotion for Repeat Purchase

Strategically, repeat purchase consumer promotions are used for more targeted, short-term objectives. Unlike trial promotions, which are designed to attract new customers to the brand, repeat purchase premiums are used to affect the *timing* of purchases by brand users. You want your customers either to buy now, effectively removing them from the market in the short term to avoid switching, or to buy continual with little or no switching. Loyalty promotions are the most effective for helping ensure consistent repeat purchase of a brand. Loading devices, sweepstakes, games, and contests are more appropriate to minimizing brand switching—drawing customers to our brand on the next purchase.

Brand Equity and Consumer Promotion

Perhaps the most important long-term benefit of building a positive brand attitude is something known in marketing as *brand equity*. Many books and articles have been written on this subject,[16] so we shall not attempt to deal extensively with it here. But it is important to understand that while the principal strength of traditional advertising is building brand attitude and thus brand equity (as we shall see in Chapter 14), effective consumer promotions should also help contribute to positive brand attitude and the resulting brand equity. This idea was recognized many years ago by R. M. Prentice, a marketer in the US who talked about something he called 'consumer franchise building' promotions.[17] The point he made was that regardless of the tactical nature of consumer promotions, you should not lose the opportunity the promotion provides for helping strengthen or build a brand's 'consumer franchise' This idea is what is generally understood today as brand equity, and what follows from a strong positive brand attitude. We are in total agreement with Chuck Middlestadt, whose long career as a managing director with the Interpublic Group of Companies included many years in Germany, that 'Promotions must be as creative as image advertising, and fully as effective in building brand equity.'[18]

How Consumer Promotions Can Help Build Brand Equity

By their very nature, coupons and refunds and rebates encourage positive brand attitude by offering the brand at a discount. But to be truly effective, they must be tied to the brand's other marketing communication, especially advertising, and *include* the brand's benefit claim as part of the promotion execution. This means the benefit claim should be *on the coupon* or refund offer, and the brand name used in such a way as to reflect the appropriate brand awareness objective. Remember, brand awareness must always be paired with brand attitude and must be as seriously considered in promotions as any other form of marketing communication. Without the appropriate link to brand awareness, there can be no brand equity building.

The use of FSIs to deliver coupons provides an excellent opportunity to underscore a brand's message, but the benefit claim must also be on the coupon itself. It is the coupon that will be detached and referred to, and that is where you want your claim. Too often coupons and refund or rebate offers rely almost entirely upon the discount. What is needed is an integration of the discount with something positive about the brand. They should not be seen as 'just a price-off deal'. It should be a part of a total effort to build positive brand attitude and brand equity. Unfortunately, especially with refunds and rebates, this is not often the case.

Most loyalty and loading devices should also automatically affect brand attitude in a positive way because you are offering a reward to your customers. When you are using a loading device such as a bonus pack there is an excellent opportunity to reinforce the brand's benefit claim in connection with the 'bonus' on the package. For example, in an advert which ran in a Swedish magazine for Flora (a non-dairy spread) the benefit claim is made in the headline, 'A simple exercise for lowering cholesterol', and the ad shows a hand lifting the lid from a container of Flora. This same illustration could be used on a bonus pack wrap, incorporating the benefit claim and the bonus via a banner such as 'Even *more* opportunities for lowering cholesterol'. In such a hypothesized example, the benefit claim and illustration is repeated from the advert, reinforcing the message *and* linking the benefit with the bonus.

If a promotion is not well planned, a negative, not positive effect upon brand attitude could result. As we mentioned, this seems to have happened with many frequent flyer programmes. Loyalty promotions work (or should work) by providing an ongoing opportunity for building positive brand attitude and brand equity through programme newsletters, as well as providing positive reinforcement through programme rewards. If the programme is not a positive and reinforcing experience, the promotion will be a failure in terms of building brand equity even if it continues to retain customers because of the perceived high cost of switching to another brand's loyalty programme.

The potential for a loading device to have a negative effect upon brand equity is not as great, but could happen. For example, if a brand has a premium image but is often seen being promoted with price packs or bonus packs, this could tend to lower its premium image. While this can happen any time price-off promotions are used too often, with loading devices the lower price is visually reinforced *on the package*.

Sampling and premiums should also in and of themselves contribute to a positive brand attitude. The consumer is getting something for nothing, or something desirable at a significantly reduced price in the case of a self-liquidating premium. When used in connection with the introduction of a new product, sampling also has the advantage of quickly establishing brand attitude, especially for fmcg's. The sample package and merchandising, and other marketing communication, associated with sampling and premium promotions also provide a good opportunity for linking the brand's benefit claim with the sample or premium reward.

Premiums are not only effective as a consumer promotion, but can also be especially strong in building positive brand attitude when the premium appeals to the same underlying motivation as the promoted brand. When premiums are offered that are congruent with the motivation driving brand category purchase this helps ensure a positive brand attitude and support for brand equity. The most common mistake with premiums is when the one selected is not related to the brand in some meaningful way, including the motivation that drives brand choice. But the biggest mistake is made when the premium offered is inappropriate or unappealing. This could actually undermine brand equity by nurturing a negative brand attitude.

Sweepstakes, games, and contests operate on brand equity in a somewhat different way from other consumer promotions. The association with positive brand attitude is largely through advertising or other marketing communication that announces the promotion. The actual sweepstakes, game, or contest should of course be created around the brand's benefit claim, but it is the *integration* of the promotion with other marketing communication that provides the basis for affecting brand equity.

Direct Marketing

To many marketing managers, direct marketing means direct mail. Although direct mail is the most popular medium for direct marketing (telemarketing is a close second[19]), it is only one of many. Direct marketing is a very specific *means* of marketing communication, and may include elements of both advertising and promotion, although historically it is thought of more in terms of promotion.

So what exactly is direct marketing? According to the Direct Marketing Association in the US, direct marketing is:

An accountable system of marketing which uses one or more communications media to effect response. It is an interactive process where responses from or about buyers are recorded in a database for building profiles of potential customers and providing valuable marketing information for more efficient targeting.

The really important parts of this definition are two interrelated terms: 'interactive process' and 'database'. We shall deal with them in more detail later when we talk about the database in direct marketing, but first we will take a more general look at direct marketing.

Implicit in the DMA's definition of direct marketing is that it is an *ongoing* process. While direct marketing may be used tactically, it must be a part of a brand's longer-term strategic marketing communication planning. This is underscored when you consider the cost of delivering an effective direct marketing programme. As an executive of a major direct marketing company has pointed out, it is hard for marketing managers to adjust to spending as much as *25 times more* per response than they are used to paying for responses to other marketing communication programmes.[20] For example, direct mail has been shown to be a very cost-effective method for direct marketing, but it is still difficult for marketing managers to budget so much more than they are accustomed to paying for other mediums on a cost-per-thousand-exposure basis. It must be remembered that effective direct marketing builds a foundation for the future, and will more than pay for itself.

There are several fundamental strategic differences between direct marketing and more traditional forms of marketing communication such as advertising. The most important of these is that rather than trying to influence brand purchase intentions over multiple exposures, direct marketing usually relies upon a single exposure to generate a response. Whether the desired response is to place an order, call for more information, or visit a dealer, the target audience is expected to *do it now*.

Target audiences are much more tightly targeted with direct marketing than with traditional advertising. You address the target audience in a more precise way about their particular needs, and never in the third person. Another difference is the way in which distribution is treated. With direct marketing, distribution itself can become a benefit claim, as in 'not available in stores'. In a very real way, direct marketing media are used *as the marketplace*, in contrast to advertising, where distribution is used to define the marketplace. These differences are summarized in Table 12.3.

Table 12.3 Fundamental Strategic Differences between Direct Marketing and Advertising

	Direct Marketing	**Advertising**
Exposure	Single exposure	Multiple exposure
Action	Immediate	Eventually
Target Audience	Tightly targeted	Widely targeted
Distribution	Media is the marketplace	Distribution defines the marketplace

Using Direct Marketing

In considering direct marketing as part of an integrated marketing communication programme, there are three questions the manager must ask (see Table 12.4). First, does direct marketing make any sense given the brand's communication objectives? We have just reviewed a number of strategic differences between advertising and direct marketing. Obviously, if you are addressing a mass audience, direct marketing is not likely to be as effective as other means of marketing communication. Also, given the tactical nature of direct marketing, brand purchase intention is the most appropriate communication objective. If brand attitude is the primary objective, (remember it is *always* an objective, along with brand awareness, even if something else is the primary objective) direct marketing is likely to be less effective than other means of marketing communication.

If direct marketing does make sense for a brand's marketing communication programme, the next question is whether or not a good database for the target audience is available. If the brand has used direct marketing in the past, then an updated database should be available. If not, you must be able to acquire or build a target list before you can even think about developing a direct marketing programme. This suggests that even if direct marketing is not currently a part of a brand's marketing communication efforts, it will still make sense to develop a database for possible future use. The importance of a good list for direct marketing cannot be understated. Studies have shown that the quality of a list accounts for some 40 per cent of the effectiveness of a direct marketing campaign, equal to the 40 per cent attributed to the headline of the message (the remainder of the message accounts for the other 20 per cent).[21] We shall look more closely at databases later in the chapter.

If direct marketing makes sense for the brand and you have a good database, the final question to ask is how you will deliver the message. There are four basic direct marketing media available: direct mail, telemarketing, mass media, and interactive media. Generally only one of these four media will be used for a particular direct marketing programme. An exception would be if various segments of the target audience are more easily reached with one medium than another. Each of these four basic types of direct marketing media are reviewed next (see Table 12.5).

Direct Mail

We have already noted that direct mail is the most popular direct marketing medium. This stems in large part from its ability to target an audience effectively while providing broad latitude for creative options in delivering the message. Direct mail can be used to

Table 12.4 Questions Managers Must Ask When Considering Direct Marketing

---

- Does direct marketing make sense given the brand's communication objectives?
- Is there a good database available for the target audience?
- How will you deliver the message?

Table 12.5 Four Basic Types of
Direct Marketing Media

- Direct Mail
- Telemarketing
- Mass Media
- Interactive

deliver almost any type of message, and through a wide variety of means: everything from flyers and brochures to videos or CD-ROMs for computers.

Telemarketing

While a close second to direct mail, telemarketing doesn't offer the same flexibility in delivering a message. What it does offer is the ability to actively converse with the consumer. This has the advantage of immediate feedback, which can be used to adjust and more finely tune a message. This interaction also enables effective telemarketing callers to deal with concerns and questions from target audience members as they come up. This, of course, requires well-trained people making the telephone calls. When we think of telemarketing, we generally think of what is known as *outbound* telemarketing, where the marketer initiates the calls, as opposed to *inbound* telemarketing, where the marketer answers calls from the target audience that have been generated by such things as toll-free numbers. A real disadvantage with telemarketing is the inability to use visual material.

Mass Media

Any mass medium could be used for direct marketing; the difference is in *how* it is used. Direct marketing is looking for the ability to target the market tightly, and to optimize *immediate response*. In the past television was rarely used in direct marketing. However, with the increasing potential for better targeting with specialized cable channels, along with the ability to run longer commercials (up to two minutes or longer) on cable, direct marketing is finding a use for television. Another growing phenomenon on cable television is the so-called 'infomercial'. This is basically a direct marketing pitch for a product lasting as long as thirty minutes, and made to look like regular programmeming. Infomercials are a growing trend, even among well-known brands, and are expected to continue.[22] In fact, there is a 24-hour cable channel in the US that shows nothing but infomercials!

Radio, as you might imagine, is not often considered for direct marketing. The obvious reason is the difficulty in generating an immediate response. Yet radio does have the advantage of tight targeting, and radio messages can be produced and aired quickly when necessary. If you can overcome the passive nature of radio with a good creative execution, radio can be effective.

Of the four principal mass media, the newspaper is probably the one used most often for direct marketing. It offers a brand the ability to insert a message of almost any length, from a single page to multi-page brochures complete with order blanks and return envelopes for posting, and it can be printed on almost any paper stock, not just newsprint. With newspapers you can also tightly control the timing of the delivery. The disadvantage is the lack of specific targeting ability beyond geographic areas, and the shrinking base of newspaper readership. Magazines offer just the opposite. They provide a highly targeted audience but lack the ability to control the timing as tightly. Magazines do not appear as frequently as newspapers, and require much longer lead times for delivering the inserts.

Interactive Media

Although they do not play a large part yet in direct marketing, interactive media are sure to be an increasingly important part of direct marketing in the future. The pace of new technology almost guarantees it. Yet without knowing what technological advances may bring, managers should be cautious about how large a role interactive media are likely to play, not only in direct marketing, but in traditional advertising as well. These media are perfect for immediate response, but difficult to control delivery of the message.

Today, CD-ROM catalogues are available for Internet shopping by those with CD-ROM-equipped computers. Almost anyone with a computer will have access to the Internet, and many big-name brands now use the Internet for direct marketing. The biggest problem for direct marketing on the Internet is how to target your market tightly enough, and creatively, how to persuade them to respond now. As one web catalogue executive has said, encouraging people to look through a catalogue on the Internet is not the problem, but 'getting them to buy is hard because they might not be direct response buyers'.[23]

Databases

The definition by the Direct Marketing Association suggests that having a database lies at the heart of direct marketing. It is important to understand, however, that although a database is necessary for direct marketing, databases can be and are used in a number of other ways in marketing (often referred to as 'database marketing'). In other words, just because you are using a database does not mean you are necessarily engaged in direct marketing. It is also important to understand that a database is not just another name for a mailing list. In direct marketing a database provides much more than a name and address. There will be details of past and current purchase behaviour and other information about each person in the database that helps better target consumers with appropriate messages. Using databases in direct marketing is also a dynamic process. Every time it is used, the database is updated and re-evaluated. Obviously, the most effective databases are computer-driven, although direct marketing used paper files on consumers for a long time before computers become so accessible and cost-effective.

To build an effective database you must begin with a list. A brand can develop its own list, or buy or rent one to get started. But a good list is not enough. It must be fully *analysed* in order to best understand how to use it most effectively. What part of the list will be most appropriate for a particular direct marketing campaign? What does the list tell you about the consumer that might influence the nature of the direct marketing effort?

Once the list has been analysed, the appropriate part is used in implementing the programme. Then, *analyse the results*. Remember one of the key parts of the definition of direct marketing is *accountability*. How effective was the information in the database in generating a response? Is there any information within the database that might help explain any unexpected response (whether good or bad)? Finally, after the results of the direct marketing programme have been analysed, use that information to *update* the information in the database. This is a perfect opportunity to track those who do not respond to a particular type of message, as well as response rates and patterns. These steps for building a strong database are summarized in Table 12.6. In following them, a brand is always building its database.

Databases are essential for direct marketing, but they are also strategically useful in identifying opportunities for direct marketing. A good database helps identify consumers who make multiple or repeat purchases. By looking at purchase patterns, if you see that purchase cycles are short, using direct marketing may not be cost-effective. On the other hand, if the purchase cycle is too long, it may not pay to use direct marketing because too few people may be in the market at any one time. Of course, if it made cost sense, you could certainly target those who *should* be in the market, based upon their past behaviour. Analysing the database in this way enables the manager to do a cost analysis relative to the likelihood of a response given known purchase behaviour. It also permits direct marketing efforts as a defensive move against competitors' promotions when you can predict times your customers are most likely to be in the market. Finally, by its very nature, a good database provides background information that might suggest opportunities for direct marketing to specific segments or market niches.

Disadvantages of Direct Marketing

There is no question that the growth of direct marketing has been fuelled by advances in technology, especially computer-driven systems and software. But there are some disadvantages that should be considered. The first is the image of some direct marketing media. Remember, consumers do not distinguish one type of marketing communication from another. Marketing managers may call a direct mail campaign a promotion, or it may be direct marketing, but the consumer is more likely to see any such mailing as 'junk mail'. The image of telemarketing is even worse. Those on the Internet are likely to see unsolicited e-mail from a brand as an unwanted intervention by 'spammers' (indiscriminate senders of e-mail). We have also pointed out that direct marketing can be expensive compared to other forms of marketing communication. Still, when carefully considered and planned, direct marketing can be an important and effective part of a brand's marketing communication effort.

Table 12.6 Steps for Building a Strong Database

1. Develop a good list for the target market
2. Fully analyse the list **before** using it
3. Analyse the results **after** using the list
4. Use the analysis to update the database

Summary

In this chapter we have considered the tactical use of promotion techniques and described the strengths and weaknesses of a variety of promotion types. In particular, we analysed the six fundamental types of consumer promotion: coupons, rebates and refunds, sampling, loyalty and loading devices, sweepstakes, and premiums. We then went on to discuss direct marketing and its use in relation to the brand's communication objectives.

Questions to consider

12.1 Why is time an important consideration in relation to promotions?

12.2 What are the three basic categories of trade promotions?

12.3 What is meant by channels marketing?

12.4 What are the six types of traditional consumer promotions?

12.5 What is the typical redemption rate for money-off coupons?

12.6 What is the objective of using Consumer Loading Devices?

12.7 What is a self-liquidating premium?

12.8 Why is it important to carefully plan and test promotions?

12.9 What is the most important strategic difference between direct marketing and advertising?

Notes

1 See Peter Simmons, 'Sales Promotion in Marketing', in N. Hart (ed.), *The Practice of Advertising*, 4th edn. (Oxford: Butterworth Heinemann, 1995), 249.

2 See L. Percy, *Strategies for Implementing Integrated Marketing Communication* (Lincolnwood, Ill.: NTC Business Books, 1997), 95.

3 See Simmons, 'Sales Promotion in Marketing', 251.

4 See ibid. 256, and Percy, *Strategies for Implementing Integrated Marketing Communication*, 96.

5 Simmons makes an interesting point in his discussion of sales promotion, pointing out that promotions are also directed toward employees, either for individual performance or for group performance; see 'Sales Promotion in Marketing'.

6 The advantages of positioning a package on the shelf at eye-level were demonstrated in a study conducted by *Progressive Grocer*, and is discussed by J. R. Rossiter and L. Percy in *Advertising Communication and Promotion Management* (New York: McGraw-Hill, 1997), 356.

7   In the US a 1995 study of consumer buying habits conducted by the P-O-P Advertising Institute found that more than 70% of brand choices are made in the store.

8   See Blattberg, Eppeu, and Lieberman, 'A Theoretical and Empirical Evaluation of Price Deals for Consumer Nondurables', *Journal of Marketing*, 45:1, (1981), 116–29.

9   See C. M. Henderson, 'Promotion Heterogeneity and Consumer Learning: Refining the Dual-proveness Construct', in C. T. Allen and D. Roedder John (eds.), *Advances in Consumer Research*, vol. 21 (Provo, Utah: Association for Consumer Research, 1994), 86–94.

10 This is a point made by Rossiter and Percy in a review of several studies dealing with the effect of displays without accompanying price reductions: see *Advertising Communication and Promotion Management*, 390.

11 See A. Krishna, F. S. Currin, and R. W. Shoemaker, 'Consumer Perceptions of Promotional Activity', *Journal of Marketing*, 55 (1991), 14–16.

12 See Chris Fill, *Marketing Communications: Frameworks, Theories, and Applications* (London: Prentice Hall, 1995), 376.

13 Paul Smith relates a number of stories of disastrous promotions in his book *Marketing Communications: An Integrated Approach*, 2nd edn. (London: Kogan Page, 1998).

14 This story of the Pepsi Philippine subsidary promotion was reported in *Precision Marketing*, 26 May 1997.

15 There are many references to this by-now-infamous Hoover promotion, including an editorial by K. Newman in the *International Journal of Advertising*, 15:2 (1993), 94, and 'Hoover and its Publicity Stunt Dive', in *Marketing* (UK), 8 Apr. 1993, 18.

16 One of the first books on brand equity, and still very good, is Dave Aaker's *Managing Brand Equity* (New York: The Free Press, 1991).

17 See R. M. Prentice, 'How to Split Your Marketing Funds Between Advertising and Promotion', *Advertising Age*, Jan. 1977, 41.

18 These comments were made in an unpublished lecture given at Yale University, 'The Coming Era of Image-Building Brand Promotion', 3 Mar. 1993.

19 Data reported for the UK in 1996 by the Direct Marketing Association listed direct mail expenditures at £1,459,000 versus £1,305,000 for telemarketing.

20 See J. W. Pickholz, 'From the Practitioners', *Journal of Direct Marketing*, 8:2 (1994).

21 See B. Lamons, 'Creativity is Important to Direct Marketing Too', *Marketing News*, 7 Dec. 1992, 10.

22 See K. Cleland, 'More Advertisers Put Infomercials in their Plans', *Ad Age*, 18 Sept. 1995, 50.

23 See C. Miller, 'Marketers Find it Hip to be on the Internet', *Marketing News*, 27 Feb. 1995, 2.

Chapter 13

Creative Execution

Many people are involved in the strategic planning and development of a marketing communication campaign, but when it comes to executing the strategy, producing the actual adverts and promotions, this is the job of the 'creatives'. For many, this is really what advertising is all about. But it is important to remember that the most brilliant creative execution, if it is *not consistent with the strategy*, cannot compete with even an average creative execution that is.

Everything we have been talking about so far in this book has dealt with the necessary tools for developing the right creative strategy for a brand. As we shall see in this chapter, all of this work is summarized in a single page, the creative brief. Once the creative idea is formed and executed, the result will (or should) be tested to ensure it is indeed on strategy.

But who is it that actually generates the creative executions used in marketing communications? Usually what comes to mind are the art directors and copywriters at advertising agencies—the 'creatives'. But we need to remember that a great deal of advertising is actually created by people who do not work for an advertising agency. Many large companies have in-house agencies where both the creation and media placement of advertising is handled by the advertiser on its own. Retail stores will frequently employ creative people to generate the many, many adverts they run in daily newspapers. Often small business advertising is created for the advertiser by the media that run it. For example, radio or television stations will develop advertising for a company, and the Yellow Pages have creative people who will develop small adverts for use in their books.

In today's advertising world, and especially in Europe, there has been an interesting trend. Many advertisers no longer use their advertising agency for traditional media planning and buying functions (as we have already seen). Rather, they are turning more and more to specialized media institutes, using their agencies only for the development and execution of creative ideas. But now it would seem that these media institutes are beginning to have a hand in overall strategic planning, and are even advising marketers on their creative product! It is almost as if the media institutes are beginning to 'morph' into traditional full-service advertising agencies.

But regardless of where the advertising is created, two basic functions will be involved: writing the copy and laying out a print advert or developing the visual content of a commercial. With smaller advertisers, the entire creative function may rest with a single individual. At large advertising agencies there may be teams of copywriters and art directors working with production experts and directors to develop and execute a campaign.

Creative executions spring from a creative idea.[1] These creative ideas may come from a variety of sources, and manifest themselves in any number of ways. But in the end, a creative idea *must be consistent* with the communication strategy and brand position. It is very important that creative thinking does not begin until a creative brief has been agreed upon. It is the creative brief, as we shall see shortly, that helps guide the *direction* the creative execution must take in order to satisfy the strategy. With the creative brief in hand, the creative team assigned to the campaign can go to work.

At its most basic level, a creative execution is simply made up of words and pictures brought together in a creative way to attract and hold the attention of a target audience, and to satisfy the communication objective. You will remember we spent a great deal of time discussing the tactics involved with this in Chapter 11. While occasionally you might find an advert with no words or one with no picture (other than radio, where it is of course not possible), all marketing communication will generally utilize both words and pictures. Obvious, of course. But this is also why it is so very important for both copywriters and art directors to work closely together in the creation of marketing communication. In fact, in some advertising agencies, creative teams may actually share the same office.

Creative teams, however, are not always completely free to execute an advert in any way they would like. Particularly with corporate or business-to-business advertising, companies may have guidelines where particular requirements for the layout and execution of advertising are given, often as detailed as the type of font that is required. Creatives, with some justification, often feel constrained by such rules. While truly good creative people will always be able to work effectively, regardless of the boundaries, these so-called 'style books' are much too restrictive, and should not be used. The reasoning behind them is usually given as ensuring a consistent look to campaigns. But as we shall see in the next section, this is not what ensures a consistent 'look and feel' to creative executions.

One of the areas that almost always falls under some advertiser restrictions, however, is the tagline, corporate signature, or logo. It is not unusual for advertisers to specify the size of the logo or tag. We do not endorse this, but at the same time you should never permit any creative licence with the tag or logo itself. Creative people should be involved in the original development of the tagline or logo, but once established it should remain consistent in all creative executions until it is changed.

Consistency in Creative Executions

One of the most important aspects of effective creative executions within a marketing communication programme and over time is *consistency*. Within a campaign, all executions must have a consistent look and feel. Whether adverts, promotions, collateral, or even packages, there should be a consistency about them that enables the target audience to recognize it immediately as coming from the brand.

Consistency and Brand Awareness

Consistency over creative executions in a campaign and over time is very important for brand awareness. You will remember from Chapter 7, when we discussed positioning, and Chapter 8, when we talked about brand awareness, the importance of establishing the appropriate link between category need and brand awareness. Consistency in creative executions enables the look and feel conveyed by the execution to quickly establish and reinforce this linkage. When a consistent look and feel to a brand's creative execution has been established, brand awareness will be triggered by the execution itself, without actual reference to the brand name. The brand name will only confirm what has been triggered by the look of the advertising.

Perhaps the best example of this is the long-running series of adverts for Silk Cut (a UK tobacco brand). For years their advertising has featured little more than some combination of scarlet silk and a 'cut'. They have now reached the point where they no longer even include the brand name. The consistent imagery of the scarlet silk and 'cut' automatically communicates the brand name. It is almost ironic to see a two-page advert in a magazine with nothing but a wave of scarlet silk and a pair of scissors . . . and a government health warning about the dangers of tobacco use.

Actually, a consistent visual or pictorial feel in marketing communication has been found to be a faster trigger for brand identification than the actual brand name or company logo, because memory for visuals is superior to memory for encoded labels or words in general. Interestingly, over half of the brain's cortex is used for the processing of visual images.[2] What we are looking for is a general recognition on the part of the target audience that the pictorial or visual execution belongs to the brand. That is what permits variation in the executions. It is not necessary or even desirable for all of the creative executions to look the 'same', only that they reflect the same overall look and feel. In fact, if the executions in a campaign are seen as too similar, the campaign will tend to 'wear out' faster. Rather, you want enough variation in the executions so that they remain fresh, and can be extended over time.

The print adverts shown in Advert 13.1 provide a good example of what we are talking about. Here are three adverts for Kenco coffee. It is freeze-dried coffee, not fresh-ground, but the imagery evokes the desired benefit of fresh-brewed (something we will be covering next). There is a good deal of variation in the executions, yet they retain the same look and feel. Note too that the same look is given both their regular coffees and their decaffeinated.

Consistency and Brand Attitude

Just as with brand awareness, consistency in the look and feel of creative executions is important for brand attitude. We briefly mentioned above the dominance of visual elements in memory. Pictures may be thought of as 'quick shots' into memory. Studies of print adverts with eye-tracking cameras have consistently shown that on average some 70 per cent of the time spent looking at an advert is spent with the picture. As you might imagine, the visual element in advertising is critical to effective communication.

Building upon this understanding of the power of visual elements in effective

13.1 Three adverts for Kenco Coffee illustrating a consistent look and feel based upon imagery associated with the benefit of fresh-brewed taste. Courtesy Kenco

marketing communication, it is desirable to find an image that the target audience readily associates with a brand's primary or key benefit. This is not as easy as it may seem at first glance. We are not looking for just any image that reflects the brand's benefit, but one that is *unique* to the brand. We know from our discussion of positioning in Chapter 7 that we should seek a unique benefit for our brand, and if that is not possible, at least to execute the benefit claim uniquely. This last is absolutely essential.

Because it is rather easy to identify 'ideal attributes', too often most brands in a category will focus upon the same basic benefit (or set of benefits). Advertisers are likely to fall back on clichés when dealing with a benefit. Truck manufacturers know truck buyers want a 'tough truck' so they all tend to show their truck travelling easily over the roughest terrain, or pulling or carrying incredible loads (or even both!). These clichés then become an image for the category, and do not help any individual 'name plate' (what automobile and truck companies call their brands) communicate that they are 'tougher' than any other.

So how can managers avoid this problem? One way is to conduct research that is designed to identify visual images that are associated with the desired benefit. This type of research was pioneered in Germany by the late Werner Kroeber-Riel.[3] In his work he looked at what he defined as three levels of schema: learned, cultural, and biological. What this means is that in our memory we have some things we have learned which tend to be restricted to a particular group to which we belong (learned schema). Some things in memory are culturally determined, and are found in such things as the myths and arts of a culture (cultural schemata), and others are there because we are human, and tend to rely upon deeply psychological responses that have a relatively strong impact upon behaviour *without* our conscious awareness (biological schema).

This means that people may react to an image in terms of things they have learned to associate with a particular group or thing, their culture, or innate psycho-biological responses. Let us look at some examples of what we are talking about. If you are a real fan of a particular football team, certain associations or images linked to that team are likely to mean something much different to you than to others who are not fans of that team, and have not learned those same associations. We all can think of cultural stereotypes, but cultural schema can be much more subtle. If a group of Eastern Europeans saw a crowd of people all pushing in a mass to enter the just-opened doors of a theatre, it would seem perfectly normal. But if an English group were to observe this, they would be surprised at the seemingly unruly behaviour because the English queue up under these circumstances. There is not a 'correct' behaviour here, the response will depend upon cultural schema.[4]

At the biological schema or human level, we all respond to particular images in the same way. Basically, these are reactions that in some way relate to latent survival responses. This is why almost everyone reacts to an infant with a warm, nurturing feeling, and with alarm to the high-pitched cry of a baby. Some very fascinating work by Jay Appleton deals with this same idea.[5] He has developed something he calls Prospect and Refuge Theory. He suggests that we respond to our environment in terms of both prospect and refuge. When humans first wandered the plains, they needed to be able to see out to the horizon (prospect). This provided a sense of opportunity as well as ample warning of danger. Humans also needed a place to hide for security (refuge). Appleton argues that we still respond to our environment in these same ways, a response based upon biological schema, and recent empirical studies support him.[6] The implication of this work is significant. When people are looking at advertising, they are *unconsciously* reacting to the visual environment depicted. If we want the target audience to feel secure, the visual image should be consistent with refuge; if the target audience is to feel a sense of opportunity, the image should be consistent with prospect.[7]

In developing creative executions you must be certain that the message and image are compatible with the target audience's schema. Images that are used must be chosen to be consistent with the brand's key benefit, and the linkage to the benefit must be easily made by the target audience. When trying to identify a visual image to correspond with a brand's key benefit, what on the surface may seem appropriate may not in fact be so. A company marketing a very high-involvement product to corporate executives wanted to associate a key benefit of relaxation with their brand. They felt a picture showing a relaxed-looking executive, leaning against a door frame without his suit jacket, holding a newspaper and cup of coffee, would embody this benefit. But the target audience did not see a man relaxing. What they saw was a man in the morning before work, contemplating the stress of the day to come. Obviously, this was not the imagery the advertiser wished to convey. It is always important to check how your target audience responds to your creative executions. We will be dealing with this in more detail later in the chapter.

An exceptionally good example of finding the right imagery and using it consistently over time to reinforce brand attitude is the long-running campaign in the UK for Oxo beef cubes. Although the campaign finally came to an end in late 1999, it ran for over sixteen years. Beginning in 1983, the advertising featured a family's day-to-day life experiences, centred around meal-time. The campaign featured the same actors over the years, and the scenarios played out in the advertising were designed to tap situations easily identified with the target audience's own family life. In terms of execution, it was a perfect example of what we have described as the critical component of low-involvement, transformational advertising: it was 'real'. The look and feel evolved in keeping with the times as the actor family grew older, but it was always internally consistent and readily identifiable as Oxo advertising. There is ample evidence that this advertising made a significant contribution to the health and growth of the brand.[8]

Another excellent example comes from Vattenfall, the Swedish power company. As in much of Europe, and especially in Scandinavia, deregulation has come to many previously state-controlled monopolies. Deregulation of the power market in Sweden began in 1995 and was completed at the end of 1999. Now, people in Sweden are free to purchase electric power from any of more than a hundred international and Swedish providers.

Vattenfall had a real challenge. Historically, they were a state-controlled monopoly. But now they were faced with creating a positive *brand* attitude for an abstract product category that is basically a true commodity, electricity. In a highly creative way, Vattenfall associated themselves with the *benefits* of electric power, and linked the brand with the means of delivery in Sweden, the two holes of a wall socket. The campaign began with the introduction of the first stages of deregulation in 1995, utilizing a billboard featuring two black dots on a clean white surface and the company logo, nothing else (see Advert 13.2). The campaign then evolved, using print outdoor, television, and even the Internet, all built around 'two holes in the wall'. As you can see with the examples of adverts from the campaign (Advert 13.3), the executions evolve, but retain a consistent look and feel.

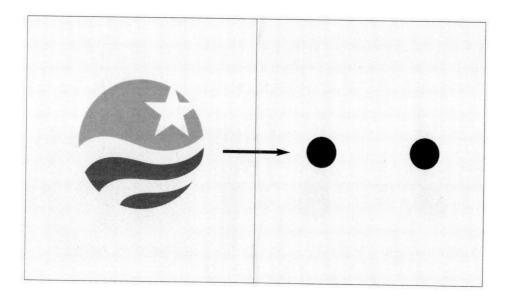

13.2 The initial advert in Vattenfall's campaign for the first stage in the deregulation of the power industry in Sweden. The two black dots represent the 'two holes in the wall' where you access electrical power. Courtesy Vattenfall

13.3 A series of adverts showing the development of the Vattenfall campaign over several years, illustrating the effective use of the 'two holes in the wall' to maintain a consistent look and feel to the advertising. Courtesy Vattenfall

The company has managed to build strong awareness *as a brand*, and to build a positive brand attitude under very difficult circumstances.

In summary, every creative execution for a brand must contribute to a consistent look and feel for that brand. While individual messages and executions may (and should) vary, the underlying theme must remain consistent, and the key to this consistent look and feel should be a visual image that is associated in the target audience's mind with the brand's primary benefit. Consistency in creative execution facilitates brand awareness and with the appropriate visual image also facilitates brand attitude. Every exposure of a brand's marketing communication, when seen within the context of a consistent, positive image, helps reinforce a favourable attitude toward the brand. This leads to a more receptive atmosphere for attending to the specific message content of the advertising.

Briefing the Creatives

Before turning our attention specifically to the creative briefing process, let us think about what O'Malley has called a contrasting style between those involved in strategy vs. those in creative.[9] He remarks that successful advertising comes from two contrasting styles of problem-solving, what psychologists have called convergent vs. divergent thinking. Convergent thinking is where you make deductions and draw logical conclusions from information. This is the type of thing we would expect from the strategist, and is inherent in most of what we have been talking about so far in this book. Divergent thinking is when you move outward from specific information to more broadly based generalization. This is the type of thing we expect from creatives. Of course, both types of thinking will be found in each group. But, overall, in our planning we are looking for convergent thinking to uncover the 'hot button' most likely to influence consumer behaviour and divergent thinking to drive creative executions that reflect this in an exciting or memorable way which will help facilitate the effective processing of the message. What we discuss next is how we transfer the fruits of the strategists' convergent thinking to the creatives in order to stimulate their more divergent thinking.

In almost every case, before creatives are asked to begin developing creative ideas, there will be a briefing. This may run from a very loosely written statement of objectives to a rather detailed, formal description of all the information which strategic people feel is important as background in understanding the nature of the consumer and advertised product.

While it is obviously quite important for those working on the creation of advertising to know as much as possible about a brand's market and the people who use the product, there is another, less tangible goal for the creative charge or brief. Creative people are always looking for the big idea, or at least some spark that will ignite the creative juices. The more a creative briefing includes unique and interesting facts about the product, brand, and consumer, the more likely the creatives will be to find that kernel of information that will spark the 'big idea' leading to effective execution. Really innovative briefings are considered so important by many advertising agencies, especially in England, that they make a point of spending a great deal of time on *how* they present the briefing. They are likely to go to great lengths in order to present the briefing to the creatives in interesting and exciting ways.

Areas that might be covered in a briefing include such things as:

- market characteristics
- consumer characteristics
- product characteristics
- brand positioning
- competitors' advertising
- communication objectives
- media considerations

Market characteristics. This is usually a background section that discusses what is going on in the market at the time. How big is it? Is it growing? Is it changing? What are the brand shares? Are attitudes changing? It is important that when creative people read this section they come away with a good feel for the market where the advertised product is sold.

Consumer characteristics. We have already spent an entire chapter talking about who makes up the target audience for a brand. This part of the creative briefing will certainly not go into that much detail, but it will provide a vivid portrait of whom we see as the most likely customers for our brand. This description will include not only traditional descriptors like age, family size, and income, but more qualitative description such as: how they feel about the product, how they go about making choices, the criteria that are important in choice, how they use the product, etc. For transformationally driven decisions, this will also include summaries of their dreams and desires—how the brand will 'transform' them.

Product characteristics. In this section the product itself will be described in detail. What can it do? How is it distributed? What are the specific attributes of the product? Are there real differences between brands? How is it packaged? How is it used?

Brand Positioning. Here you are interested in how the market sees your brand as well as its competition. This is very important information, because the advertising created must be consistent with the brand's current image in the market (as we have just seen in the last section); unless, of course, the strategy is to change it. But to change the brand's image is a very serious decision, and a very difficult job to accomplish. Generally speaking, radical departures from a brand positioning creates uncertainty in the market, and can erode the equity a brand has built over the years.

Competitors' advertising. It is very important to include a review of current and recent competitors' advertising in the charge to the creatives. This provides them with an idea of the general themes and executions that comprise the 'noise' or the environment within which the advertising they create will be seen. This review of competitors' advertising will also ensure that the new advertising which is created is different from their advertising in execution.

Communication objectives. As we learned in Chapter 8, creative work cannot begin until the communication objectives are set. It is the communication objectives that reflect where and how advertising and other forms of marketing communications will fit within the overall marketing plan.

Media considerations. While it is usually not necessary to restrict the creative department in terms of what media they should consider, often it is necessary to request specific media that they may not otherwise have considered. This is particularly true when your model of consumer decision-making has identified points within the decision process where such things as point-of-purchase collateral or direct mail might be effective, but also when something other than television or print is desired (for example outdoor or even radio, which is not often considered).

Other areas may also be covered in the creative briefing, but this outline should provide a guide to some of the more typical kinds of information that will be included. In addition to the creative briefing, a summary document should be provided that acts as the 'blueprint' for the creative executions. This is the creative brief.

The Creative Brief

Most advertising agencies, and many marketers as well (especially of fmcg's), have a specific outline they use for preparing a creative brief. There is no one 'correct' way of preparing a creative brief, but there are certain key areas that should be covered:

- What is the task at hand?
- What are the specific objectives and strategy?
- What, if anything, *must* the executions contain?

We shall now present a general outline for a creative brief that addresses these questions (see Fig. 13.1). It is important to understand that even though creative briefs are generally only associated with traditional advertising, they are equally necessary for promotion planning. In fact, a creative brief should be the basis for the development of all marketing communication. The outline that follows includes ten points, and while specific creative briefs used by advertising agencies and marketers may not look exactly like this, in general these areas will be addressed in their briefs.

Task Definition

The first four areas covered in our outline for a creative brief help you define the task at hand for the creatives. Here is where you are primarily concerned with important insights into the market and target audience. First, we want to identify a *key market observation.* What one point can be made about the market that will help those developing the creative execution understand and believe the brief? Next, what is the *source of business?* Where specifically does the brand expect to get business? This should not be general, but provide a quite specific definition. For example, a creative brief for a luxury sports car might see their source of business as current owners of competitors' luxury cars who are looking for something more exciting. You can see that for a creative brief you are trying to create *images* for the creatives. The third area seeks to provide a specific *consumer barrier or insight.* What one thing do you know about your target audience that would help reach

Brand:

Task Definition

Key Market Observation:
Source of Business:
Consumer Barrier or Insight:
Target Audience:

Objectives and Strategy

Communication Objectives and Tasks:
Brand Attitude Strategy:
Benefit Claim and Support:
Desired Consumer Response:

Execution

Creative Guidelines:
Requirements or Mandatory Content:

Fig. 13.1 Creative Brief

them; or is there something about them that we may need to overcome in order to communicate successfully with them? Finally, you will want to provide a vivid description of the *target audience*. You should provide enough information here so that the creatives can form a true understanding of whom they are to address.

Objectives and Strategy

The next section of the brief contains four points that are primarily concerned with developing the creative execution. Here is where you are laying out the creative objectives and strategy, the positioning, and the key benefits and support, along with the *one benefit* that, if communicated, will achieve your desired objective. First, what are the specific *communication objectives, and tasks*? Then, what specifically is the *brand attitude strategy*? Is the decision we are dealing with high- or low-involvement, positively or negatively motivated? Next, what is the *benefit claim and support*? This is by far the most difficult, and often contentious, area of the creative brief. Here is where the fruits of your positioning work are put into a few words that link the brand to the motivation. The benefit claim takes the benefit, what the consumer wants, and puts it in terms of the emotional response desired. This will be the heart of the creative execution. Finally, you address the *desired consumer response*. You want to provide a brief summary of what you expect to happen if the target audience successfully processes the message.

Execution

The last two areas covered in our creative brief deal with specific executional factors. Here is where you provide any specific *creative guidelines* that you want to be certain are considered in the execution. For example, this is a place where the look and feel of the brand's advertising may be detailed. The last area covered in the creative brief contains any *requirements or mandatory content*. Often companies have specific requirements for their logos or other layout constraints (although constraining creative layout or production technique is rarely a good idea, as we have mentioned) and these would be detailed here, along with any legal requirements.

Fig. 13.2 provides an actual example of a creative brief for a bank's telephone banking services that follows this outline. Perhaps the most important thing to notice about the brief is its size. It is complete on *one page*. In preparing a creative brief, there are really only two areas where a lot of detail may be needed: the description of the target audience and the *support* for the benefit claim. Otherwise, keep the creative brief to the bare essentials. There will always be plenty of backup available from the marketing plan and the communication strategy plan if the creatives want more. The key to an effective creative brief is that it is *brief*. This helps ensure that the information provided has been carefully considered.

Creative Research

With the creative brief in hand, the job of developing the creative execution begins. More often than not, creatives will come up with ideas on their own, although there are a number of research techniques available that can aid this process. If any research is likely to be done at the creative development stage, it will be to explore or screen concepts. Again, there are a number of procedures available to help here as well.[10] The most important thing to remember if you do conduct creative-ideation or concept-screening research is to conduct the research among a sample of the brand's target audience.

Once a concept has been agreed upon, one or more test executions will be developed. Actually, the more test executions created, the better, within reasonable constraints of time and cost.[11] While research may not have been involved in the development of the concept, it is *essential* that the test executions be pre-tested. A great deal of money will go into the production and media exposure of the final executions, and you will want to be as certain as possible that the creative execution satisfies the brief, meets the communication objective, and delivers the benefit claim in an understandable manner.

Many agencies and even marketers often do not feel it is necessary to pre-test their creative execution, feeling they can rely upon their experience and knowledge of the

Product	Job	Date
Telephone Banking		

Key Market Observations
Potential customers are probably going into branches to conduct business that could be done over the phone
Source of Business
Current bank checking account/current account customers
Consumer Insight
They are willing to use electronic devices, and are heavy users of ATMs
Target Audience
Loyal and vulnerable, profiled as young and middle-income 'full nest' households with busy lives
Communication Objectives and Tasks
Brand attitude primary objective—to reinforce overall IMC convenience positioning
Brand Attitude Strategy
Low-involvement/informational brand attitude strategy driven by motivation of incomplete satisfaction
Benefit Claim and Support
Telephone banking is more convenient. Support: pay bills almost any time as well as transact basic banking business at any time
Desired Consumer Response
See that telephone banking really is more convenient than branch banking and try
Creative Guidelines
Tie 'inconvenience' of banking to awareness of telephone banking (recall); consider exaggeration in execution
Requirements/Mandatory Content
Required legal identifications

Fig. 13.2 Creative Brief for a Telephone Banking Service

brand and market to guide their decision. But regardless of how experienced or know-ledgeable someone is about a brand and market, it is foolish not to pre-test. In fact, one's very experience and knowledge can actually be a handicap in evaluating one's own creative executions. Because managers are so familiar with the brand and the creative execution, they 'see' and process it in a much different way than the target audience possibly could. They naturally make connections between the brand and benefit claim *because* of their knowledge, connections that may not be possible without that knowledge. It just makes sense to pre-test so you are certain of how the target audience will respond to the creative execution.[12]

Pre-testing Creative Executions

The job of pre-testing creative executions requires original primary research, custom-tailored to reflect the appropriate creative strategy. Relying solely on a standardized pre-testing procedure offered by a research institute or syndicated service may not be appropriate for the execution you are testing. Flexible procedures based on *the brand's advertising communication objectives* provide a much better fit and provide the manager with a better understanding of the execution's potential.[13]

The reason you pre-test creative executions is to improve the chances that the advertising will work as planned when placed in the media. Whether or not it will work depends on three factors:

- the creative content of the executions;
- correct media placement and scheduling;
- competitive advertising activity.

Pre-testing deals only with the creative content of the execution. Tracking a campaign over time evaluates all three factors. Pre-testing a creative execution ensures it is consistent with strategy. It lets you know if the execution is likely to achieve the communication objectives set for the brand, and enables you to predict how it will 'work' in the market. A good pre-testing system also provides the manager with understanding that can be used to revise or improve the execution if necessary. In fact, in a summary of 75 top British advertising agencies the reason given most often for pre-testing was for 'learning' and to improve future campaigns.[14]

Methods Unsuitable for Pre-testing Creative Executions

Before we begin to examine the best ways of pre-testing creative executions, we want to discuss three methods often used in pre-testing that the manager should avoid: using focus groups to test executions, using advertising recall measures, and using physiological measures.

First, never use focus groups to pre-test creative executions. While focus groups are very helpful for formulating the communication strategy prior to the development of the execution, they are totally inappropriate for pre-testing executions. There are at least two compelling reasons for this. The first problem is that focus groups vastly over-expose the execution compared with how it will be seen in the market. In a group setting, they are thoroughly discussed, a far cry from the 30 seconds or so that a TV advert has to communicate in the real world or the 1 to 2 seconds that a print or outdoor advert has in which to gain the consumer's attention. The second concern is a validity problem. By their very nature, focus groups encourage group interactions that largely prevent individual reactions to the executions from occurring as they would normally. People process advertising as individuals, even if they are watching TV with others.

Second, advertising recall is *not* a valid predictor of communication effectiveness. The most that can be said about recall measures, especially day-after recall (DAR) testing, is that they may be a rough measure of attention to the advertising. But the fundamental flaw is that recall procedures are *advertising*-recall based, not *brand*-recall based. We are looking for *brand*-associated communication effects. *Brand* awareness and *brand* attitude are the fundamental communication objectives, not advertising awareness or attitudes toward the advertising. No *pre-test* measure based upon advertising recall that we are aware of has ever been shown to predict advertising effectiveness, and this is because the media vehicle (as in DAR) or the test situation (as in the case of most syndicated recall measures) are cues that are irrelevant to the consumer's decision process.

Finally, physiological measures on their own are not particularly effective in pre-testing creative executions. Physiological measures generally only measure attention to an execution. EEG, or 'brain-wave', measures certainly record the fact that something is going on when you are exposed to an execution, but the interpretation of this response in terms of advertising effects is not clear. Eye-tracking techniques have shown some relationship to brand recognition, but not to either brand recall awareness or brand attitude.[15]

Pre-test Measures

One of the most important considerations in pre-testing creative executions is the *order* in which the test questions are asked. Basically, you want to order the questions so as not to sensitize or bias later questions. For example, brand purchase intention and brand attitude should be measured before brand benefit beliefs, because measuring the beliefs first could lead a person to form new or revised attitudes or intentions as a result of thinking about the benefit beliefs presented. Brand awareness should be measured on a delayed basis, because if you measure it immediately after exposure to the test execution the result is likely to be much higher than it would likely be in the real world, where delays occur between seeing an advert and an opportunity to purchase the brand.

Attention Measures

Print adverts and Internet banner adverts must arrest the reader's attention so that they do not continue turning the page or surfing before the message can register. Research has shown that about 50 per cent of all print adverts fail to gain the reader's attention. On the other hand, because radio and television adverts rely upon reflexive attention, an attention measure is not necessary when they are pre-tested.

Eye-tracking experiments by Kroeber-Riel and von Keitz have shown that it takes about 1.75 seconds to process an illustration in a print advert and about 0.25 seconds to process each word in a headline.[16] Since the illustration and headline is the minimum input required if the execution is to communicate anything, when pre-testing print adverts you should compute the time necessary for minimally processing the test execution and then use a timed portfolio test as the first measure in your pre-test. The time spent looking at the test execution should be recorded and compared with the time needed to actually process the picture and headline in order to establish a measure of the number of people likely to pay attention to the execution. The remaining pre-test measures of communication effects should then be corrected for the proportion of attention achieved by the test execution.

Processing Measures

Processing reflects a person's immediate responses to the execution. These responses are transient, so they must be measured immediately following exposure to the test execution. If you were to try to measure them during processing, as some pre-testing procedures do, this would of course disrupt processing and provide a poor measure of the actual effect. An immediate retrospective measurement of reactions to an execution does not affect subsequent brand-related measures. The two types of processing measures that should be taken at this point in the pre-test are acceptance for high-involvement brand attitude, and learning for low-involvement brand attitude.

Acceptance. If the brand decision is high-involvement, then as we have learned, the consumer must *accept* the brand's benefit claims. What matters in high-involvement strategies is the extent to which the consumer willingly agrees with the message. The most valid measure of high-involvement processing is something called cognitive response measurement, which requires post-coding or scoring the test subjects' comments about the message. Mention of the brand should also be recorded because the comments should reflect opinions about the brand. Failure to mention the brand could indicate a possible brand awareness problem with the execution.

Learning. With low-involvement brand decisions, you are looking for rote learning responses. While learning is also necessary for brand awareness, this cannot be measured until after the other measures are taken. In low-involvement strategies, what counts is the perceived message about the brand. It doesn't matter whether the target audience fully accepts or is convinced by the message, as long as it is understood correctly. A successfully registered low-involvement attitude shift will show up on the communication effect measures of intention to try the brand (low-involvement informational advertising) or brand attitude image (low-involvement transformational advertising).

Measuring low-involvement attitudinal learning is rather straightforward. It consists of the following type of question: 'In this advert, aside from trying to convince you to try the brand, what do you think the advertiser is trying to *tell* you?' Verbatim playback or accurate paraphrases of the advert-proposed brand benefit (usually there is only one main benefit proposed in low-involvement advertising) are scored as successful learning during processing, with one important qualification. If the brand name has not yet been mentioned, the interviewer should ask: 'What was the brand advertised?' This is because the association to be learned is between the brand (awareness) and the benefit (attitude) and not the benefit in isolation. After the open-ended acceptance measures for high-involvement advert pre-tests or the learning measures for low-involvement ones, for diagnostic purposes you may wish to include some more structured questions.

Communication Effects Measures

On those occasions when category need is a communication objective and you have to remind the prospective buyer of a latent need, you will want to measure *category* purchase intention. If the category need objective is to 'sell' the category, two other measures will be needed: category benefit beliefs, and a delayed measure of category awareness. The addition of a category benefit belief measure is to assess whether in fact the execution generated a perceived interest in the category. The need for a *category awareness* measure is to ensure that once someone forms an interest in the category they remember it. This category-level awareness occurs within the context of competing purchase categories. Once these category measures are taken, you can then go on to the brand measures.

Brand Purchase Intention Measures A measure of brand purchase intention is not necessary for low-involvement transformational advertising. The reason is that in a pre-test situation, it is not reasonable to expect an immediate effect on purchase intention. Instead, the effectiveness of low involvement transformational advertising should be *inferred* from increases in the brand benefit beliefs, because this is the only reasonable effect that can be expected during the pre-test. Once such advertising is running in the market, you will measure both brand purchase intention and overall brand attitude because the transformational advertising should have had a sufficient number of exposures to work.

Measures of brand purchase intention must pay attention to the wording of the intention question in terms of 'try' or 'use' and include a time frame for the intention. Paying attention to the wording of questions should go without saying, but too often important distinctions are ignored. For example, with new product categories (and brands), consumers are more willing to state intention to 'try' a brand, which implies less commitment, than they are to state intentions to 'buy' it. The wording of the intention measure should precisely reflect the purchase or purchase-related action objective.

The time frame for a brand purchase intention measure is satisfied by making the intention conditional on category need. For example:

- Suppose you were going to add to your investment portfolio. How likely is it that you would consider Alliance Leicester?

- The next time you buy a candy bar, how likely is it that you will buy Bounty?

Brand Attitude Measures Next comes the overall measure of brand attitude, except when testing low-involvement transformational executions as explained above. Measuring brand attitude helps to interpret the ultimate pre-test criterion measure, brand purchase intention given awareness of the brand. For brand purchase intention we measured how likely someone is to try, buy, or use the brand after exposure to the creative execution. For overall brand attitude we measure how favourably the brand is evaluated *relative to other brands*, regardless of whether there is interest in buying or considering the brand at the next purchase opportunity. The main thing to remember in a brand attitude measure, as with the intention measure earlier, is to specify the *situation* for which the brand is to be purchased or used. This should directly reflect the purchase motivation. For example, someone's attitude toward brands of coffee may differ depending on whether it is for their own breakfast or for serving to guests at a formal dinner. An attitude measure should be situation-specific and provide the opportunity to evaluate your brand relative to competing brands when the same question is posed of them.

After this overall measure of brand attitude, you will want a measure of a brand's perceived delivery on the specific benefit or benefits presented in the execution. These benefit claims are there to influence brand attitude and measuring them serves as a diagnostic method for interpreting the overall brand attitude result. It also serves as the *sole* measure of brand attitude for low-involvement transformational executions. The measures of the brand benefit claim should follow the overall brand attitude rating to avoid contamination. You do not want those evaluating the execution to form a spurious attitude based on benefits suggested in the measures rather than on benefits spontaneously processed from the advertising.

Brand Awareness Measures Why is the brand awareness measure delayed until the end of the pre-test? Brand awareness is the key communication effect, without which nothing else really matters. It plays a gate-keeping role vis-à-vis the other communication effects, and is critical for purchase of the brand. If the prospective buyer does not recognize or recall the brand it will not be purchased, no matter how well established or how favourable the other communication effects of the brand are for the consumer.

Only in the special case of direct-response broadcast advertising, such as the 'call or write now' type of adverts that appear on TV or radio, should you measure brand awareness at the beginning of the pre-test. For all other types of advertising, in the real world there will be a delay between advertising exposure and the next purchase decision opportunity. This may range from an hour or so for 'same-day' retail advertising, to a week or more for other products.

Unfortunately, brand awareness measures taken during the pre-testing session itself (or as much as ten minutes later in some syndicated tests of TV commercials) do not provide a reliable measure of a creative execution's ability to generate or increase awareness for the brand. Short-interval measures should never be interpreted as absolute measures of an execution's ability to create or increase brand awareness. This is especially true for recall brand awareness, which declines significantly over time due to other advertising's competitive interference in memory. The only reliable way to estimate brand awareness is to administer a delayed test. This is obviously more costly and time-consuming than attempting to assess brand awareness during the pre-test. But as you should now realize, to include the measure in the pre-test will be unreliable.

For recall brand awareness, the measure can be taken by phone by calling back those interviewed after an appropriate time interval has elapsed, and asking what brands in the product category they recall and comparing the response with that of a sample which did not see the test execution. For recognition brand awareness the measure is more difficult, because it requires a personal re-interview in which those interviewed are shown a photograph of brand packages and asked which brands they recognize at a glance. Two-way TV methodologies may eventually facilitate brand recognition measurement, but for now a personal follow-up interview will be required.

Tracking Creative Executions

A carefully considered pre-test should help ensure that the creative execution will deliver the desired message effectively, assuming it has proper exposure among the target audience and proper attention is paid to the advertising. Whether or not the advertising works, however, is another question.

Once the finished executions have been placed and are running in the market, to be certain they are actually working requires *tracking*. Tracking a campaign is a good idea even if every indicator you have suggests the advertising is working well. Without tracking you can never be sure if it is the *advertising* which is causally responsible for sales or usage in the market, or whether other factors in the marketing mix, such as competitors' activity or even unusual market conditions, are mediating sales. Tracking can be expensive, but it is money well spent.

For tracking to be successful you must measure not only responses to your own advertising and other marketing communication (such as promotions or direct marketing activity), but responses to your competitors as well. Unlike pre-testing, when we are only concerned with specific executions, now we are concerned with how executions perform within the overall context of the market. This means that we must also measure not only our brand and competitors' brand advertising, but any marketing activity that might influence target audience behaviour. This includes such things as promotions, your brand and competitors media spending, and even trade activity. For example, your advertising may be communicating very well, but if your competitor has just secured a special trade promotion for their brand, this could seriously affect overall market share.

There are basically four ways to track advertising campaigns. Some marketers simply monitor sale activity, correlating it with known advertising and promotion spending for their brand vs. competitors. The problem here, of course, is that you are assuming the advertising is *directly* responsible for any observed sales results. This can lead to serious misinterpretations because you simply cannot know what may be causing the activity observed in the market.

Another way of tracking advertising is to utilize a panel of consumers who are questioned about their purchases and recall of advertising. This does have the advantage of measuring causality at the individual level, but it has its own problems. Using a panel of consumers may sensitize those participating and influence their purchase behaviour over time.

The most common way of tracking the effectiveness of a campaign is to take a series of measures over time, 'tracking' the results. With waves of interviews, a benchmark is established prior to a campaign and additional measures are taken at various points in time. These measures generally correspond to the end of major periods of advertising, providing a 'before–after' comparison. The biggest problem with taking periodic measures is that you do not know what is going on between the measurements.

Look at Fig. 13.3. If this represented what was actually going on in the market, periodic measures would significantly underestimate the effectiveness of the advertising

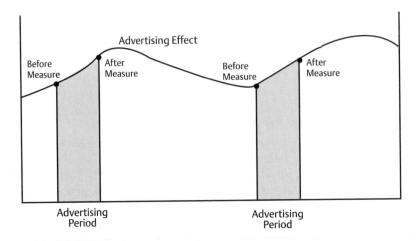

Fig. 13.3 Potential Problem with Before–After Effectiveness Measures: Advertising Effects Continue to Build After the End of the Advertising Period

campaign. What the graph suggests is that it takes a while for the advertising effect to build, and by taking a measure at the end of the advertising flight you are missing the true effect of the campaign. Fig. 13.4 illustrates another possible scenario. By measuring the results at the end of the advertising flight, in this case you completely miss the advertising's effect, and in fact show no effect at all!

The best way to track advertising is with *continuous tracking*.[17] Continuous tracking utilizes on-going interviewing of small samples of consumers, 'rolling' the results, with moving averages for weekly, bi-weekly, or four-week periods. This permits a relatively continuous measure of what is going on in the market, offering a sensitive measure of actual advertising effects. Because the measures are ongoing, it is possible to read the result for any period, at any time. This provides the manager with a powerful diagnostic tool, and avoids the danger inherent in other methods of misreading the effects of a campaign.

Of course, even with continuous tracking, the results will only be as good as your measures and analysis.[18]

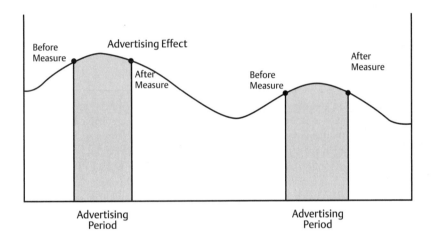

Fig. 13.4 Potential Problem with Before–After Effectiveness Measures: Advertising Effects Peak Before the End of the Advertising Period

Summary

We have now considered in detail the creative execution of a communications strategy, emphasizing the importance of consistency related to the brand's primary benefit. We examined the creative briefing process and the content of the creative brief itself. We then went on to discuss creative research, looking at the appropriateness of various pre-testing measures and then at tracking studies, where we highlighted the important role of continuous tracking of advertising effects in providing the manager with diagnostic information.

Questions to consider

13.1   Why is consistency in creative executions very important?

13.2   Why should a creative briefing include a review of current and past competitive advertising?

13.3   Why should a creative brief include unique and interesting facts about the product, brand, and consumers?

13.4   What four areas should be covered in the task definition section of a creative brief?

13.5   Why is the benefit claim and support the most difficult part of the creative brief?

13.6   Why is it essential that creative executions be pre-tested?

13.7   Why is advertising recall not a valid predictor of communications effectiveness?

13.8   How can advertising campaigns be tracked?

Notes

1   While a creative idea of some kind is obviously needed before advertising can be developed, it is probably impossible to describe where a creative idea comes from. Many authors and researchers have tried, and although there is a general understanding of some of the things that nurture creativity, it is far from complete. A good introduction to the vagaries of creativity is Arthur Koestler's *The Act of Creation*. Creative ideas spring up in different ways with different people. However, successful creative ideas will adhere to some basic guidelines. They will be interesting, unique, and *workable* ideas that enable the creatives working on the advertising to present a brand's positioning engagingly to the target audience. It should also be *extendable*. As Roderick White put it in *Advertising: What it is and How it works*, 3rd edn. (London: McGraw-Hill, 1993), 51: 'Ideas that can be developed beyond a single campaign into a campaign that will run for years are really worth their weight in gold.'

2   See L. R. Squire and E. R. Kandel, *Memory: From Mind to Molecules* (New York: Scientific American Library, 1999).

3   The work of Kroeber-Riel, who was Director of the Institut für Konsum- und Verhalternsforschung at the University of the Saarland, represents perhaps the most productive research into understanding the effects of visual imagery in advertising. Unfortunately, much of his work is not available in English, including his important book on pictorial communication, *Bildkommunikation* (Munich: Vahlen, 1993). However, an introduction to his ideas on emotional elements in advertising can be found in W. Kroeber-Riel, 'Nonverbal Measurements of Emotional Advertising Effects', in J. Olson and W. K. Sentis (eds.), *Advertising and Consumer Psychology*, vol. 3 (New York: Praeger, 1986).

4   Perhaps the best work available on the effects of culture on how we react to our everyday encounters may be found in the writings of Edward Hall. His classic works

are still well worth reading: *The Silent Language* (New York: Doubleday and Co. 1959) and *The Hidden Dimension* (New York: Doubleday and Co. 1966).

5 See Jay Appleton, *The Symbolism of Habitat: An Interpretation of Landscape in the Ark* (Seattle: University of Washington Press, 1990) and *The Experience of Landscape*, revd. edn. (Chichester: John Wiley and Sons, 1996).

6 See L. Percy, 'An Introduction to the Theory of Symbolism of Habitat and its Implication for Consumer Behavior and Marketing Communication', in F. Hansen (ed.), *European Advances in Consumer Research*, vol. 2 (Provo, Utah: Association for Consumer Research, 1995).

7 In an interesting and fascinating example of this, Grant Hildebrand discusses how Frank Lloyd Wright's houses reflect this idea of prospect and refuge. Practically, Wright's houses are very difficult to live in, but the sense of well-being enjoyed as a result of his innate understanding and use of prospect and refuge in design make people overlook the inconveniences. See G. Hildebrand, *The Wright Space: Pattern and Meaning in Frank Lloyd Wright's Houses* (Seattle: University of Washington Press, 1991).

8 A detailed case history of the Oxo brand is reported in C. Baker, *Advertising Works 7* (London: NTC Publications, 1992).

9 See O'Malley, 'Creative Briefing', in D. Cowley (ed.), *How to Plan Advertising* (London: Cassell, 1987), 77–85.

10 See Cowley (ed.), *How to Plan Advertising*, and J. R. Rossiter and L. Percy, *Advertising Communication and Promotion Management* (New York: McGraw-Hill, 1997).

11 See Rossiter and Percy *Advertising Communication and Promotion Management*.

12 An excellent review of the measures used to evaluate the effectiveness of advertising in the UK and Sweden may be found in two papers by Lars Bergkvist: 'Competing in Advertising Effectiveness: An Analysis of the 1996 British Advertising Effectiveness Award Case Histories', unpublished paper presented at the AEJMC annual convention, New Orleans, 4–7 Aug. 1999; and 'Swedish Awards', unpublished paper presented at the 15th Nordic Conference on Business Studies, Helsinki, Finland, 19–21 Aug. 1999.

13 See L. Percy, 'The Importance of Flexibility in Pre-testing Advertising', *Admap*, 381 (Feb. 1998), 29–31.

14 See M. P. Flandin, E. Martin, and L. P. Simkin, 'Advertising Effectiveness Research: A Survey of Agencies, Clients and Conflicts', *International Journal of Advertising*, 41 (1990), 203–14.

15 See L. Weinblatt's 'New Research Technology for Today and Tomorrow', in *Copy Research* (New York: Advertising Research Foundation, 1985), 180–92, and 'Eye Movement Testing', *Marketing News*, 5 June, 1987, 1.

16 See W. Kroeber-Riel, 'Effects of Emotional Pictorial Elements in Ads Analyzed by Means of Eye Movement Monitoring', in T. Kinneau (ed.), *Advances in Consumer Research*, vol. 11 (Ann Arbor, Mich.: Association for Consumer Research, (1984), 591–7 and B. von Keitz, 'Eye Movement Research: Do Consumers Use the Information they are Offered?', *European Research*, 16 (1988), 217–24.

17 An excellent discussion of continuous tracking is to be found in Max Sutherland,

Advertising and the Mind of the Consumer (St Leonard's, Australia: Allen and Unwin, 1993). Paul Feldwick also discusses tracking in his article 'Tracking Studies', in John Philip Jones (ed.), *How Advertising Works: The Role of Research* (London: Sage, 1998), 234–43.

18 An excellent review of advertising effectiveness testing may be found in a paper by Flemming Hansen, 'Testing Communication Effects', to appear in the *Handbook of Marketing and Opinion Research*, edited by Colin McDonald for ESOMAR. Also, Jones (ed.), *How Advertising Works* provides a number of informative chapters on research in advertising.

Chapter 14

Integrating Advertising and Promotion

Putting together a marketing communication program requires a full understanding of the strengths and weaknesses of both traditional advertising and promotion. There are strengths and weaknesses to all aspects of marketing communication, which is why a truly integrated *planning* approach is so important to effective mass communication. Different media have different strengths in different situations. This is one of the things that developing a consumer decision-making model helps isolate. Various target audience roles at different stages of the decision process are better suited to some forms of marketing communication than others.

What we want to look at now are the basic ways in which traditional advertising and promotion as we have been discussing them in this book differ in terms of their appropriateness in specific marketing and communication situations. Remember, when we are talking about *traditional* advertising and promotion, we are referring to their basic functions. Traditional advertising is marketing communication used primarily for long-term brand equity *delivered* via such media as print, broadcast, direct mail, and packaging, as opposed to traditional promotion, which is marketing communication used primarily for short-term tactical goals, regardless of whether it is delivered via print, direct mail, point-of-purchase collateral, or broadcast media.

Optimizing the Communication Objectives

One of the fundamental decisions a manager will be charged with is whether to use traditional advertising or promotion in order to meet specific communication objectives. Depending upon the communication effect, advertising and promotion will have different strengths. For marketing communication to be effective, it is important to understand the relative strengths and weaknesses of traditional advertising and promotion in contributing to the four basic communication effects. These relative strengths and weaknesses are discussed below.[1]

Category need. Neither advertising nor promotion is especially strong in stimulating category need. Category need generally springs from some felt need, the result of a particular consumer motivation. Advertising would have a hard time trying to *create* a motivation. Its strength would be in positioning a category so that it is seen as satisfying an existing motivation. Promotions have the ability to *accelerate* category need, but again are not likely to actually generate category need. As a result, neither advertising nor promotion is likely to have a major impact upon creating category need. (In fact, this is a case where publicity can make an important contribution.)

Brand awareness. Brand awareness is a traditional strength of both advertising and promotion. However, the manager must remember to consider what type of awareness is involved. While advertising can deal effectively with both recognition and recall brand awareness, promotions are likely to be more effective for recognition brand awareness.

Brand attitude. Here we have the traditional strength of advertising. By its very nature it offers the message flexibility that is so very well suited for brand attitude objectives. But good promotions should also work on brand attitude, as we saw in Chapter 12. If proper attention is paid to how a promotion is executed (especially in terms of the words and images in the message) it will be able to contribute something to brand attitude. Nevertheless, advertising is still the strongest contributor to brand attitude communication effects.

Brand purchase intention. This is the traditional strength of promotion. Because of their generally short-term, tactical nature, promotions are geared to immediate action on the part of the consumer. Advertising can contribute to brand purchase intention, but if it is truly an advertisement, and not a hybrid advertising message that includes a promotion, it is unlikely to make as strong a contribution.

Marketing Considerations Affecting Advertising or Promotion Emphasis

As we can see, the relative strengths of advertising and promotion are directly related to communication effects. But aside from this, perhaps the next most important guide to the relative emphasis placed upon the use of traditional advertising vs. promotion in marketing a product is where the product falls in the product life cycle.[2]

Product Life Cycle Influence Upon Relative Emphasis

The product life cycle is generally presented in four parts, as shown in Fig. 14.1. There is an introductory phase, followed by a period of growth. After a certain point the product reaches maturity, and in the long run most products will decline. One of the key determinants of the shape of this curve is the effectiveness of the overall marketing effort. Ideally, a company would like to accelerate the early stages of the cycle, quickly introducing the brand and growing to a position of strength in the market. At this point it is possible to scale back marketing expenditures, while at the same time experiencing

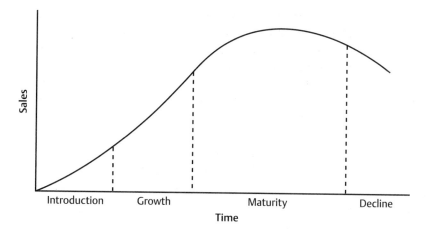

Fig. 14.1 Product Life Cycle

manufacturing efficiencies. This is the period of greatest profit from the brand, and every effort is made to prolong this period before the forces of the ever-changing market eventually push the brand into decline.[3]

Where does advertising and promotion fit in relation to the various stages a brand experiences over its life? If you were to ask yourself where you would probably need to spend the most marketing monies over the life of a product, the obvious answer is during its introductory phase. This is the time when you must make potential consumers aware of the new brand, and teach them something about it in order to interest them in trying it. A very high level of spending is required here, both for advertising and promotion. The high advertising expenditure goes into helping make people aware that the brand exists and just exactly what kind of product it is. The high expenditure for promotion is needed to help make the target audience aware of the brand, and to induce them to try. Both the advertising and promotion efforts must be carefully integrated here in order to provide the consistent image we talked about in the last chapter.

As the brand moves from the introductory stage into the growth stage, the proper distribution of advertising vs. promotion expenditure will depend upon the nature of the product itself, or upon the marketing strategy undertaken for the brand. If the new product is a leader in the category or has a readily apparent difference that makes it more desirable than competitive brands, you will want to spend heavily on advertising. Why? Because with advertising you are able to underscore your competitive advantage and maintain high levels of awareness for the brand. Promotions really do not make a lot of sense here, since potential consumers should be interested in trying your brand because of the benefits associated with it, not because of some incentive.

On the other hand, if there is really not much to differentiate your brand from others in the category, you will probably spend less on advertising because you are counting on competitors' advertising to help maintain interest in the category. But, if you adopt this strategy, you must invest in promotional expenditures in order to entice consumers to try or switch to your brand once the category need has been established and maintained by the overall advertising expenditures in the category. However, you must be *very* careful not to overuse promotions to the point where your target audience anticipates them, effectively lowering the brand's price point.

In the growth stage of a product's life cycle, you can see that the relative roles of advertising and promotion will differ, depending upon the nature of the product. This same situation occurs when a product reaches maturity, only in this case the difference in expenditure will vary as a function of brand loyalty. If you enjoy a high degree of brand loyalty, it makes very little sense to spend much money on promotion, since all you would be doing, in effect, is lowering the price of your product because most of your users would be buying the brand anyway. On the other hand, if there was very little brand loyalty in the category, with a great deal of switching among brands, you will spend less on advertising but more on promotion. In this case advertising is primarily used to maintain awareness for the brand, while promotion is used to attract and hold customers.

Finally, once a product begins to decline, both advertising and promotion spending should drop too as the marketing manager begins to phase out support for the brand. Soon there will be no spending at all on advertising, and only minimal spending on promotion to the trade (not the consumer) in order to maintain distribution for the product until the company has used up its inventory of the brand. All of these relationships between the amount spent on advertising vs. promotion during different stages of the product life cycle are summarized in Table 14.1.

Additional Marketing Considerations Affecting Relative Emphasis

In addition to the inherent strengths of advertising and promotion as they relate to communication effects, various characteristics in the market also suggest emphasizing either advertising or promotion. These market characteristics may be grouped into four categories, and are reviewed below (see Table 14.2).

Table 14.1 Relating Advertising and Promotion to the Product Life Cycle

Product Life Cycle Stage	Utilizing Advertising	Utilizing Production
Introduction	Drive up awareness	Generate initial trial
Growth		
Differentiated Brand	Underscore brand's advantage	Unnecessary
Undifferentiated Brand	Rely upon category spending to maintain interest	Encourage switching to brand
Maturity		
High brand loyalty	Maintain loyalty	Avoid because it effectively lowers price point
Low brand loyalty	Maintain brand awareness	Use to attract and hold customers
Decline	Unnecessary	Maintain distribution until inventory is gone

Table 14.2 Advertising vs. Promotion Emphasis under Specific Market Considerations

Market Consideration	Emphasis
Product Differentiation	Advertising
Strong Market Position	Advertising
Poor Performance	Promotion
Competitive Activity	Respond Accordingly

Product Differentiation

Generally speaking, if a brand has a positively perceived difference over its competitors, there should be an emphasis on advertising in its marketing communication programme. Two potential differences to consider are quality and price. If you have a brand that consumers see as high-quality you will be likely to spend more on advertising in order to communicate its quality benefits and support its 'quality image', reinforcing positive brand equity. If your brand is seen as lower-quality you will tend to spend more on promotion in order to persuade people to 'trade down'. Quality generally relates to price, so you will tend to find high-priced brands spending more on advertising in order to build and sustain a strong brand equity to justify their higher price. Lower-priced brands generally spend more on promotion, and usually price promotion, in order to appear to offer consumers a better value. Price promotion could certainly help tactically in the short term, but it will not help justify a higher price in the long term.

If your brand is seen by consumers to have special benefits not found in other brands in the category, you will be more likely to spend money on advertising in order to inform your target audience about unique benefits associated with the brand. On the other hand, 'commodity' brands are thought of as similar and as a result tend to compete more on a promotion basis. Brands can be differentiated on the basis of obvious benefits, such as taste, but also on the basis of attributes that the consumer never really sees, such as special whitening ingredients in a detergent or the presence or absence of caffeine in colas. As long as a brand is perceived as different, advertising can have a greater effect than promotion.

Products that have a real risk associated with them, not just high-priced brands or ones with perceived psychological risk (i.e. high involvement), tend to employ advertising to reassure consumers that they are making a safe choice. Such potentially high-risk products, for example those needed for very serious health problems, are unlikely to use promotion.

Market Position

If a brand has a strong market position, based upon either a high market share or frequent purchase, advertising should be emphasized over promotion. The key again is advertising's ability to help build and reinforce a positive brand attitude, especially in a market where there may be a lot of switching behaviour. Promotion, of course, can be used tactically, but to sustain a strong position in the market requires an advertising emphasis.

Poor Market Performance

If a brand is having problems in the market, promotion should be emphasized over advertising because of its more immediate impact. This emphasis makes sense at both the consumer and trade levels when a brand is in need of a 'quick fix'. It is assumed, of course, that there is not an inherent product problem, or other serious marketing mix problem, because promotion will not provide a long-term cure.

Competitive Activity

A final and obvious factor in the relative expenditure of marketing monies for advertising vs. promotion is the activity of your competitors. Suppose a direct competitor increases its advertising spending. If you are to maintain your relative position in the market it will probably be necessary for you to increase your advertising spending. Likewise, if your major competitor turns to heavy use of promotion, it will probably be necessary for you to increase your promotion spending at least somewhat as well, in order to minimize the likelihood of people switching from your brand as a result of your competitors' promotions. Then again, this may not be in your brand's best interest. It is important to study each situation carefully and respond accordingly.

As we shall see in the next section, one of the advantages of a good marketing communication programme that effectively utilizes the strengths of both advertising and promotion is that strong brand equity can help minimize the effect of a competitor's promotions. And again we caution that you must guard against falling into the trap of regularly using promotions, effectively telling your target audience to make their choice on price.

Another area to consider is the strength of private labels in your brand's category. If there is a strong private label presence in the market, it makes sense to emphasize advertising and not try to compete on price with promotion.

It should be clear now that in marketing a brand you must make strategic use of both advertising and promotion. You should not think in terms of advertising vs. promotion, but rather whether advertising *or* promotion is most likely to satisfy a communication objective, and whether or not certain market conditions suggest *emphasizing* either advertising or promotion. These are not unrelated. The market conditions discussed above will suggest the need for a particular communication effect, which will guide the selection of the communication objectives.

So we can see that depending upon the desired communication effect (which could be a function of more than the market characteristics just discussed) there will be advantages to emphasizing either advertising or promotion. It is not enough to regard advertising and promotion as independent parts of the marketing communication mix. Rather, traditional advertising and promotion each have special characteristics that make them more or less appropriate to achieve particular marketing and communication ends. The decisions as to where you place your emphasis will be a function of specific circumstances in the market.

While it is certainly possible to use only advertising or only promotion since both are able to produce each of the four basic communication effects, this is generally not desirable. The best course is an integrated marketing communication programme that builds upon the individual strengths of advertising and promotion, and the advantage of using them together, which is discussed next.

Advantages in Using Advertising and Promotion Together

There is no doubt that using advertising and promotion together offers real advantages over using advertising or promotion alone. Nevertheless, while a brand's marketing communication profits from using advertising and promotion together, for most brands traditional advertising will almost always be more important. This stems primarily from advertising's brand attitude strength, and the fact that brand attitude should be the central communication effect for all brand marketing communication. This may seem surprising given the fact that traditional advertising receives only about one-third of all marketing communication spending. Unfortunately, too often brands get caught up in short-term competitive marketing and rely too heavily upon promotion.

What makes using advertising and promotion *together* so strong is the interaction between the long-term effects of brand attitude on building brand equity, and the tactical advantages of promotion. Without a strong brand attitude, promotion effectiveness suffers. When advertising has been effective in generating a strong brand attitude, all of the brand's uses of promotion become that much more effective. There are two principal reasons for this:

- When a strong positive brand attitude is developed through advertising it means that when a brand does use promotion the target audience will see the promotion as a better value, and

- The strong positive brand attitude also means that when a brand's competitors use promotion, the brand's target audience will be less likely to respond.

The logic here is straightforward. If consumers have a strong positive attitude toward a brand they will be less likely to switch simply because of a competitor's promotion; and when a brand consumers like does offer a promotion of its own they will be that much more pleased. Additionally, a promotion in that light will also tend to reinforce consumers' already held positive brand attitude.[4]

There is another thing to consider here. What we have been discussing are the reasons why advertising and promotion work so well together in terms of communication effects. You might well be thinking that if advertising does such a great job building brand attitude and brand equity, and tends to immunize your target audience against competitive promotions, why promote at all? The reason is simple. Even with a positive brand attitude, most consumers will occasionally switch brands. If they were always loyal to your brand, there would be no need to promote. But most consumers tend to use more than one brand in a category, at least on occasion. That is why some promotion will almost always be needed for tactical support of the brand. We want to maintain as large a share of our customer's purchases as possible, and the effective use of promotion helps accomplish this task.

While advertising is of critical importance to a brand, because without advertising it is very difficult to maintain strong brand equity, the overall strength of a brand is increased when it is used along with promotion. When advertising and promotion are used together, the overall communication effects are stronger.

The Ratchet Effect

A good explanation of how this mutual reinforcement between advertising and promotion works has been offered by Bill Moran, a marketing consultant. He calls his explanation a 'ratchet effect' and it reflects the discussion we have been having.[5]

One of the behavioural consequences of most promotions is that they 'steal' purchases, either by moving forward a purchase by a consumer who would eventually be buying the brand anyway, or by taking a regular purchase away from a competitor. As just discussed, one of the reasons for a brand to promote, even when it enjoys a strong positive brand attitude, is to maximize the brand's purchase by the occasional brand-switcher. As a result, when a brand promotes it should generate more sales than usual. But our objective is not to increase sales temporarily (except for an occasional short-term tactical reason), but *permanently*. Without advertising, after the promotional period sales will drop below average levels for a while, then slowly return to normal as consumers return to their regular purchase patterns.

This is where advertising comes in. When advertising is used together with promotion, the effect of a promotion within or following a period of advertising is to stimulate the overall growth rate for the brand faster than with advertising alone. This is what is meant by a 'ratchet effect'. A well-conceived promotion, one that also addresses brand attitude, helps to reinforce the positive brand attitude of regular users. The occasional user of a brand who is attracted by the promotion will be more likely to stay with the brand, buying it more often after the promotion because of the effect of the advertising that ran along with or after the promotion, building upon the advertising-driven brand attitude that existed prior to the promotion. As this cycle continues, the regular base of consumers grows, 'ratcheting up' with each advertising–promotion cycle.

You can see how this happens by looking at the charts in Fig. 14.2. When only promotions are used, a brand experiences a short-term spike in sales, followed by a steady decline until sales return to relative equilibrium and normal purchase cycles resume. Unless the promotion attracts new *loyal* users, the promotion will not have added incremental business. Over time, nothing has been gained. When only advertising is used, we see that sales generally build steadily if not dramatically over time as the effect of positive brand attitude develops more interest in the brand. But when advertising and promotion are used *together* we experience Moran's ratchet effect. Promotion accelerates purchase, but ongoing advertising helps sustain and build a customer base so that over time the overall effect on sales is greater than when advertising is used alone.[6]

Moran has suggested that this ratchet effect can be explained in terms of two kinds of demand elasticity: 'upside' and 'downside' elasticity. These are important considerations in communication planning, because they help focus a manager's thinking on *how* the

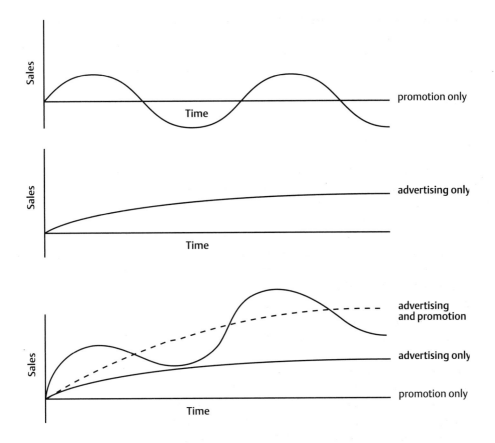

Fig. 14.2 The Effects Over Time of Using Promotion vs. Advertising and Promotion

relationship between advertising and promotion that we have been talking about influences sales, and not simply on the overall price elasticity of a brand. These notions of upside and downside elasticity relate to a brand's pricing strategy as well as *competitor brand* pricing strategy. When prices are cut, either directly or via promotion (our interest here) and sales go up, we have upside elasticity; when sales decline as a result of a price increase we have downside elasticity. It is important for the manager to remember that when competitors aggressively promote, they in effect 'raise' the price of our brand.

As this discussion should make clear, the best defence against an aggressive promotion campaign by a brand's competitors is *not* necessarily to match their promotion spending, but to maintain a strong advertising presence to ensure a strong brand equity, while promoting *tactically* as necessary. Effective advertising stimulates high upside and low downside elasticity by building and maintaining strong brand equity through positive brand attitude.

Once again we are back to the importance of understanding communication effects and which communication effects are necessary for the effective marketing of our brand.

And at the heart of this understanding is how to deal with the important and essential communication objective of brand attitude.

Integrated Marketing Communication (IMC)

One of the most talked-about ideas in marketing during the 1990s was the notion of integrated marketing communication (IMC). And while marketing managers (especially in the USA[7]) still clearly feel it is a valuable concept, and one that will play an increasingly more important role in their companies, there is unfortunately a great deal of evidence to suggest that *truly* integrated marketing communication is the exception rather than the rule.

There are a great many reasons for this, which we shall deal with later in this chapter. One problem is that too often IMC is thought to be nothing more than using several means of delivering a message. If a brand manager uses direct mail, television, and print advertising, along with some promotions, this is likely to be considered an IMC campaign. But, simply using a variety of marketing communications does not necessarily mean an *integrated* marketing communication campaign.

Defining Integrated Marketing Communication

If using a variety of marketing communications doesn't define IMC, what does? You might briefly consider IMC as the *planning* and execution of all types of marketing communication needed for a brand, service, or company in order to satisfy a common set of communication objectives; or put more specifically, to support a single positioning. It is our feeling that IMC means *planning*, and the ability to deliver a consistent message.

Without planning, it is impossible to have IMC.[8] Centralized strategic planning is the very heart of IMC. The job of a marketing or advertising manager is to use whatever combination of marketing communication options is available to them in order to achieve the desired communication objective. But the use of these options must be *centrally planned and coordinated*, utilizing a systematic strategic planning process. In a very real sense this book has provided a detailed description and understanding of the tools involved in delivering an effective IMC campaign.

In our example above, if a brand manager uses a direct mail programme that is not tied into the advertising, that does not have the same 'look and feel', that is not developed from the same umbrella creative brief, it is not a part of an integrated campaign. If the promotions are not extensions of the advertising's message, they are not a part of an IMC campaign.

In fact, it is quite possible to have an IMC campaign that utilizes *only* direct mail or *only* advertising or *only* some promotion. How? If the manager went through a thorough strategic communications planning process and came to the decision that only one form of marketing communication was required to effectively meet the brand's marketing communication objectives, then the result is indeed an IMC campaign. Why? Again, because IMC is in the *planning*. All possible options were considered, even if only one was needed.

Traditional Advertising and Promotion in IMC

We must never forget that *all* forms of marketing communication may be considered in IMC planning: everything from product packaging to store signs to more familiar forms of advertising and promotion. But from a practical standpoint, it is easier to talk about marketing communication options in the traditional terms of advertising and promotion, our long-term strategic and short-term tactical marketing communication, as we have done throughout this book.

As we saw in the first chapter, to understand the fundamental distinction between traditional forms of advertising and promotion, we need only look at the Latin roots of the two words. You will remember that the Latin root of advertising is *advertere*, which may be roughly translated as 'to turn towards' ; and the Latin root of promotion is *promovere*, which may be roughly translated as 'to move ahead'. This summarizes nicely the difference between the communication contribution of each: advertising contributes to long-term attitude while promotion contributes to short-term action.

We have emphasized, and will continue to emphasize, that IMC is all about planning. The word 'integrate' comes from the Latin verb *integrare*, and is defined by the *Oxford Dictionary of Current English* as 'combine [parts] into a whole'. In IMC planning, we are looking at all our available options in terms of their ability to satisfy the communication objectives of our brand. The parts that are 'combined' are various forms of traditional advertising and promotion, and the 'whole' is a consistent marketing communication programme.

You may be wondering why we have been using the adjective 'traditional' throughout this book in referring to advertising and promotion. This is to remind us of the *strategic* roles each plays in planning marketing communication. But in today's world of marketing communication it is often not easy to tell an advertising execution from a promotion execution. Television commercials include direct response toll-free numbers or ask consumers to look for coupons in newspapers or magazines, and actually show the coupon. FSIs (those 'free-standing inserts' that clutter up Sunday newspapers and other print media), which are traditional promotion vehicles for delivering coupons, are often very advert-like in their appearance. Look at Advert 14.1. Is this a promotion or an advert for Findus's Les Papillotes? It ran in *marie france*, a French magazine, so you might assume it is an advert. But it also includes a 5-franc coupon, so you might think it is a promotion. From the consumer's standpoint, it really doesn't matter because they look at all marketing communication as 'advertising'.[9]

In the past there was a rather clear-cut difference between advertising and promotion media. Advertising was delivered via 'measured media' in such things as television, radio, newspaper, magazines, and outdoor. Today, however, it is not unusual to find advertising messages being delivered through direct marketing and channels marketing (trade-oriented marketing programmes similar to 'co-op' where the marketer and the retailer cooperate on marketing communication programmes, and discussed back in Chapter 12), which in the past were only used for promotional messages.

"Les Papillotes" de Findus :
Laissez-vous mener
par le bout du nez

Avec "Les Papillotes" de Findus, nul besoin de résister. Laissez-vous troubler
par l'harmonie des arômes, la couleur gourmande des petits légumes coupés
comme à la maison, la saveur des filets de poisson à la chair moelleuse.
Vos papilles vont en fondre de plaisir. Et avec 5 Francs de réduction immédiate

14.1 Is this a promotion or an advert? It is not always easy to determine, as this example illustrates.
Courtesy Findus

In addressing this issue of traditional advertising vs. promotion, Rossiter and Percy[10] have made two important points. Talking about the increase in the marketing monies going into promotion relative to advertising in recent years, they point out that in spite of this swing there has nevertheless been an *increase*, not a decrease, in the use of general advertising media because of an increase in the number of media options available for advertising (as we mentioned above). They also note that most of this growth in promotion spending, apart from all-but-required promotions to the trade, has been *additional* spending, and most of this increase has gone into *advert-like* promotions.

A second point they make is very important. Familiar forms of promotion (things like sweepstakes, coupons, and samples) are not growing. What is growing is the use of promotion-oriented messages that are very much like advertising. As they point out, the fastest-growing forms of marketing communication are direct mail and telemarketing, which have traditionally been thought of as 'promotion' rather than 'advertising'. But both direct mail and telemarketing are as much 'advertising', in the traditional sense of 'turning toward' (e.g. in terms of building brand awareness and brand equity), as they are 'promotion', in the traditional sense of 'moving ahead' some short-term action objective such as sales. As we have already discussed, even FSIs, which are by far the most widely used way of delivering coupons, are more and more advert-like in how they are being used to help build awareness and brand equity at the same time they offer a coupon.

As the old distinction between advertising and promotion becomes more blurred, thinking in terms of IMC is all the more important. What has in the past been thought of as traditional 'advertising skills' now play a critical role across the board with IMC. Planning an effective marketing communication programme with IMC requires a manager to address the creative and media questions that have always been addressed with traditional advertising. These same principles are simply being applied to a wider range of options.

Here would be a good place to revisit some of the points we made back in Chapter 4 when we were discussing the strategic planning process and introducing the Marketing Communication Task Grid (see Fig. 4.2). In fact, you might want to go back and re-read the discussion of Step Five in the strategic planning process. You will see that this summarizes a major part of the *planning* required to *integrate* a marketing communication campaign.

In the Marketing Communication Task Grid, for each important stage of the decision process involved in choosing a product or service, it provides an opportunity to summarize:

- what we want to accomplish with our marketing communication at that stage in the decision process,

- whom we want to reach with our marketing communication at that stage,

- how we can best reach them at that stage, and

- the best media available to accomplish the task (remembering that 'media' includes everything from direct mail to packaging to collateral, not just the usual print and broadcast media).

By now you should be able to see the potential this has for IMC strategy. In effect, the

Marketing Communication Task Grid provides a single source for reviewing all of the ways it is possible to positively affect the decision to purchase a brand or use a service.

Rarely would you be able to implement all the possibilities suggested from the Marketing Communication Task Grid, but they will certainly inform your thinking as you integrate the available options into an optimum strategic plan. It also will remind you of the need to be consistent in the look and feel of the message and execution, *regardless* of the marketing communication options selected to meet the communication tasks needed for positively effecting specific steps in the decision process.

With IMC we are setting communication objectives and selecting media to maximize our ability to reach our target market effectively. Unlike in the past, when managers considered various ways of using advertising, and independently considered using some form of promotion, the planning and execution of all marketing communication must be *integrated*.

Problems in Implementing IMC

We mentioned earlier that although most managers agree that IMC is the best way to approach their company's marketing communication needs, in reality true integrated planning for marketing communication is rare. Why should this be the case given such general acceptance of its value? Unfortunately, there are a number of potential roadblocks to the implementation of IMC.[11] Perhaps the single biggest problem involves the decision-making structure of most companies. The structure or organizational make-up of a company, and the way managers think or approach marketing questions, often create problems in trying to implement IMC programmes. While the decision-making structure is by far the biggest problem, there are at least three other areas that can cause problems: managers' perceptions of IMC, compensation considerations, and current marketing trends (see Table 14.3).

The Decision-making Structure

IMC requires a central planning expertise in marketing communication. However, with widely dispersed resources, individual manager relationships with marketing communi-

Table 14.3 Problems in Implementing IMC

Decision-Making Structure	Organizational structure too often is not conducive to sharing information
	Too often marketing communication has a low priority, and is peopled by specialists with a narrow focus
	Organization character inhibits a common culture
Manager Perceptions of IMC	Resistance to change and politics associated with power inhibit sharing
Compensation	Worries about position and salaries in a re-structured IMC-oriented group
	Compensation is based upon individual budgets, not contribution to total good
Trends in Marketing	Belief company already implements IMC
	Niche and micromarketing are thought to not need common themes

cation agencies and vendors, and (critically) a lack of incentive to cooperate, it is no wonder there are problems when it comes to trying to develop and implement IMC.

A number of aspects of a company's decision-making structure contribute to these problems. Basically they reflect organizational structure and what we might call organizational character, or the way an organization 'thinks'.

Organizational Structure

We have noted that there is broad agreement among marketing managers over the need for IMC, but the very organizational structure of many companies stands in the way of effective implementation. At the heart of this problem is an organization's ability to manage the interrelationships among information and materials between the various agencies and vendors involved in developing and creating marketing communication. There are a number of specific structural factors that can make this difficult.

The Low Standing of Marketing Communication in an Organization

Unfortunately, for too many companies, marketing communication has a very low priority within the organization. For many in top management, spending money on marketing communication is seen as a luxury that can be afforded only when everything else is going well. One of the fastest ways for a company to send a lot of money to the bottom line is to not spend budgeted marketing communication money. When companies frequently employ this tactic, it is not surprising that those most responsible for marketing communication occupy lower-level positions within the organization.

Specialization

To manage IMC effectively, those in charge should ideally be marketing communication generalists. Unfortunately, there are very few people like this holding marketing communication positions. In fact, what you are most likely to find are people specializing in particular areas; and, even more problematic, these specialists rarely talk with each other. They have their own budgets and their own suppliers, and jealously guard the areas they control.

Given the narrow focus and understanding of such specialists, it is very difficult to bring them together in the first place, let alone expect them to have the broad understanding and appreciation of the many marketing communication options necessary for effective IMC planning. But even if they did have this understanding, getting them to give up control, especially when it is unlikely to be financially advantageous (which we shall discuss more specifically later), is a lot to ask. Yet this is precisely what is necessary if IMC is to work.

How the Organization Thinks

In addition to the problems inherent in the way most marketing departments are structured, there are less tangible aspects of an organization's thinking and behaviour that also pose problems for implementing IMC. Because of the structural barriers we have just been talking about that can impede the flow of information, it is very difficult for an entire company to share a common understanding of that company's marketing communication.

But it is very important for everyone working at a company to understand and communicate the image being projected by the company's marketing communication.

Anyone who has any contact with customers must reflect this image. This means store clerks, sales force, telephone operators, receptionists; all are a part of a company's marketing communication, and hence in many ways are IMC 'media'. Unfortunately, all too often only those directly involved with the marketing communication programme are familiar with it, and this can be a serious problem.

Manager Perceptions of IMC

How managers perceive IMC is something that can hinder the implementation of effective IMC. Managers with different backgrounds or different marketing communications specialties, either within the company organization or at marketing communication agencies or vendors, are likely to have different perceptions of what constitutes integrated marketing communication and what roles different people should play in the planning and implementation of IMC.

Resistance to Change

Different perceptions of IMC will certainly influence its effective implementation. But even more troubling is the natural resistance to change that the idea of IMC is likely to trigger, making it difficult if not impossible to implement even though IMC's benefits are generally accepted.

Perhaps the most serious problem associated with this is a fear that the manager responsible for IMC planning will not fully appreciate someone else's area of expertise. This is compounded when advertising takes the lead (which it should in most cases), because of long-held feelings that advertising managers simply do not understand or even consider other means of marketing communication (which, unfortunately, is all too often the case). This is aggravated by the conflict, for example, between the short-term tactical experience of those working in promotion and the longer term thinking of advertising managers.

Politics and Power

Another way of looking at this tendency to resist change is in terms of both intra-organizational and inter-organizational politics. It doesn't matter if the motivation is individual self-interest or an actual belief by managers or employees in the superiority of their way of doing things: the result is the same. People, departments, and organizations want power and the rewards that go with it. Too often managers and their staff believe they will be giving up too much personal responsibility if they are part of more broadly based IMC planning. Compensation (which is discussed next) is only one part of the problem. When lines of responsibility are blurred, it is easy for individuals to feel that their prestige and position, in many cases hard-won, is threatened. This can be very difficult to overcome.

Compensation

While compensation issues are less of a direct problem with companies than with agencies and vendors working in marketing communication, they can still be a problem. When managers are worried about the importance of their positions in a realigned IMC-oriented marketing communication group, this leads quite naturally to worries about salaries and promotion, which lessens interest in IMC.

But the real concern about compensation is with agencies and vendors involved in the marketing communication needs of the company. Management at agencies working in the marketing communication field are traditionally rewarded on the basis of the total size of their business with companies. This means they are very unlikely to suggest to their clients that they might be better off spending more of their money on some other form of marketing communication.

Somehow these managers must be compensated in terms of their contributions rather than of how much is spent on their particular speciality. Without such a scheme, effective IMC is impossible because those managing one type of marketing communication will be more concerned with 'selling' it, not with how their speciality will best contribute to an overall IMC programme.

Trends in Marketing

Surprisingly, several trends in marketing have also created problems for effectively implementing IMC. Perhaps the most perplexing is the trend toward IMC! When many managers are asked about IMC, they are likely to report that their company is indeed implementing it. But this is unlikely, at least in the way we have been discussing IMC. If a company is in fact implementing IMC in some limited way, or feels that it is, this makes it very difficult to get managers to think in different ways, or to acknowledge that they still have a way to go before they are effectively implementing IMC.

One recent trend in marketing is niche or micro-marketing, an increasingly popular way of addressing complicated markets. One of the problems here is that too often managers feel that each segment or niche requires its own distinct communication programme. But if a single *brand* is involved, the most effective course is still likely to be one IMC programme. The *executions* will not necessarily be the same, but the overall look and feel must be if you are to maximize the impact of your communication expenditure. Even if it may be better to position a brand differently to different segments under certain circumstances, within each segment you should still be approaching the strategic development of the communications within the same IMC framework.

Summary

In this last chapter we have looked at the differences between traditional advertising and promotion, and how they can be integrated for optimal effect. We outlined their relative strengths and weaknesses in relation to the four basic communication effects, and then went on to discuss the way in which a product's position in the product life-cycle can guide the relative emphasis placed on traditional advertising vs. promotion. We examined the ratchet effect of combined advertising and promotion activity, but suggested that although advertising and promotion used together offer real advantages over using only one or the other the emphasis should almost always be on using advertising due to its ability to build brand attitude strength. We went on to discuss integrated marketing communications and related it to the use of the Marketing

Communication Task Grid, emphasizing the need for all communications to be driven by strategy.

Questions to consider

14.1 Which of the four basic communication effects is most appropriate for traditional promotions and which is most appropriate for traditional advertising?

14.2 When in the product life-cycle is it most appropriate to use advertising rather than promotions?

14.3 Why is advertising most appropriate for brands which position themselves as high in quality?

14.4 Why do products with real risks tend to use advertising rather than promotions?

14.5 Why might promotions be appropriate if a brand is performing poorly in the market?

14.6 What is the 'ratchet effect'?

14.7 Why is centralized strategic planning the heart of integrated marketing communications?

14.8 How can the Marketing Communications Task Grid be used to develop integrated marketing communications?

Notes

1 When J. R. Rossiter and L. Percy first introduced their notion of communication effects in their 1987 text *Advertising and Promotion Management* (New York: McGraw-Hill), they also went into considerable detail discussing the relative strength of advertising and promotion in generating those effects.

2 See R. A. Strang, *The Practical Planning Process* (New York: Praeger, 1980).

3 Lodish and others have found that advertising elasticities are dynamic, and decrease during the product life cycle. See L. M. Lodish, *et al.* 'How Advertising Works: A Meta-analysis of 389 Real World Split Cable TV Advertising Experiments' *Journal of Marketing Research*, 32 (May, 1995), 125–39.

4 A number of case histories supporting the idea that effective advertising leads to better promotions are discussed by W. T. Moran in a paper presented to the Association of National Advertisers' research workshop in New York on 9 Dec. 1981. This paper was summarized in 'Use Sales Promotion Yardstick ANA Told', *Advertising Age*, 14 Dec. 1981, 12.

5 See W. T. Moran, 'Insights from Pricing Research', in E. B. Bailey (ed.), *Pricing Practices and Strategies* (New York: The Conference Board, 1978), 7–13.

6 There is a great deal of empirical research which supports this notion. Lodish and his colleagues have found that short-term effects in marketing communication are

necessary for long-term effects, as they point out in 'A Summary of Fifty-five In-market Experimental Estimates of the Long-term Effects of Advertising', *Marketing Science*, 14 (1995), 6133–40. A more specific conclusion has been reached by John Philip Jones, who notes that short-term promotional effects are longer than advertising effects, and that short-term advertising effects diminish rapidly. See his paper 'Exposure Effects under a Microscope', *Admap*, 30 (Feb. 1995), 28–31, and his book *When Ads Work* (New York: Lexington Books, 1995).

7   A number of US studies conducted in the early 1990s that researched marketing manager's opinions of integrated marketing communication all suggested a positive response to the idea. A study reported by C. E. Caywood, D. E. Schultz, and P. Wang, *Integrated Marketing Communication: A Survey of National Consumer Goods* (Evanston, Ill.: Department of Integrated Advertising Marketing Communications, Northwestern University, 1991), found that senior marketing executives of major fast-moving consumer good (fmcg) advertisers believed IMC to be a sound idea with real value to their company; and two-thirds said they now practiced IMC. In another study reported by T. R. Duncan and S. E. Everett, 'Client Perceptions of Integrated Marketing Communication', *Journal of Advertising Research*, May/June 1993, 30–9, communications and marketing managers overwhelmingly reported feeling that IMC was 'very valuable'.

8   A useful discussion of the need for planning in IMC can be found in L. Percy's *Strategies for Implementing Integrated Marketing Communication* (Lincolnwood, Ill.: NTC Business Books, 1997), and in J. Moore and E. Thorson's 'Strategic Planning for Integrated Marketing Communications Programmes: An Approach to Moving from Chaotic towards Systematic', in E. Thorson and J. Moore (eds.), *Integrated Communication* (Mahwah, NJ: Lawrence Erlbaum Associates, 1966), 135–52.

9   In a fascinating study reported by Don Schultz, in 'What is Direct Marketing?', *Journal of Direct Marketing*, 9:2 (1995), 5–9, when people were presented with a list of 100 various forms of marketing communication—everything from bumper stickers, checkout coupons, and refund offers to obvious forms of advertising such as print adverts and a TV commercial–94 were described as 'advertising'

10   J. R. Rossiter and L. Percy, *Advertising Communication and Promotion Management* (New York: McGraw-Hill, 1997).

11   A more in-depth discussion of potential problems in implementing IMC may be found in two papers in Thorson and Moore (eds.) *Integrated Communication*: D. Prensky, J. A. McCarty, and J. Lucas, 'Integrated Marketing Communication: An Organizational Perspective', 167–84; and L. A. Petrison and P. Wang, 'Integrated Marketing Communication: Examining Planning and Executional Considerations', 153–65.

Index